FORD MADOX FORD

FORD MADOX FORD

THE ESSENCE OF HIS ART

by R. W. Lid

University of California Press
Berkeley and Los Angeles 1964

PR6011
.O53
.2 73

UNIVERSITY OF CALIFORNIA PRESS
BERKELEY AND LOS ANGELES, CALIFORNIA

CAMBRIDGE UNIVERSITY PRESS
LONDON, ENGLAND

For Kenneth Millar

PREFACE

Ford Madox Ford wrote thirty novels. The reader coming upon Ford for the first time is apt to ask why it is that, until the recent (1962) publication of the *Fifth Queen* trilogy, only *The Good Soldier* and the four books that comprise *Parade's End* have been in print. And faced with Ford's subterranean and, to the general public, seemingly baffling reputation, he is apt to ask with some justice why he should read Ford at all. These questions this book attempts to answer.

This study of Ford's principal novels is intended for the general reader of Ford, as well as the serious student. It focuses on his whole literary output through the final achievements of his two masterpieces, *The Good Soldier* and *Parade's End*. Unlike other recent studies of Ford, which deal with scholarly thoroughness with his entire voluminous output, the central feature of this study is the examination of the sources and development of Ford's narrative style, which is the essence of his art.

Ford was both a germinal and a transitional figure in the history of twentieth-century literature. His story is part of the elusive and recent past which literary chroniclers have yet to place in full perspective. He was one of those novelists who considered it part of his art to try to write a true history of the subtle shifts in English culture. This and other considerations forced him to be a technical innovator. His unique vantage point between two centuries allowed him a clarity of vision which foresaw in broad outline the consequences of our nineteenth-century inheritance and the cultural tragedies yet to come. His fiction, in its double allegiance to the Victorian and the modern novel, reveals and illuminates the radical changes in the novel since the turn of the century. These changes reflect in part our changing conceptions of character and time, in part our changing conception of what a novel is and can be. Ford played a major role in widening the dimensions of twentieth-century sensibility and taste, and a knowledge of both his merits and his limitations is necessary to anyone who wants to comprehend the history of the modern novel.

*   *   *

For their kind permission to quote copyrighted passages from Ford's works, thanks are due to the following:

The Executors of Ford Madox Ford for *The Brown Owl, The Shifting of the Fire, The Benefactor, An English Girl, England and the English, Memories and Impressions, Thus to Revisit, Some Do Not . . ., Joseph Conrad: A Personal Remembrance, No More Parades, A Man Could Stand Up—, Last Post, The English Novel, Return to Yesterday,* and *It Was the Nightingale.*

Alfred A. Knopf, Inc., for *The Good Soldier* and *Parade's End.*

The Bodley Head Ltd for *The Bodley Head Ford Madox Ford, Volume I (The Good Soldier).*

George Allen & Unwin Ltd for *The March of Literature* and *Mightier than the Sword*; Bobbs-Merrill Company, Inc., for *Ring for Nancy*; Chatto & Windus Ltd for *A Call*; Dodd, Mead & Co. for *Henry James: A Critical Study*; Martin Secker & Warburg Ltd for *Collected Poems.*

Acknowledgements are also due to the following for permission to quote from the books named:

The Executors of Ford Madox Ford and Collins Sons & Co., Ltd, for *Drawn from Life* by Stella Bowen; William Morrow and Company, Inc., for *Those Earnest Victorians* by Esmé Wingfield-Stratford; New Directions and Arthur V. Moore for the lines from "Piere Vidal Old" and "Hugh Selwyn Mauberley," from *Personae* by Ezra Pound; Charles Scribner's Sons and The Bodley Head Ltd for *The Great Gatsby* by F. Scott Fitzgerald; Charles Scribner's Sons, the Executors of the Ernest Hemingway Estate, and Jonathan Cape Ltd for *The Sun Also Rises* by Ernest Hemingway; Charles Scribner's Sons and John Farquharson Ltd on behalf of the Henry James Estate for *The Wings of the Dove* by Henry James.

Thanks are also due to the author and the *Sewanee Review* for permission to quote from "A Diamond of Pattern: The War of F. Madox Ford," by Ambrose Gordon, Jr.

Parts of the book appeared in somewhat different form in *Kenyon Review, First Person, Prairie Schooner, Jubilee, English Literature in Transition, Spectrum,* and *Critique.*

Numerous people have aided me during the preparation of this book. I owe a special debt of thanks to Janice Biala, Ford's literary executor, and also to Ford's daughter, Mrs. Julia Loewe, who allowed me free access to Ford letters and manuscripts. I also wish to thank Mrs. Joan Bennett of Girton College, Cambridge, who located for me the passage from George Eliot quoted in chapter 5.

A final and special debt of thanks is owed Professor Robert F. Haugh, of the University of Michigan, who a number of years ago gave me wise counsel on an earlier draft of sections of this book.

R. W. L.

CONTENTS

INTRODUCTION

ONE

Return to Yesterday

"Who are you, Sir Knight?" she asked; "and where
do you come from?"
"I am the Knight of London, your majesty."
"London, London; where's that? — I've never heard
of it."
"London is the capital city of England."
"But where *is* England?" she asked.

THE BROWN OWL

On a trip to the United States in the 1920's, Ford Madox Ford
was interviewed in Chicago by Samuel Putnam, who later recalled
the interview in *Paris Was Our Mistress* (1947). At one point
the middle-aged Ford, speaking very close to his true thoughts,
said: "When George Moore dies, I believe I shall be the dean of
English novelists."[1] Then, the interview over, he hired a cab and
went on a pilgrimage to Oak Park, the Chicago suburb which had
given birth to Ernest Hemingway. It was characteristic of Ford
that, years younger than Moore and years older than Hemingway,
he considered himself a contemporary of both; and in one sense
he was—he had come of age in the decade in which Moore published his greatest work, and he had been among the first to
recognize Hemingway's talent. In another, truer sense, Ford was
a contemporary of neither. He had a foot in both centuries, and
during his lifetime he was destined never to receive the homage
that he saw given Moore and which he longed for. Perhaps for
this reason, among others, he composed endless memoirs of his
childhood and literary life in which he linked himself with the
great and near-great of the nineteenth and twentieth centuries.

The facts of his early life were almost as remarkable as his elaborate fantasies about it.[2] He was born Ford Hermann Hueffer, at eighteen baptized as a Roman Catholic and given the name Joseph Leopold Ford Hermann Madox Hueffer; after the first World War he changed his last name to Ford. His father was the German-born music critic of the London *Times,* a champion of Wagner, an ex-pupil of Schopenhauer, and a close friend of William Morris. His mother was the daughter of Ford Madox Brown, the Pre-Raphaelite painter. By marriage the Rossettis— Dante Gabriel, William Michael, and Christina—were part of the family circle. It was a brilliant literary and artistic world. But it was also a world of foreigners, of people outside the mainstream of English culture; and just as he later fabricated an Eton and Oxford background for himself, so over and over again Ford impressed his personal fantasy of landed gentry upon his fiction, until it reached mythic proportions in the Tietjens saga.

As a very small boy with long golden hair, he was on occasion dressed in a Pre-Raphaelite "suit of greenish-yellow corduroy velveteen with gold buttons, and two stockings of which one was red and the other green."[3] More than once he posed for his painter-grandfather; a portrait of a flaxen-haired child of eight now hangs over the fireplace in the home of his daughter Julia. He played with his precocious Rossetti cousins, the children of William Rossetti, who lived but one door down from his grandfather's, and acted in their home-produced Greek dramas; later he published his first poem in their anarchist magazine, *The Torch.*

Much of his childhood was spent in the house described by Thackeray in *The Newcomes,* the gloomy, cavernous dwelling of Madox Brown in Fitzroy Square, where over the porch balanced a funerary urn with a ram's head. Under this precariously situated urn passed many of the Victorian great, Morris, Burne-Jones, Swinburne; poetesses come to tea in four-wheelers; art critics and buyers, painter-poets, poet-craftsmen, and painter-musicians. There, in his studio, with the walls covered in gilded leather, the doors painted dark green, Madox Brown painted his great pictures "Work" and "The Last of England." "With a square white beard, with a ruddy complexion, and with thick white hair parted in the middle and falling above the ears," he reminded his grandson exactly of "the king of hearts in a pack of cards."[4] Romantic by nature, benevolent and generous, he could on occasion be irascible, temperamental, a roarer in his rages, and nothing aroused him more quickly than some injustice he had heard of. "He would rage over an injustice to someone else to the point of being bitterly unjust to the oppressor." Madox Brown was also a great talker, and at night, in the immense old Georgian mansion, the lights in the studio lit, the fire glowing, he "would sit with his glass of weak whisky-and-water in his hand, and would talk for hours." His young grandson sat on the other side of the rustling fire and listened.

Madox Brown "had anecdotes more lavish and picturesque than any man" Ford ever knew. He talked of Beau Brummel, of Paxton who built the Crystal Palace, of the mysterious Duke of Portland; "he would revive the splendid ghosts of Pre-Raphaelites, going back to Cornelius and Overbeck and to Baron Leys and Baron Wappers, who taught him first to paint in the romantic grand manner"; and, William Rossetti come in from down the street, he would go on to talk with him "of Shelley and Browning and Mazzini and Napoleon III." Something of the genius of the grandfather seems to have presided over the career of the grandson. A later Ford not only wanted to be a storyteller; his passionate desire became to write as well as Madox Brown and a few others talked.

Ford grew up in an age when, in one way or another, the artistic community was in retreat before modern industrial society. Dante Gabriel Rossetti and the Pre-Raphaelite Brotherhood had turned to medieval, mystical, and romantic themes. So had William Morris, immersing himself in Arthurian legends and Icelandic sagas and old tapestries. The influence of Ruskin was widespread, Art for Art's sake was having its day, and Pater had somewhat reluctantly become the leader of the Aesthetic Movement. The pagan god Pan held sway over the *Yellow Book*. Fauns with hoofs and slanted eyes cavorted on the general literary scene. Fairy tales were popular, and Kenneth Grahame was writing *The Wind in the Willows*. Oscar Wilde, dressed exotically, was insisting that life imitated art. Max Beerbohm was drawing his impish caricatures. Whistler was in his Japanese period. Decadence was in vogue, cynicism popular, and a host of *fin de siècle* isms (naturalism, determinism, hedonism, nihilism, atheism) seemed to indicate the bankruptcy of romanticism.

The hallmarks of the artist were fantasy, whimsy, eccentricity.

A belated Ruskinite wore "garments of prismatic hues—a mustard-coloured ulster, a green wide-awake, a blue shirt, a purple tie, and a suit of tweed."[5] The contemporary aesthete was satirized by Gilbert and Sullivan in the person of Reginald Bunthorne, the Fleshly Poet who sang:

> Though the Philistines may jostle, you will rank as
>   an apostle in the high aesthetic band,
> If you walk down Piccadilly with a poppy or a lily
>   in your mediaeval hand.

It was also considered aesthetic to be radical. Simple-lifers, utopian socialists, Fabian socialists, anarchists, quietists, and pacifists mingled with occultists, theosophists, and spiritualists. But the programmatic dreams of such men as William Morris, who tried to plan the merger of the new society and the new art, somehow tended to exclude living people, especially those who dropped their aitches.

This cultural milieu of Ford's childhood determined his dreams as well as his later realities. Personal fantasy, the fairy tale of the adult, became the mode of his fiction, and all his novels seemed to grow out of a single conflict: an inner strife in which the desire to retreat from society is at war with the humane desire to better it.

Ford's first novel, *The Shifting of the Fire,* already exhibited what Graham Greene has called "the unmistakable Hueffer stamp—the outrageous fancy, the pessimistic high spirits,"[6] and from first to last his works revealed a social idealism which sought outlet in the fables he constructed. A young American becomes the richest man in the world and tries to spend the money for purposes of social improvement (*An English Girl,* 1907). The god Apollo comes back to earth disguised as a man and mingles with do-gooders among the lower classes (*Mr. Apollo,* 1908). A mental injury in a train derailment temporarily sends a man backward in time to the fourteenth century, allowing the author to compare medieval institutions with those of the twentieth century (*Ladies Whose Bright Eyes,* 1911; revised 1935). In each case the contemporary world falls far short of the Fordian dream, and the impossibility of significant action dominates the fable. Even Ford's rich young American, in *An English Girl,* finds his money so entailed by the corporate structure to which it is bound that he is not free to use it. Ford was always highly critical of Morris, feeling that he "had never looked mediaevalism, with its cruelties, its filth, its stenches, and its avarice, in the face."[7] Yet he himself kept turning backward, sometimes satirically, sometimes sentimentally, but never self-deceptively, searching for the pastoral dream.

As a young man, Ford wrote some poetry but thought he wanted to be a composer. His father died and he and his mother and brother and sister moved in with Madox Brown. According to the *Times,* the Queen sent a messenger with 300 pounds to the widow of Dr. Hueffer, but Madox Brown sent him back with the message that his daughter was not yet destitute. Ford talked of a career in the Indian Civil Service or the Army. He wore a blue shirt and red satin tie and the Inverness cape of Dante Gabriel Rossetti which Madox Brown passed on to him. Then, in 1892, at the age of nineteen, he published his first book, *The Brown Owl,* a fairy tale written for his sister. According to Ford, his grandfather ordered the publisher's reader Edward Garnett, who was sitting for him, to have it published. " 'Fordie has written a book, too. . . . Go and get your book, Fordie.' . . . and the manuscript at the end of Mr. Garnett's very thin wrist disappeared into his capacious pocket. . . ."[8] A second tale and a novel followed within a year. He had discovered his amazing facility with words.

At twenty he eloped with Elsie Martindale, the seventeen-year-old daughter of a well-known manufacturing chemist. Her mother had been matron of a Dublin hospital. The young couple met at Praetoria House, a private school in Folkestone. After their marriage, they settled in a country cottage furnished in the manner of William Morris. There Ford wrote poetry, inherited 3,000 pounds, and took up golf. By 1896 he had six books to his credit. But already there were signs of the restlessness and neurasthenia that eventually drove him to the spas on the continent, estranged his wife, separated him from his children, and made him a literary vagabond.

He had been, to use his own words, "trained for genius." But what kind of genius, and how was he to become it? He had written fairy tales because it seemed to be the natural thing to do in his milieu. He had written poetry because he had been brought up in the "hot-house atmosphere of Pre-Raphaelism."[9] He had written a book about his painter-grandfather because he was the man most readily available to do the job. He had written a topographical study of the "five ports" because Rye, Hythe, and Winchelsea were his historical hunting ground in those years. And he had written a novel—but exactly why is hard to say. Except for the same general reason: all these early books appear as finger exercises by which he unsuccessfully tried to find a place for himself in the literary world. He became the polished man of letters long before he had anything really important to say in the pages he turned out so rapidly. In his haste to set down words, phrases, sentences, Ford seemed reluctant to stay over a page a moment longer than necessary, as if pausing would reveal the vacuity of what he was saying.

Ford Madox Ford wrote over seventy books of fiction, poetry, propaganda, criticism, biography, and history. Among his thirty novels were the classic, *The Good Soldier* (1915), a depth study of English manners, and the four Christopher Tietjens books, collected as *Parade's End* (1924-1928), a history of private passion and public disaster during World War I. There were also novels with utopian and medieval themes, and a trilogy revolving around Katherine Howard, the "Fifth Queen" (1906-1908), which has since become a classic of historical fiction. He satirized social reform in *The Simple Life Limited* (1911) and surveyed the contemporary political scene in novels such as *The New Humpty-Dumpty* (1912)and *Mr. Fleight* (1913). There were also farces, such as *The Panel* (1912; published in America as *Ring for Nancy,* 1913), and novels with Jamesian themes: *An English Girl* (1907) and *A Call* (1910).

In addition to this vast artesian flow of novels, good, bad, and indifferent, Ford also engaged in major editorial and literary activity. Having collaborated as a young man with Joseph Conrad, he later wrote a book about their association. He wrote the first full-length study of Henry James. He was founder and editor of two famous literary magazines, the *English Review* and the *transatlantic review.* The first issue of the *English Review,* in 1908, contained contributions by Thomas Hardy, Henry James, Joseph Conrad, John Galsworthy, W. H. Hudson, and H. G. Wells. In the 'twenties the pages of the *transatlantic review* were a sounding board for such *avant garde* writers as James Joyce, Gertrude Stein, and e. e. cummings. But Ford was not a celebrity-hunter, and he was a generous mentor to younger writers. He was the first to recognize and publish D. H. Lawrence, Norman Douglas, and Wyndham Lewis, and in Paris he hired as his subeditor an unknown young writer: Ernest Hemingway. Ford's two careers as editor were to leave him financially exhausted. He lost the *English Review* within a year through insolvency; the *transatlantic review* lasted barely longer.

In the decade before World War I he lived the life of a literary dandy, writing four hours a day, taking a morning constitutional at eleven, "wearing a very long morning coat, a perfectly immaculate high hat, lavender trousers, a near-Gladstone collar, and a black satin stock."[10] He carried a malacca cane with a gold knob. His personal affairs became complicated, and he attempted to divorce his wife and to marry Violet Hunt, an English bluestocking eleven years his senior. He went to Germany where he tried to establish citizenship in order to obtain a divorce. But all efforts failed and finally he and Violet Hunt returned to England claiming to be married, and caused something of a scandal. Many of Violet Hunt's friends cut her. They lived together at South Lodge, 84 Holland Park Avenue, the house of Mrs. Hunt, Violet's mother, who was the original of Tennyson's "Margaret" and a prolific and successful novelist. Wyndham Lewis painted a mural and decorated a room for Violet and the "flabby lemon and pink giant."[11] Ezra Pound came to play tennis, and Gaudier-Brjeska's stone bust of Pound stood in the garden. Through it all Ford wrote his four hours a day, never taking a complete day's rest. Looking back at his literary production, he was to remark:

My record in the British Museum Catalogue fills me with shame; it occupies page on page. . . . I do not say that I am proud of the record. If I had written less I should no doubt have written better. Of the fifty-two separate books there catalogued probably forty are out of print. There is only one of those forty that I should care to re-publish and of the remaining twelve there are not more than six of which I should much regret the disappearance.[12]

Among Ford's voluminous writings are some dozen books of

memoirs. His finest volume of reminiscence is *Joseph Conrad: A Personal Remembrance,* written in the immediate shock of Conrad's death. In the decade after the turn of the century Conrad had become Ford's principal literary mooring, and Ford's memories of those years fill the book with a poignant sense of loss. When it was published, however, Ford was accused of lying about the extent of his role in their mutual undertakings, *The Inheritors* (1901) and *Romance* (1903). Only today has scholarship begun to demonstrate the justness of Ford's claims to originality in the partnership.

Like Conrad, Henry James proved a circuitous detour in Ford's career. Ford made James his teacher, and in his efforts to be his equal he wrote imitations of his work, unable to escape James's pervasive influence and discover his own artistic range. When he finally broke free, to write *The Good Soldier,* he was forty; by the time he wrote his finest books, the Tietjens tetralogy, he was clearly a tired man and his prose shows it.

Ford's reminiscences of James and Conrad and other literary figures—in such volumes as *Return to Yesterday, It Was the Nightingale,* and *Mightier than the Sword* (published in America as *Portraits from Life*), and his memories of his childhood among the Pre-Raphaelite great, particularly in *Ancient Lights* (published in America as *Memories and Impressions*)—all contain elements of fantasy. "Impressionist memories," he called them. "I don't really deal in facts; I have for facts a most profound contempt. I try to give you what I see to be the spirit of an age, of a town, of a movement."[13] Beautiful reading: accurate in tone, characterization, image (Conrad rolling on the floor of a railway carriage in the agonies of correcting proofs; Henry James carrying on an elaborate discourse with a "tweeny" maid who fails to understand him); seemingly inaccurate in everything else. Yet there is a factual basis for many of his anecdotes, even if the truth is glossed over by the manner of his telling. Did Queen Alexandra hold him on her knee at a concert, and was the Abbé Liszt persuaded to play the first movement of the *Moonlight Sonata* for the small boy present in the drawing room, and did a drunken Swinburne feed the child jujubes? They are not unlikely happenings, and it may well be that, as in his relationship with Conrad, his Pre-Raphaelite memories will prove in time to be more accurate than anyone has suspected.

Ford did not enjoy being young. Clearly those years, at the turn of the century, when he was associating with Conrad, James, W. H. Hudson, and Stephen Crane—his literary elders, as well as his betters—were hard ones for the young man "trained for genius." One suspects that he was glad when they were over and he could look back in reminiscence. Stephen Crane, apologizing for an incident at Brede Place, wrote Sanford Bennett: "You must not be offended by Mr. Hueffer's manner. He patronizes Mr. James. He patronizes Mr. Conrad. Of course he patronizes me and he will patronize Almighty God when they meet, but God will get used to it, for Hueffer is all right."[14] Eccentricity, whimsy, and fantasy were the hallmarks of the artist. But others, like H. G. Wells, took offense at his manner. "A great system of assumed personas and dramatized selves,"[15] he called him. Yet ultimately it was such self-dramatization, adopted as fictional strategy, that earned him a place beside James and Conrad.

Ford's meeting with Conrad in 1898 has been described by Jocelyn Baines, in what is likely to be the standard biography of Conrad, as "the most important event in Conrad's literary career."[16] It was just as important to Ford, though their collaboration meant something different to each. Conrad, then forty-one, had written and published *Almayer's Folly, An Outcast of the Islands, The Nigger of the Narcissus,* and *Tales of Unrest.* But he was slow at construction, and the English language occasionally still troubled him. He was also in financial straits, and with the aid of the verbally facile young man he hoped to write a rapid series of popular novels. Ford, twenty-four, was at loose ends, his career adrift. Up to this point in his life he had written fairy tales, poetry, a novel, and a biography of his grandfather. There seemed little direction behind his career except the compulsive need to write. Conrad gave him the example of a man who, only a few years earlier, had given up the sea as a source of livelihood, burned all his boats on the shore, and dedicated himself solely to the art of fiction. It is hard to measure the price Ford paid for their collaboration, in money and energy and time spent, in nervous breakdown, ultimately in clouded reputation. On the other hand, it was Conrad who turned Ford into a serious novelist, who in effect "talked" him into the mainstream of twentieth-century literature.

Deep in the English countryside, the collaborators spent their evenings before the fire at Pent Farm. They talked about the day's work, about novel writing, about Flaubert, whom they both admired. They talked about construction, style, *le mot juste* at a time when, as Ford put it, the mere mention of the word "technique" was "sufficient to goad many writers into frenzies."[17] Out of the talk grew a theory of the "Impressionist novel." Life does not narrate, they argued—it makes *impressions* on our brains. Memory, the recording instrument, arranges events in a psychological, not a chronological, order. The fictional pattern that would emerge from novels written under such a theory would reveal truths otherwise hidden by the encumbrances of conventional plot. But to write such novels of psychological insight they needed a new method, new techniques. As in Flaubert, the author would be impartial, impersonal, hidden. Narrative would be broken into fragments of remembered events, and such shards of meanings, set side by side, would produce an additional impact, often of irony, always of psychological suspense, upon the reader.

It is easy to see now that they were beguiled by technique. Both would have been better writers if they had not had to rely so heavily on it. Their convention of time rearranged by a narrator was no more true to life than that of events viewed by an omniscient author. Ford and Conrad were each in their way aliens to England, and their fictional strategy gave each of them a mask, a "persona," behind which to hide when necessary; it also gave them, when they needed it, the advantageous position of insider. Conrad's narrator Marlow and Ford's Dowell and his Christopher Tietjens help to figure and justify the author's personal disinvolvement from the society that is his subject matter. Marlow provided Conrad with a safe English persona combined with the opportunity to make philosophical speculations. Unlike Ford, Conrad tried additionally to isolate his characters, to separate them from society. Ford immersed his characters in the flux of society, and in so doing made more significant and more skillful use of the technique of remembered events.

Perhaps not surprisingly, there is little in their two major collaborations to show the real trend of Ford's talent. As Joseph Warren Beach pointed out in *The Twentieth Century Novel*, (1932), the curious thing is "how little use of this method

[Impressionism] Conrad and Ford made in their novels written in collaboration, compared with the novels of Conrad alone written at about the same period or later, and the novels of Ford written since the war."[18] The first significant use Ford made of their mutually held theories involved the "time-shift," or the technique of "chronological looping," by which events are re-ordered in the narrator's memory. In his second independently written novel, *The Benefactor* (1905), he developed a thirty-three-page section (pp. 187-219) in which time shifts backward and forward over a three-month period. These pages are unified by a framing device, or envelope: a walk on the beach by two of the major characters. But this method, which he also used in the Katherine Howard books, is much more closely aligned to the flashback in both its formality and its obviousness.

Particularly in his later years, Ford talked a good deal about the time-shift, and its major role in his art. "My friend on the New York *Times*," he remarks in *It Was the Nightingale*, "calls me a master of the time-shift. He adds that a great many people dislike my books because I use that device. But he is mistaken. It is me they dislike, not the time-shift which is a thing that delights everybody."[19] It is not easy to describe the literary mechanics of the time-shift or its effect in a novel. Basically, it allows the writer to give full play to all tenses of memory, to move backward and forward over a series of events without following an order based on calendar time. This device frees him from any obvious chronological narrative base and allows him to achieve kaleidoscopic effects by juxtaposing events separated in time. It differs from the flashback both in complexity and in the frequency with which it is used. Also, of course, the ordering within a flashback is usually simply chronological; whereas within the time-shift the author may turn to either the past or the future to explain an event being handled in the novelistic present. The flashback is one-dimensional; the time-shift, many dimensional.

In *The Good Soldier,* for example, Ford used a dazed narrator remembering the events of the past. The chronological sequence is broken into fragments of meaning; event is juxtaposed to event, conversation to conversation, impression to impression. Ford breaks up time the way Seurat broke up light. Paraphrasable plot disappears, and linear action loses its significance. The novel embodies two extremes—that of a man overwhelmed by passion (Captain Ashburnham, the "good soldier") and that of a man incapable of passion (Dowell, the narrator). Two plot strands, running parallel, tell the stories of the two men and their wives, then join for a series of events leading to a denouement centering on the Ashburnhams' ward, Nancy Rufford, then separate again. The actual structure of the book, however, is something other than such a plot outline makes it appear, for by shifting through the tenses of memory as the narrator reconstructs events, Ford creates a masterpiece of psychological tension. Gradually the pieces of the story pull together. The deceptions, the appearances of the past nine years, the placid surface of the happy life Dowell thought the two couples led, is replaced by the realities of those years—adultery, malice, cruelty, deceit. It is the time-shift that makes possible Dowell's slow but passionate reconstruction of their lives.

Reminiscence was the characteristic mode of Ford's thought, in his fiction as well as his memoirs. The time-shift became the device that allowed him to give memory full play. At its most brilliant, it captured "the shimmering, the haze," the complexity, of life. At its most ordinary, it revealed the calisthenics of a tired mind. Like all techniques mastered, the time-shift became for Ford the natural way to proceed. Yet for all of Ford's talk about the time-shift, and for all the attention paid it by recent critics, its discovery and use by Ford is not sufficient to explain the development of his narrative art or the literary effects he achieved. The real basis of his narrative skill, if less flashy and seemingly more simple, lies in the more profound art of the sentence, and in the art of connecting sentences: the imaginative movements, the transitions, which accompany such shifts-in-time as Ford in his reminiscences or the narrators in his novels choose to make. In 1913, reviewing the first edition of Ford's *Collected Poems,* Ezra Pound commented: "It is he [Ford] who has insisted, in the face of a still Victorian press, upon the importance of good writing as opposed to the opalescent word, the rhetorical tradition. Stendhal had said, and Flaubert, de Maupassant and Turgenev had proved, that 'prose was the higher art'—at least their prose."[20] And years later, in *Parade's End,* a fatigued Christopher Tietjens comes close to revealing Ford's own thoughts. During a brief period of calm in the trenches in France, he imagines himself for the moment as "walking near Salisbury in a grove," with the spire of the church of George Herbert visible through the foliage. "One ought to be a seventeenth-century parson at the time of the renaissance of Anglican saintliness . . . who, wrote, perhaps poems. No, not poems. Prose. The Statelier Vehicle."[21]

Ford's passionate desire was to learn to write as well as he and a few others talked. It is not surprising, then, that he was to gravitate toward Henry James, whose novels continually derive from overheard speech. James and Ford knew each other in the English countryside. James was living at Rye, Ford at Winchelsea, and the young collaborator of Conrad found himself drawn into the sphere of writers who have been influenced by the example of the master. If Conrad's example gave Ford the courage to become a serious novelist, and if their mutual theories gave him the necessary ballast to get under way, it was nevertheless James, not Conrad, who played the larger role in the development of his art. Even as early as *The Benefactor* (1905) Ford was imitating Jamesian dialogue.

"Mr. James is the greatest of living writers and in consequence, for me, the greatest of living men."[22] There is little doubt that Ford was sincere when he wrote these words in his 1913 book on James immediately before *The Good Soldier*. How, then, are we to interpret the conduct of a character of Ford's named Major Teddy Brent in *The Panel* (a farce of 1912) who goes around saying: "So that there we all, in a manner of speaking, are"?[23] When asked for an explanation of why he talks this way, he replies that it is a habit acquired from reading James. James's characters are perpetually making such remarks. "And, of course, as you can never make out where they are, it's extraordinarily strengthening to the brain to work it out. That's why I'm the youngest major in the British army."

It is not necessary to suppose that Ford was hostile to James. On the contrary, *The Panel* is in part a satire on the mentality that cannot understand the novels of the master. But there is an ambiguity in Ford's attitude toward James which needs explanation.

A good part of the explanation lies in Ford's self-imposed tutelage under James, for in his book on Conrad he remarks casually that in the past he had written "two pastiches in the manner of Mr. James."[24] The one was *An English Girl* (1907),

Ford's attempt to handle "the international theme." Much like James's Lady Barberina, Ford's heroine, Eleanor Greville, is set down in the alien environment of America, where she must accommodate herself to a different cultural and moral pattern. Ford complicates this Jamesian situation by introducing into the novel a young hero who is filled with aesthetic idealism and social purpose but helpless to act. *A Call* (1910) contains such Jamesian characters as Etta Stackpole, who later becomes Lady Hudson, and Madame de Mauvesine. Its opening chapter is a more Jamesian beginning to a novel than any Henry James ever wrote, and the prose style reveals how accomplished Ford has become in the Jamesian manner. The novel's superstructure, however, collapses as Ford's subject matter, which is basically un-Jamesian, fights the manner of the telling.

Ford's relationship with James was largely confined to the period of time he spent in the country near Rye. The perceptive James used him as a model for Merton Densher in *The Wings of the Dove,* the "longish, leanish, fairish young Englishman" whose "difficulty" was "that he looked vague without looking weak—idle without looking empty."[25] In his reminiscences, Ford says that he acted the role of a *jeune homme modeste* in his relationship with "the old man." He also remarks that their intimacy was "a wholly non-literary intimacy,"[26] and there is no reason to doubt him. Nor is their personal relationship important compared to the influence of James on Ford's work. When the relationship came to a close, it was largely because of Violet Hunt, whom James knew as well as, if not better than, he knew Ford.

Ford's early borrowings from James are both derivative and imitative. The later works show a new imprint: *The Good Soldier* develops the latencies of the international theme to make a sexual tragedy out of the materials of social comedy, and the Tietjens tetralogy makes a new and surprising use of the Jamesian technique of developing nodal situations almost totally by dialogue. One cannot help seeing Ford in his early novels as a kind of Ulysses, held captive by Polyphemus, the Cyclops whose name meant "much fame." At one point during his captivity Ulysses is asked *his* name by the giant. He replies, "Noman"; but later, after he has put out Polyphemus's eye and escaped to sea, he taunts the giant by saying that his name is Ulysses, his home

Ithaca, and so forth. With this ceremony he regains his identity. And, similarly, Ford was to regain his identity from his Cyclops, for he was to break free of James and write *The Good Soldier.* Yet that novel is at the same time a testimony to what Ford learned from James, for it is the Jamesian novel that Henry James was incapable of writing.

For a number of years Ford apparently thought that both James's subject matter and his method could be his. Like James, he wanted to be the historian of manners. He wanted, as he put it, "to register my own times in terms of my own time."[27] And it is from this desire that a large part of his admiration for James stems, for the greatness of the master, "to put it succinctly, is that of the historian—the historian of one, of two, and possibly of three or more, civilizations."[28] "He, more than anybody, has faithfully rendered his observations for us."[29] But neither James's perspective nor his rendering of society could be Ford's. And the lesson he finally learned from James was just that. Jamesian dialogue, which in the novels of the master produced conflict, only impeded conflict in the novels of the pupil. The ceremonial nature of the talk was inhibiting. Ford's characters were never able to broach the complex sexual matters that they faced. Finally, with the introduction of his narrator Dowell in *The Good Soldier,* Ford was able to achieve his characteristic tone of passionately well-informed gossip, and with that step he left behind him the pallid and thinly ethical Jamesian descriptions of society which marked his early novels.

As Graham Greene has remarked, *The Good Soldier* and *Parade's End* are "almost the only adult novels dealing with the sexual life that have been written in English. They are almost our only reply to Flaubert."[30] James, writing in the *Notebooks* of his plans for *The Wings of the Dove,* had said: "But one can do so little with English adultery—it is so much less inevitable, and so much more ugly in all its hiding and lying side."[31] Ford's answer is *The Good Soldier* and *Parade's End.* Influences, Ford once remarked, "are queer things, and there is no knowing when or where they may take you."[32]

Ford began writing *The Good Soldier* on his fortieth birthday, December 17, 1913. Up to this point in his life, he tells us in a

Dedicatory Letter to a 1927 edition, he had "written rather desultorily a number of books—a great number—but they had all been in the nature of *pastiches,* of pieces of rather precious writing, or of *tours de force.*"[33] He had, in fact, published thirty books. Roughly one-half of them had been novels. Now he was to try to put all he knew into one book: "I sat down to show what I could do—and *The Good Soldier* resulted." The novel was a technical achievement he was never again quite to match. "Judged as a technical feat alone," Walter Allen comments in *The English Novel,* "*The Good Soldier* is dazzling, as near perfection as a novel can be."[34] In his Dedicatory Letter, Ford remarks, ". . . I was astounded at the work I must have put into the construction of the book, at the intricate tangle of references and cross-references." *The Good Soldier* is the classic well-made novel—no dangling plot strands, no word that does not contribute to the story—and it represents Ford's achievement in novelistic form at its highest.

When war broke out in 1914, Ford with patriotic fervor hastily wrote two books of propaganda, *When Blood is Their Argument: An Analysis of Prussian Culture* and *Between St. Dennis and St. George: A Sketch of Three Civilizations.* Then he obtained a commission in the Welch Regiment (not the Coldstream Guards, as his Letter implies). *The Good Soldier* was published in 1915 while he was in the service. He had originally entitled it "The Saddest Story," but John Lane, his publisher, objected that the title was a bad one for a book in wartime. Ford half-jokingly suggested "The Good Soldier." The title stuck.

Ford's 1927 Dedicatory Letter was addressed to Stella Bowen, the Australian painter with whom he lived for nine years. Ford first met Stella in London nine months before the Armistice. She was a young art student from Adelaide, and a member of a loosely knit group of writers, painters, and musicians for whom Ezra Pound was a chief mentor. Ford was then a forty-four-year-old captain. By 1919 time was running out on him in England, though he did not quite yet realize it. Not merely his personal life with Violet Hunt, but his English literary life, was drawing to a close. The literary establishment, which had in the past confined itself to a show of hostile levity toward him, now turned its back completely. "I was no longer a literary figure," he remarks in *It Was the Nightingale,* "and I was battered and mournful." "At the literary teas," he goes on, "I must have been as a ghost. Occasionally a man—presumably a writer—would address a word to me. They would even ask me if I hadn't once written something."[35] "Poor Ford," Stella Bowen comments in her biography, *Drawn from Life* (1941). "If ever a man needed a fairy godmother, he did."[36] They went to live together in the English countryside, first at Red Ford, Sussex, in what Ford described as "a leaky-roofed, rat-ridden, seventeenth century, five-shilling a week, moribund labourer's cottage,"[37] prompting Ezra Pound to write:

> Beneath the sagging roof
> The stylist has taken shelter,
> Unpaid, uncelebrated,
> At last from the world's welter.

> Nature received him;
> With a placid and uneducated mistress
> He exercises his talents
> And the soil meets his distress.

> The haven from sophistication and contentions
> Leaks through its thatch;
> He offers succulent cooking;
> The door has a creaking latch.[38]

Later Ford and Stella pooled their money and bought a cottage at Bedham. Violet Hunt and her friends journeyed to Sussex to peer at them over a fence.

Ford "wanted to dig potatoes and raise pigs and never write another book. Wanted to start a new home. Wanted a child." Stella made these possible for him. She even gave him the courage to write again, and he began *The Marsden Case.* "He was a writer —a complete writer—and nothing but a writer. And he never even felt sure of his gift."[39]

Their daughter Julia was born in 1920. They spent two more years in Sussex. Then Harold Monro offered his small villa at Cap Ferrat at a nominal rent, and the sale of *The Marsden Case* enabled them to say goodbye to England. In Provence Ford began

the first of his four Christopher Tietjens books. Within a year
they settled in Paris. Here he continued to write his tetralogy and
began the *transatlantic review.*

Ezra Pound put him again in contact with the literary world.
In 1923 T. S. Eliot, then editor of the *Criterion,* wrote him express-
ing interest in publishing a section of Ford's unpublished "History
of British Literature." In the course of one letter, Eliot modestly
remarks: "There are *I* think about 30 good lines in The Waste
Land. Can you find them? The rest is ephemeral."[40] His next letter
thanks Ford for his "flattering remarks" on the poem.

It is a great deal to find that there is one person, and that person
yourself, who regards the poem as having pretensions to coherence
and unity at all. It has been unfavorably received in this country; the
critics here are too timid even to admit they dislike it. As for the lines
I mention, you need not scratch your head over them. They are the
29 lines of the water-dripping song in the last part.[41]

We assume that Mr. Eliot was writing with the critical license of
one poet corresponding with another.

Stella and Ford began to hold open house on Thursday in the
various apartments in which they lived. Sisley Huddleston later
described "the parties in the studio of the rue Notre-Dame-des
Champs," the apartment of Dorothy and Ezra Pound, later of
Stella and Ford. "A phonograph was set going and the guests
danced to their heart's content." Ford "was indefatigable: a trifle
heavy, but enthusiastic." Pound was "a supreme dancer." "If it
is not too disrespectful, I used to think of Ford and Pound, when
they danced, as the Elephant and the Mule."[42] Ford and Stella
also made arrangements with the owner of a *bal musette* so that
they and their friends could have the place to themselves one
night a week. Hemingway describes it in the early pages of *The
Sun Also Rises,* putting Ford and Stella into the novel as Mr.
and Mrs. Braddocks. According to Gertrude Stein, "it was Ford
who once said of Hemingway, he comes and sits at my feet and
praises me. It makes me nervous."[43]

Other young men also came and sat at his feet, as his daughter
Julia remembers: "the aspiring unknowns, hungry but vital,
with whose work Ford was ever prepared to take endless trouble."[44] She also remembers being allowed, as a child of seven

or eight, to "help" Ford prepare for his daily stint of writing. In Paris "this usually took the form of sitting beside him while he played game after game of solitaire." She "had to be absolutely quiet, because it was understood this was just an occupation to keep his hands busy while he thought out his next chapter or article." She was, however, allowed silently to point out possible moves that she thought he had missed. In Provence, some years later, he prepared in another way: irrigating his vegetable patch at the Villa Paul early in the morning. "The social amenities were for later in the day, when his writing was done—that terrible, all-consuming writing that had to be completed whatever the cost."

His daughter remembers him as "very fair, and large, and quiet, his voice soft and his movements gentle and slow. His hair was so fair that when it finally turned white, nobody really noticed, his eyes were very blue and he had that white English skin that turns ruddy when exposed to the sun. His voice was somewhat breathless and low." He was no longer the "longish, leanish, fairish young Englishman" described by Henry James. But he was once more the center of literary activity. Meanwhile, the Tietjens series was coming to a close, as were his years with Stella.

The basic situation of *The Good Soldier* is one psychological progression involving two women and a man. This is the characteristic situation of all of Ford's novels. In *The Good Soldier* a series of such situations makes the plot complex and gives depth to meaning. Edward Ashburnham, the "good soldier," is a lachrymose rake, and his dilemma, profound and tragic, is that he is caught in a vise between public codes and private passion, between social and moral restraints and, as he puts it near the end of the novel, his "mad passion to find an ultimately satisfying woman." From such an intensely personal affair Ford creates a "tale of passion" which ends by being a depth study of English manners and of the sexual conscience of nineteenth-century England.

Parade's End is another matter. Its subject is no less than the advent of the twentieth century, and within its pages lies one of the great tales of modern love to appear in fiction. It also reveals the personal history of a man broken by the war and by society, reflecting not merely the predicament of its major figure, Christopher Tietjens, but also that of its author. Yet Ford, like his hero, survived both the fatigues of war and the hostile acts of

society. Indeed, he was one of the few established prewar writers
to come through 1914-1918 with his imaginative faculties strained
but intact.

As in *The Good Soldier,* the basic situation in *Parade's End*
revolves around two women and a man. Christopher Tietjens'
desires and his sense of duty are caught between his wife Sylvia,
a Catholic, and Valentine Wannop, the young woman he has
come to love. Again, as in *The Good Soldier,* the plot can be said
simply to be the ruin of one man's "small household cockleshell."
Christopher's civilian life crumbles: his marriage founders on his
wife's adultery; his friendships crack under friends' duplicities;
his government post of trust is undermined by betrayal. But events
here are not merely personal; they are interwoven with the events
of the Great War and the cataclysm affecting an entire civilization as its ruling class crumbles. Domestic melodrama is made to
seem a reflector, an index, of the break-up of order and tradition.
We are watching the disappearance not only of the sacred vows
of marriage but of all ceremonies: all rites, drills, routines,
"parades" by which society preserves its health. The stately
Edwardian world, with its leisure, its culture, its hereditary ruling
class, disappears in the aftermath of the Great War.

With an almost paranoid intensity Ford captures the flux of
this moral and social disintegration: its inconsistencies, its petty
persecutions, its major disasters. With the breakdown of codes of
decorum, tradition, fair play, idealism embodied in social forms,
the ruling class proves itself unfit to rule. A class of opportunists
arises to take its place, no better, perhaps worse. The *nouveaux
riches* appropriate as well as scatter culture. Civilization is driven
underground.

The pattern of *Parade's End* is epic: four novels unfold a history
of England during the years 1912-1920. The cast of characters is
large. The settings include a railway carriage occupied by two civil
servants, a golf course with a prime minister and invading suffragettes, the parsonage of an insane clergyman, a horse cart moving
through the foggy English countryside, the command hut of a
supply depot in France, an English girls' school, the trenches in
France, the London of Armistice Day, and a farm in the English
countryside with a paralyzed man lying beneath an open thatched
shelter. Yet for all these settings, the major scenes are really

few in number. Time in the novels is also strictly limited. *Some Do not . . .* covers a long weekend in the country plus a day four years later; *No More Parades* encompasses less than twenty-four hours at a supply depot in France; *A Man Could Stand Up*— spans an hour in the trenches in France and several hours in London on Armistice Day; and *The Last Post* incorporates roughly one hour of present time. But the major unity of the four novels comes through the figure of Christopher Tietjens, Ford's mytho-poeic hero.

Christopher is by birth one with the ruling class, but he does not share in its derelictions. Ford deliberately places him on the periphery of society—"the last English Tory," the last representa-tive of tradition, in effect an anachronism. "He's so formal he can't do without all the conventions there are, and so truthful he can't use half of them." If Sylvia cannot divorce Christopher because she is Catholic, Christopher is equally bound to her by his code of "some do not." For his honesty Christopher is hounded —by Sylvia, who accuses him of wanting "to play the part of Jesus Christ"; by Brownie, a bank official who refuses to honor his gentleman's overdraft; by a myriad of equally petty persecu-tors. His goodness is translated as immorality, his fidelity viewed as witless behavior.

Like Dowell, the narrator of *The Good Soldier,* who is left dazed by events, Christopher suffers mental agonies, first because of the conduct of Sylvia, who refuses to tell him whether their child is his, and who goes off with another man, only to demand to be taken back; then because of events in the war in the trenches and behind the lines where he is responsible for feeding, housing, equipping, and transporting troops. He suffers so intensely from Sylvia's actions that he wonders if he has had a stroke; events so crowd him that he questions his sanity, but it is the world, not Christopher, that is going insane. Then in the war, his brilliant memory is damaged and he has to reconstruct the past. So too he will have to reconstruct his life, and with it Valentine Wannop's, in a world that is falling apart.

No easy summary can do more than suggest the plot of *Parade's End,* for the thread of narrative runs in Christopher's mind, which like a seismograph records the shocks and quakes of personal and public disaster. It is a mind very much like Ford's own—weary, sensitive, sentimental; above all, intelligent. But though Christopher is Ford's fictional counterpart, his dramatized self, reflecting in his story many of Ford's concerns, including Catholicism, he is not merely the author thinly disguised. Such a figure is found in the poet Gringoire in *No Enemy,* a semiautobiographical "reconstructionary tale" which reveals many of the same attitudes and some of the events of *Parade's End.* The point is worth making, for Ford's imaginative cast of mind was such that in his fiction he transcended the limitations of personal fantasy. If, like Christopher, Ford longed for the pastoral world, for the seventeenth century and the sanctuary of Herbert's "Sweet day, so cool, so calm, so bright / The Bridal of the earth and sky," he also knew that for himself only one return to yesterday was possible.

In the last decade of his life Ford divided his time between America and France. With him was Janice Biala, the American painter, who illustrated his two volumes of memoirs, *Provence* (1935) and *Great Trade Routes* (1937). He still had his dream of buying a small house in his beloved Provence, and in one of his last letters to his daughter, written from Olivet College in Michigan, where he was visiting lecturer in literature during 1937-1938, he said: "We are desperately trying to save up enough to buy a cottage by Lyon where they are cheap and not too far from Paris, and yet still in the Midi . . . About Valence ou le Midi commence. We are tired of wandering for ever without a home. . . ."[45]

At Olivet College Ford completed *The March of Literature* in July of 1938. In the Dedicatory Letter to the volume he calls himself "an old man mad about writing—in the sense that Hokusai called himself an old man mad about painting." To the end of his life Ford believed what today is too easily forgotten: that there is a community of letters and that literary production is essentially a communal process. Indeed, his own career, as critic and guide to the young, but more especially as novelist, is a testimony to that belief.

Ford spent freely of himself as a teacher—in his endless volumes of literary criticism and reminiscence, in his constant association with young writers—novices learning a profession—and in his final gift to the young, *The March of Literature.* In his last years he was the *cher maître* of a group of American writers, including Allen

Tate and Caroline Gordon. At Olivet College he strolled the campus, as Robie Macauley has said, "like a pensioned veteran of forgotten wars."[46] The elder statesman of English letters was in eclipse. But he was still associating with the young, and he was still talking, "lecturing" as he had all his life.

Thirty years earlier his voice was already being heard, for it was Ford's talk in 1908 that kept Ezra Pound daily climbing Campden Hill to visit him. Pound had gone to England to learn from Yeats. In his own words, he "stayed to learn from Yeats and Ford."

Ford himself never forgot what he learned from Conrad and James. The community of letters was for him a tangible community in which one man helped another. "For a quarter of a century," he remarked in 1916, "I have kept before me one unflinching aim—to register my own times in terms of my own time, and still more to urge those who are better poets and better prosewriters than myself to have the same aim."[47] For over twenty years more, wherever there was talk of literature in the English-speaking world, there was also the voice of Ford. And now that the voice is quiet, there remain *The Good Soldier* and *Parade's End*.

"THE GOOD SOLDIER"

TWO

The Art of Narrative

"Is there any point to which you would wish to draw my attention?"

"To the curious incident of the dog in the night-time."

"The dog did nothing in the night-time."

"That was the curious incident," remarked Sherlock Holmes.

THE MEMOIRS OF SHERLOCK HOLMES

"From the death of Swift to the publication of the 'Way of All Flesh,'" Ford once said, "there is very little to be found in the English novel that is not slightly unworthy of the whole attention of a grown-up man—say a grown-up Frenchman."[1] Ford's admiration for Butler stemmed from the realism of his portrayal, basically from his ability to see behind the Victorian proprieties and to record what he saw. V. S. Pritchett has called Butler's novel "one of the time-bombs of literature," remarking that it lay unpublished for thirty years, "waiting to blow up the Victorian family and with it the whole great pillared and balustraded edifice of the Victorian novel."[2] *The Way of All Flesh* was published in 1903, two years after Queen Victoria's death and one year after the author's. In his story of a Victorian clergyman's family Butler attacked the sanctimonious inhumanity, the creeping spiritual and emotional paralysis, the dry rot he found beneath the decorous facade. Twelve years after the publication of *The Way of All Flesh* Ford turned his attention upon another British institution, the country gentleman. *The Good Soldier* was published in 1915, the year in which Joyce began *Ulysses* and Virginia Woolf embarked on her literary career with *The Voyage Out.* There was nothing quite like it in earlier English fiction—either in complexity of treatment or depth of awareness or in the probing of a subject matter that in England had been reserved for the smoking room or small-hour confidences between husband and wife.

The Good Soldier is a *Madame Bovary* told from the viewpoint of the deceived husband. For John Dowell, the deceived narrator, there is domestic tragedy: a desultory courtship, an elopement in which his bride keeps him waiting two hours at the foot of a rope ladder while she packs her trunks, an unconsummated marriage, twelve years of bondage to a feigned illness, cuckoldom. But *The Good Soldier* is more than the story of the American John Dowell and his wife Florence. It is also the story of their relationship with three other people: Captain and Mrs. Ashburnham, the "better sort" of British couple—"good country people"—with whom they associated on the continent and in the German bathing towns; and the Ashburnhams' ward, Nancy Rufford. There is an international episode of nine years' duration, which is an ironic modulation on the moral and cultural antinomies of Henry James. Again the ingredients are those of melodrama: sexual imbroglios, lechery, adultery, a second feigned illness, blackmail, a gambling debt, an incurable infatuation, two suicides, one case of insanity. The result, however, is anything but melodrama. It is a comic spectacle filled with pathos, a "tale of passion" told by a narrator who is ill-equipped to tell of passion and enacted by people whose lives, one would say, were very little concerned with passion. It is also, one should point out, the story of an author who cannot accept traditional definitions of evil.

In his 1927 Dedicatory Letter Ford remarks that he wanted "to do for the English novel what in *Fort comme la Mort* Maupassant had done for the French."[3] Maupassant's novel is the story of Oliver Bertin, a portrait painter, who falls in love with the Countess de Guilleroy and has an affair of years' duration with her. As time passes, the daughter of the countess, Annette, grows up to resemble the mother so closely in appearance that Bertin begins to fall in love with her. Realizing what is happening, and also aware that it is largely the image of the mother and not the girl herself he is falling in love with, he tries to master his feelings and desires. In the end he becomes emotionally disturbed and is accidentally run over by a carriage while in this condition.

The obvious parallels to *The Good Soldier* are the triangle situation spanning two generations and Edward Ashburnham's ruling passion for his ward, Nancy Rufford, which drives him eventually to suicide. Ashburnham's desires, like those of his French counterpart, derive from conventionally hidden and habitually suppressed feelings which lie in the recesses of the heart, and which, aroused by sexual passion, are circumscribed by moral ambiguity. "The heart of another is a dark forest," Ford was fond of quoting, and he originally intended "Another Dark Forest" to be the title of *The New Humpty-Dumpty*.[4] It would have been more appropriate as the title of *The Good Soldier*.

Finally, there is Ford's intention, underscored by his reference to Maupassant, to explore his subject matter in terms of manners and customs and cultural patterns peculiarly English. Ford comments in his Dedicatory Letter that he had the novel "hatching" within himself for a decade and that it is a true story. In an earlier book on the character of the English, *The Spirit of the People* (1907), he told the story of a married couple—"good people"—with whom he stayed in the country. The husband had fallen in love with his ward and between the two an attachment had developed. "P—— had not merely never 'spoken to' his ward; but his ward, I fancy, had spoken to Mrs. P——. At any rate the situation had grown impossible, and it was arranged that Miss W—— should take a trip around the world with some friends who were making that excursion." P—— asked Ford to accompany them to the station on the morning of departure because he was afraid of a "scene." What Ford goes on to describe is the incident from which he derives the final parting of Ashburnham and Nancy. They ride to the station in a dog cart, Ford seated behind. The conversation is desultory, casual, without any reference to what has happened. At the station the two part without any show of emotion; he does not even say goodbye to her. But after the train has pulled out P—— goes into the station to pick up a package and then drives off without his rider. "He had forgotten me," Ford comments, "but he had kept his end up."

Now, in its particular way, this was a very fine achievement; it was playing the game to the bitter end. It was, indeed, very much the bitter end, since Miss W—— died at Brindisi on the voyage out, and P—— spent the next three years at various places on the continent where nerve cures are attempted. That I think proved that they "cared"—

but what was most impressive in the otherwise commonplace affair, was the silence of the parting. I am not concerned to discuss the essential ethics of such positions, but it seems to me that at that moment of separation a word or two might have saved the girl's life and the man's misery without infringing the eternal verities. It may have been desirable, in the face of the verities—the verities that bind and gather all nations and all creeds—that the parting should have been complete and decently arranged. But a silence so utter: a so demonstrative lack of tenderness, seems to me to be a manifestation of a national characteristic that is almost appalling.[5]

Behind Ford's true life account of denied sexuality, as behind his complex restatement of this same relationship in *The Good Soldier,* lie the typical attitudes and gestures, the social assumptions, the class mentality of the nineteenth century. As one critic of the period put it, it was an age in which broad appearances were imposing and everyday facts sordid. The Victorians averted their eyes from the ugliness and the injustices before them. Concealments were fostered by the social graces, the amenities and urbanities, the decorum so highly prized. Yet, as Osbert Sitwell has remarked, "the indictment against the Victorian age is not that it was not comfortable, or, in spite of its many cruelties, kindly; but that it left its debts, mental, moral, and physical, to be paid by a later generation."[6] It is this legacy of his own generation that Ford examines in *The Good Soldier.*

In his treatment of the post-Victorian gentleman, Ford was not concerned with writing a propagandistic attack, as Samuel Butler was in *The Way of All Flesh.* And although he seems to have created the immediate situation of *The Good Soldier* from the resources of his own life, his relationship with his subject matter was on a different plane from Butler's. In the course of his literary career Ford was involved for largely personal reasons in a long romance with the concept of the English gentleman. Yet in his hero, Edward Ashburnham, the "good soldier," Ford portrayed a figure that Butler would have sanctioned and that today has become the common property of contemporary novelists. "You meet an English gentleman at your golf club," Ford remarks in his book on Conrad.

He is beefy, full of health, the moral of the boy from an English Public School of the finest type. You discover, gradually, that he is hopelessly neurasthenic, dishonest in matters of small change, but unexpectedly self-sacrificing, a dreadful liar, but a most painfully careful student of lepidoptera and, finally, from the public prints, a bigamist who once, under another name, hammered on the Stock Exchange. . . . Still, there he is, the beefy, full-fed fellow, moral of an English Public School product.[7]

The moral and psychological contradictions in the character of Ford's public-school figure, though mere illustrative examples, are essentially of the same kind as those of his Captain Ashburnham.

Ashburnham is one of a long line of Ford heroes who are "gentlemen of honor," kind, gentle, generous, idealistic men. He differs in an important way from Ford's earlier heroes by being one with his social milieu, instead of an eccentric alien (Robert Grimshaw in *A Call*), a social reformer (Sergius Macdonald in *The New Humpty-Dumpty*), or a conscious meddler in the lives of others (George Moffat in *The Benefactor*), though significantly he shares with them the same vaguely defined feelings of good will and social purpose.

To realize such a figure as Ashburnham in fiction, you need a method. As Ford says in the Conrad book: "You must first get him in with a strong impression, and then work backwards and forwards over his past. . . ."[8] The immediate context of Ford's remarks on disrupted chronology is Conrad's and Ford's mutually held theory of Impressionism, with its emphasis on psychological realism: "it became very early evident to us [Conrad and Ford] that what was the matter with the Novel, and the British novel in particular, was that it went straight forward, whereas in your gradual making acquaintanceship with your fellows you never do go straight forward."[9] Other contexts as meaningful and significant suggest themselves. By moving backward and forward with the tenses of memory, Ford achieves an ordering not so much of events as of their meanings. Gradually he peels off, layer by layer, the protective covering of civilization—manners, public action, lip service to codes—to reveal the passionate duplicities underneath.

Such freedom in arrangement permits the writer to elongate the moment and thus to accommodate all the particulars of psychological experience, much in the same way the stream-of-consciousness suspends time to clinically analyze an experience. It allows the juxtaposition of imaginative syntax. And juxtaposition produces what Ford chose to call *progression d'effet* (gallicized English for "progression of effects"). Such climactic arrangements of effects and such controlled psychological revelation became possible for Ford only when he introduced a first-person narrator into his fiction.

That wise old romancer of the novel, Henry James, once remarked that, for the writer of fiction, the use of the first-person narrator opens the backdoor on "the darkest abyss." It invites the author to be self-indulgent: to introduce material that interests him but is irrelevant to his story, and to construct episodes for their own sake. "The first person, in the long piece, is a form foredoomed to looseness."[10] But James wrote before Ford proved him wrong in *The Good Soldier*. In Ford's hands first-person narration produces tightness of form and the means of penetration into the heart of man. In his early novels the omniscient point of view had often encouraged Ford to improvise recklessly. In *The Good Soldier* his first-person narrator, the American John Dowell—like his hero Ashburnham created out of the resources of Ford's own personality—enabled him for the first time to view his hero objectively (in effect he had to silence him) and to build his story around crucial psychological episodes.

The form of *The Good Soldier*—disrupted chronology and emergent psychology—evolves from the narrator's conscious attempt to recall a sequence of events, the meanings of which were veiled from him as they occurred. For nine years Dowell was unaware of the adulterous liaisons of his wife; he read only the surface of her relationship with Captain Ashburnham. Now, facing the ruin of his "small household cockleshell," Dowell reconstructs the past, shifting backward and forward over those years during which he and his wife Florence associated with Edward and Leonora Ashburnham. The very first paragraph of the novel sets the conditions of the narrative to follow:

This is the saddest story I have ever heard. We had known the Ashburnhams for nine seasons of the town of Nauheim with an extreme intimacy—or, rather, with an acquaintanceship as loose and easy and yet as close as a good glove's with your hand. My wife and I knew Captain and Mrs. Ashburnham as well as it was possible to know anybody, and yet, in another sense, we knew nothing at all about them. This is, I believe, a state of things only possible with the English people of whom, till today, when I sit down to puzzle out what I know of this sad affair, I knew nothing whatever. Six months ago I had never been to England, and certainly, I had never sounded the depths of an English heart. I had known the shallows. [p. 3] (p. 15)*

Here we have the nexus out of which the story grows as it moves backward and forward through a maze of events. We have its duration and its locale, and we know something of the outcome: "This is the saddest story I have ever heard." Then in one image Ford creates a picture of the society these four inhabited; theirs was "an acquaintanceship as loose and easy and yet as close as a good glove's with your hand." This image drastically shrinks the limits of the relevant world. We are in a society where one is judged by the social graces, by good manners and grooming; by one's luggage and the tie one wears and the newspaper one reads. Its people inhabit a world of convention in which they are judged as much, if not more, by what they *do not* say as by what they do say. There is an opposition, even a polarity as it is finally adumbrated in *The Good Soldier,* between appearance and reality. For the Dowells knew the Ashburnhams "as well as it was possible to know anybody, and yet, in another sense, we knew nothing at all about them."

It was Ford's belief that, above all, necessity must dominate the pattern of a work of fiction. This is what he meant when, in *Joseph Conrad: A Personal Remembrance,* he spoke of "justification":

Before everything a story must convey a sense of inevitability; that which happens in it must seem to be the only thing that could have happened. Of course a character may cry, "If I had then acted differently how different everything would now be." The problem of the author is to make his then action the only action that character could have taken. It must be inevitable, because of his character, because of

---

*Dual page references are provided throughout for *The Good Soldier.* In *all* instances the *first* reference is to the American edition (New York: Knopf [Vintage Book], 1957) and the second to the English edition, *The Bodley Head Ford Madox Ford, Volume I* (London: Bodley Head, 1962).

his ancestry, because of past illness or on account of the gradual coming together of the thousand small circumstances by which Destiny, who is inscrutable and august, will push us into one certain predicament.[11]

Narrative necessity demands that Ford justify the contradiction between appearance and reality. The latter part of the first paragraph of *The Good Soldier* contains a half-stated syllogism based on the classic cliché of British reticence ("This is a state of things only possible with the English people . . ."). So this early in the novel Ford begins to establish the plausibility of a deceived narrator who must piece together his story bit by bit.[12] Dowell "had never sounded the depths of an English heart"; he "had known the shallows." The entire novel is a tissue of such "justifications" involving difficult premises.

The second paragraph of *The Good Soldier* is even more carefully reasoned. Above all, Ford wants to establish the actuality of the world he is to describe.

I don't mean to say that we were not acquainted with many English people. Living, as we perforce lived, in Europe, and being, as we perforce were, leisured Americans, which is as much as to say that we were un-American, we were thrown very much into the society of the nicer English. Paris, you see, was our home. Somewhere between Nice and Bordighera provided yearly winter quarters for us, and Nauheim always received us from July to September. You will gather from this statement that one of us had, as the saying is, a "heart," and from the statement that my wife is dead, that she was the sufferer.   [pp. 3-4] (p. 15)

The logic of the paragraph stems from the emphasis behind the double use of "perforce," the intimacy of "you see," and the credit for deduction given in "you will gather."

The ensuing paragraphs give a logic of a different order—to use Ford's words, of past illness and age and ancestry and, finally, of character. Captain Ashburnham also "had a heart." The ostensible reason for his illness was "too much hard sportsmanship in his youth." The reason Florence gave was a storm at sea upon their first crossing to Europe; doctor's orders confined her to the continent. And so on, through the ages of the four principal characters and their family trees. All of this presents the smooth surface of habitually accepted fact.

By the time the eight compactly written pages of the first chapter are over, Ford has given us the counters, the indices, to which the narrator will refer again and again throughout the novel. We know that Edward Ashburnham and Florence Dowell are dead and that there has been an affair between them. We know too that the narrator, John Dowell, has been deceived. We have gleamings of the character of Florence Dowell and Leonora and Edward Ashburnham. We know something too of the character of the narrator, John Dowell. We have a suggestion of the future life of Leonora. It is almost as if Ford had made true his statement about the form of the *nouvelle* in his book on James: "The whole of the story, of the murder, of the liaison, of the bequest, might well be related in the opening of the first paragraph. The author might then devote the whole of the rest of the 'action' to the consideration of the mental states of the various characters affected."[13] But Ford's narrative improves on this theory—because the whole of the affair is never really given until the very last word of the novel.

As sophisticated and complex as it may seem, Ford's art bears broad resemblances to the traditional art of storytelling. Ford asks us to imagine a storyteller seated before a fire with a group of people around him. As Dowell tells his tale he tries to reconstruct it as he has heard parts of it from the mouths of different people; this is the narrative convention established in Chapter II. The ostensible excuse for the fragmentation of plot is the imperfection of human observation and memory; the story came to Dowell in bits and pieces. The process of remembering is necessary for the story to be told at all, for like all good storytellers, Dowell claims that his story is true; in this case, as we know from what Ford has said, part of it really was. But more important than the factual events from which the story arose is the delicate interplay of various devices. Ford's version depends less on its factual basis than on its psychological telling point by point. Governing the meaning is the insistence of the narrator on verisimilitude, on the limitations of his knowledge.

That of course is only conjecture but I think the conjecture is pretty well justified. You have the fact that. . . .   [p. 116] (p. 107)

I am not going to make up speeches. To follow her psychological development I think we must allow that. . . .   [p. 213] (p. 185)

Such a handicap becomes in Ford's hands an advantage. He fashions into a subtle instrument of moral probing Conrad's device of narrative by conjecture.

The method of the traditional storyteller was to tell his story by chronological sequence. By a gradual unfolding of events, and by a withholding of vital information until the proper moment, he aroused his listener and held his interest. Hero and obstacle clash, the impending crisis arrives, actions resolve. Complication, rising action, denouement, falling action: all these occur in the simplest tale. But they do not occur in *The Good Soldier,* at least not in this order. What Ford does constantly is to cut the ground from under any narrative sequence of physical action. He dislocates time, rearranges events, foreshadows in outline actions to come. Few incidents are related at length; many are nothing but pluperfect summaries. Dialogue is minimal. Significance lies not in the events themselves but in the unfolding of their substratum: a series of clues leading to the discovery of the inner nature of man.

The suspense of *The Good Soldier* is the suspense of human deception, of a narrator who has been deceived and who now, through the process of writing, is trying to reconstruct what happened and to reëxamine events in the shifting light of his belated awareness. As he learns more about the events, we learn more about the disparity between the appearances of this society (tradition, fair play, idealism shown in social forms) and some of its underlying realities (adultery, malice, cruelty, deceit).

It is the slow but passionate act of reconstruction that occupies the foreground of a reader's attention and gives plausibility to an increasingly implausible series of events. Forestalling the reader's refusal to believe, there is the narrator's doubting voice, his incredulity that what has happened could really have happened.

Good God, what did they all see in him?—for I swear that was all there was of him, inside and out; though they said he was a good soldier. Yet Leonora adored him with a passion that was like an agony, and hated him with an agony that was bitter as the sea. How could he rouse anything like a sentiment, in anybody?

[p. 26] (pp. 33-34)

Dowell, aware that he has been cuckolded by Ashburnham, baffled that he could be, angry that he has been, is unable to understand what it was *they all* saw in him. It is his questioning that helps sustain a willing suspension of disbelief as the story becomes more and more unbelievable.

It might almost be said that Ford has heightened the implausibility of his story for artistic purposes which transcend realism. Here is a man who was almost farcically gulled: who eloped with a bride who kept him waiting two hours at the foot of a rope ladder while she packed her trunks, who was tricked by his bride's feigned illness into twelve years of unconsummated marriage, and who, for nine years, was oblivious to the sexual imbroglios surrounding him. Underneath the relationship of Dowell with the Ashburnhams and their ward, Nancy Rufford, there was lechery, adultery, suicide, insanity. "It is melodrama; but I can't help it" (p. 110) [p. 103], the narrator says at one point. But Ford can help it. The emphasis is not on events themselves but on the tension between past and present, between what was thought to be and what is now seen to have been. The form of *The Good Soldier* frees the story of its melodramatic content, the stage properties which accompany the liaisons, just as it takes the "strain" off the style.

Permanence? Stability! I can't believe it's gone. I can't believe that that long, tranquil life, which was just stepping a minuet, vanished in four crashing days at the end of nine years and six weeks. . . . No, indeed, it can't be gone. You can't kill a minuet de la cour. You may shut up the musicbook, close the harpsichord; in the cupboard and presses the rats may destroy the white satin favours. The mob may sack Versailles; the Trianon may fall, but surely the minuet—the minuet itself is dancing away into the furthest stars, even as our minuet of the Hessian bathing places must be stepping itself still. Isn't there any heaven where old beautiful dances, old beautiful intimacies prolong themselves? Isn't there any Nirvana pervaded by the faint thrilling of instruments that have fallen into the dust of wormwood but that yet had frail, tremulous, and everlasting souls?

No, by God, it is false! It wasn't a minuet that we stepped; it was a prison—a prison full of screaming hysterics, tied down so that they might not outsound the rolling of our carriage wheels as we went along the shaded avenues of the Taunus Wald.

And yet I swear by the sacred name of my creator that it was true. It was true sunshine; the true music; the true plash of the fountains from the mouth of stone dolphins.   [pp. 6-7] (pp. 17-18)

Dowell is able to speak with a *de haut en bas* voice impossible under the conventions of the ordinary novel, for the limits of tone are normally the limits of social milieu. Nor is Dowell bound by the limitations of circumstance. He is not "talking" in a scene but ranging in time and space as he talks.

As Ford's narrator in the opening pages of the novel shifts his focus from one to another of the major participants in the drama to follow, he sustains his tone of incredulous bewilderment. First there is Florence, who Dowell believes must not have been out of his sight except when sleeping—and yet she must have been, "to carry on the protracted negotiations which she did carry on between Edward Ashburnham and his wife." Then the "model couple," Edward and Leonora, who ironically in all that time never spoke a word together in private: Edward, "with such honest blue eyes, such a touch of stupidity, such a warm good-heartedness!"; and Leonora, "so tall, so splendid in the saddle, so fair!"

Yes, Leonora was extraordinarily fair and so extraordinarily the real thing that she seemed too good to be true. You don't, I mean, as a rule, get it all so superlatively together. To be the county family, to look the county family, to be so appropriately and perfectly wealthy; to be so perfect in manner—even just to the saving touch of insolence that seems to be necessary. To have all that and to be all that! No, it was too good to be true.   [pp. 8-9] (p. 19)

Yet Leonora once did try to take a lover. Riding home in a carriage in the dark from a hunt ball she had a chance, but she had been unable to go through with it. " 'And I burst out crying and I cried and I cried for the whole eleven miles. Just imagine *me* crying! And just imagine me making a fool of the poor dear chap like that. It certainly wasn't playing the game, was it, now?' " (p. 9) [p. 20].

And then there was Edward, who did not even like smoking-room stories. ("Fellows come in," Dowell remarks, "and tell the most extraordinarily gross stories—so gross that they will positively give you a pain. And yet they'd be offended if you suggested that they weren't the sort of person you could trust your wife alone with.") Ashburnham was "the cleanest-looking sort of chap; an excellent magistrate, a first-rate soldier, one of the best landlords, so they said, in Hampshire, England." Dowell trusted Ashburnham with his wife—"and it was madness."

Finally there is Dowell himself, with his insistent questioning. How could Florence "have known what she knew? How could she have got to know it? To know it so fully. Heavens!" And what of Leonora's remark that she failed "the poor dear chap" in the carriage? "I don't know; I don't know; was that last remark of hers the remark of a harlot, or is it what every decent woman, county family or not county family, thinks at the bottom of her heart? Or thinks all of the time, for that matter? Who knows?" ". . . But perhaps that is what all mothers teach all daughters, not with lips but with eyes, or with heart whispering to heart." And what of Teddy Ashburnham, whom Dowell does not want to dismiss as "a brute"? Dowell doesn't believe he was. "God knows, perhaps all men are like that." But if that is true, what is Dowell to make of himself?

And yet again you have me. If poor Edward was dangerous because of the chastity of his expressions—and they say that that is always the hallmark of a libertine—what about myself? For I solemnly avow that not only have I never so much as hinted at an impropriety in my conversation in the whole of my days; and more than that, I will vouch for the cleanness of my thoughts and the absolute chastity of my life. At what, then, does it all work out? Is the whole thing a folly and a mockery? Am I no better than a eunuch or is the proper man—the man with the right to existence—a raging stallion forever neighing after his neighbour's womankind?

I don't know. And there is nothing to guide us. And if everything is so nebulous about a matter so elementary as the morals of sex, what is there to guide us in the more subtle morality of all other personal contacts, associations, and activities? Or are we meant to act on impulse alone? It is all a darkness.   [pp. 11-12] (p. 22)

It is Ford's rhetoric of narrative that produces the highly suggestive and richly textured nuances of tone in *The Good Soldier*: a rhetoric that complexly derives both from Ford's weighted structure and from the seriocomic situation of his deceived narrator, Dowell. It is through Dowell's mind that the pattern of *The Good*

Soldier develops. Basically it is a pattern of sexual conflict, both
ludicrous and tragic, pressed to the limits of credibility and controlled both by Dowell's ironic skepticism and by his fantastic
belief that he himself can somehow propitiate and correct the
tragic comic universe that surrounds him.

The strategic effectiveness of placing Dowell at the center of the
narrative can be seen in the almost Shakespearean range of diction and allusion which his presence allows Ford to employ.

> You may well ask why I write. And yet my reasons are quite many.
> For it is not unusual in human beings who have witnessed the sack
> of a city or the falling to pieces of a people to desire to set down
> what they have witnessed for the benefit of unknown heirs or of
> generations infinitely remote; or, if you please, just to get the sight
> out of their heads.   [p. 5] (p. 17)

The seemingly loose precision of *quite many,* its tone of cultured
small talk, is juxtaposed to the grand metaphor which controls
the meaning being conveyed.

> Someone has said that the death of a mouse from cancer is the whole
> sack of Rome by the Goths, and I swear to you that the breaking up
> of our little four-square coterie was such another unthinkable event.
> Supposing that you should come upon us sitting together at one of the
> little tables in front of the club house, let us say, at Homburg, taking
> tea of an afternoon and watching the miniature golf, you would have
> said that, as human affairs go, we were an extraordinary safe castle.
> We were, if you will, one of those tall ships with the white sails upon
> a blue sea, one of those things that seem the proudest and the safest
> of all the beautiful things that God has permitted the mind of men
> to frame. Where better could one take refuge? Where better?
>   [pp. 5-6] (p. 17)

Ford's language, both personal and poetic, conveys the disparity
between events, private, sexual, sordid, and their larger significance; for *The Good Soldier* is a microcosmic version of the
downfall of a highly civilized society. Hence Ford's metaphors
of civilization. "No, indeed, it can't be gone. You can't kill a
minuet de la cour. You may shut up the music-book, close the
harpsichord; in the cupboard and presses the rats may destroy
the white satin favours. The mob may sack Versailles; the
Trianon may fall . . ." (p. 6) [p. 17]. Such images, at first sug-

gestive of dimensions seemingly incongruous with the story Ford has to tell, become ultimately precise equivalents for the outcome of the tragic action to follow.

Chapter II of *The Good Soldier* presents the reader with a seemingly random selection of times and places and incidents associated in one way or another in Dowell's mind with the story he has to tell. Behind such randomness lies the calculation of art. The earliest chronological incident is Dowell's first meeting with Florence, in America; the latest incident, and the one on which the chapter closes, is Dowell's arrival, three months before the action of the novel ends, at Branshaw Teleragh, where he has come at the insistence of Leonora, who greets him as if he had "run down to lunch from a town ten miles away, instead of having come half the world over at the call of two urgent telegrams."

> The girl was out with the hounds, I think.
> And that poor devil beside me was in agony. Absolute, hopeless, dumb agony, such as passes the mind of man to imagine.
>
> [p. 20] (p. 29)

We know nothing of why Edward is in an agony—indeed, we know nothing at all yet about the situation which forms the culminating action of the book—though an inference can be drawn from the juxtaposition of Dowell's statement just before that "the girl was out with the hounds." The entire chapter is composed of equally significant clues about later events in the novel, while the overall effect of bridging time in this fashion is to unite the novel's two major "affairs" (Florence and Edward, and Nancy and Edward) into one continuous "progression of effects." The chapter begins with Dowell establishing the narrative convention on which the novel rests.

> . . . I shall just imagine myself for a fortnight or so at one side of the fireplace of a country cottage, with a sympathetic soul opposite me. And I shall go on talking, in a low voice while the sea sounds in the distance and overhead the great black flood of wind polishes the bright stars. From time to time we shall get up and go to the door and look out to the great moon and say: "Why, it is nearly as bright as in Provence!" And then we shall come back to the fireside, with just the touch of a sigh because we are not in that Provence

where even the saddest stories are gay. Consider the lamentable
history of Peire Vidal. Two years ago Florence and I motored from
Biarritz to Las Tours, which is in the Black Mountains.
                                                    [pp. 12-13] (pp. 22-23)

Provence has made the narrator think of Peire Vidal, and the
Provençal troubadour has in turn made him remember a trip
made by Florence and himself two years before to Las Tours,
where Vidal flourished. It was Florence who wanted to go to
Las Tours. She was inquisitive and interested in culture—"a
graduate of Vassar"—and she liked to talk.

She would talk about William the Silent, about Gustave the Loqua-
cious, about Paris frocks, about how the poor dressed in 1337, about
Fantin Latour, about the Paris–Lyons–Mediterranée train-de-luxe,
about whether it would be worthwhile to get off at Tarascon and go
across the windswept suspension-bridge over the Rhone to take another look at Beaucaire.   [p. 13] (p. 23)

The logic behind the inclusion of the story of Peire Vidal is never
formally stated, and we are left to make the deduction ourselves
from the paratactic construction; for the narrator learned of
Peire Vidal on one of the numerous trips he and Florence took
to historical sites, trips on which they were often accompanied
by the Ashburnhams. The story is one such as she might have
told Teddy Ashburnham while Dowell and Leonora stood listening. "I have heard her lecture Teddy Ashburnham by the hour
on the difference between a Franz Hals and a Woovermans and
why the Pre-Mycenaic statues were cubical with knots on the
top" (p. 15) [p. 25]. But this is no Isabel Archer lecturing a
Lord Warburton, as we learn shortly later, in Chapter IV,
when the two couples make a trip to the historical sites at
M——. Ford's use of the "international theme" ironically reverses both the nationality and the sex of the Jamesian innocent,
while the deportment of both sexes suggests a dimension James
no more than hinted at in his Anglo-American stories and novels.
    The effect of the opening pages of Chapter II is one of
general time, that is, of repeated action: this is how they lived
together in Europe. "Is all this digression or isn't it digression?"
Dowell asks. "Again, I don't know. You, the listener, sit opposite
me. But you are so silent. You don't tell me anything. I am, at

any rate, trying to get you to see what sort of life it was I led with Florence and what Florence was like" (p. 14) [p. 24].

Ford's rhetoric of narrative is such that nothing in this chapter is digression. Dowell only appears to ramble. Both his apparently eccentric elaboration of the story of Peire Vidal, the Provençal poet, and the odd assortment of facts he relates about Florence's family, her aunts, the Misses Hurlbird, and her Uncle John, are central to Ford's design. The flow of Ford's narrative unites these strands of meaning, together with the Jamesian motif, into a richly complex pattern. One result of such technical maneuvering is ironic juxtaposition: thus, for example, a trip at sea meant the preservation of health for Florence's Uncle John, who had heart trouble, and the destruction of health for Florence, who developed heart trouble on her wedding voyage to Europe. Thus Dowell's task was to keep Florence alive, and it was a difficult task lasting for years—yet Florence's aunts used to say that he must be the laziest man in Philadelphia. Florence was interested in culture, for which Dowell was grateful, since it kept her off exciting topics —and yet culture, to use the example of the story of Peire Vidal, meant exactly the emotions she was to avoid.

For twelve years I had to watch every word that any person uttered in any conversation and I had to head it off what the English call "things"—off love, poverty, crime, religion, and the rest of it. Yes, the first doctor that we had when she was carried off the ship at Havre assured me that this must be done. Good God, are all these fellows monstrous idiots, or is there a freemasonry between all of them from end to end of the earth? . . . That is what makes me think of that fellow Peire Vidal.

Because, of course, his story is culture and I had to head her towards culture and at the same time it's so funny and she hadn't got to laugh, and it's so full of love and she wasn't to think of love. Do you know the story? [p. 16] (p. 25)

Peire Vidal, the troubadour poet, paid court to the Chatelaine of the Lord of Las Tours who was also known as La Louve, the she-wolf, but she would have nothing to do with him. He even dressed himself in wolfskins in honor of her and went up into the mountains, but the shepherds and their dogs mistook him for a wolf and he was bitten by the dogs and beaten with clubs. So he was carried back to Las Tours and his wounds cared for. La Louve, however, was not impressed by his gesture, even though her husband remonstrated with her that it was not right to treat a great poet with indifference. Peire Vidal then tried other paths to his lady's heart, but they also failed. He declared himself Emperor of Jerusalem, but she failed to kneel and acknowledge him. Then he went off to the crusades in the Holy Land; but he never reached there. His ship went aground and the husband of La Louve had to fit out an expedition and send for his return.

And Peire Vidal fell all over the lady's bed while the husband, who was a most ferocious warrior, remonstrated some more about the courtesy that is due to great poets. But I suppose La Louve was the more ferocious of the two. Anyhow, that is all that came of it. Isn't that a story?   [p. 17] (p. 26)

Peire Vidal's harlequinade, his gestures and posturing, provides Ford with one of the novel's major cultural referents, for the tradition of courtly love gives dimension and meaning to events to follow. "And so the whole round table is begun" (p. 33) [p. 39], Florence is made to remark the first time the two couples sit down to dine together. But more important than this casual reference to Arthurian legend is the identification of Ashburnham as the knight-errant of courtly romance and the interpretation of his conduct in the light of this tradition. "He was the Cid; he was Lohengrin; he was the Chevalier Bayard" (p. 226) [p. 195], Dowell remarks in Part Four of the novel. A series of such references informs Edward's story, and his actions gain depth of meaning in the light of these suggested parallels to Romance literature.

Behind the Provençal story of Peire Vidal lies humor and pathos—for in Provence even the saddest stories are gay. But the story Dowell is telling is unrelieved by any liberating force— "yes, this is the saddest story"—unless it is that of irony: "Forgive my writing of these monstrous things in this frivolous manner. If I did not I should break down and cry" (p. 61) [p. 61]. Ultimately even the preposterous story of Peire Vidal is ironic in the context of *The Good Soldier,* for Dowell, though he lacked awareness of the true nature of events during the years the action of the novel took place, might as well have been the lord of

Las Tours waiting upon Edward Ashburnham, urging him on in his adulterous liaison with Florence. But Las Tours was a "ferocious" knight who acted from principle and his Chatelaine was a great lady worthy of a great poet's love. Dowell, on the other hand, was passionless and did nothing; Florence was hardly the ideal lady of romance; and Edward was simply an English gentleman with an uncontrollable taste for women—or was he more than that? Was there perhaps true nobility in his conduct? Was his passion for women a reflection of the religious idealism such as flourished among some of his medieval counterparts? The reader, like Dowell, can only search for the truth among possible explanations of Ashburnham's actions.

Finally, in Chapter II, there is the narrative strand of Dowell's courtship of Florence and of her family background. Again the events chosen seem at first sight merely reflections of Dowell's fancy, the results of the free play of memory and association. But, as by now the reader expects, behind the randomness lies the selection of art.

Most of Dowell's information is relayed as he tells an "anecdote" (pp. 17-19) [pp. 26-28] to give the reader some idea of what Uncle John was like. The old gentleman had heart trouble. He ran a factory in Waterbury, Connecticut, and he wanted to retire, but he was afraid of being called "the laziest man in Waterbury." So he took a trip around the world in the company of Florence, then healthy and single, and a young man named Jimmy whose job it was to attend him. Wherever he went Uncle John gave presents of oranges to people (Ford first used such a voyager in 1907 in *An English Girl*); he had crates of them taken along on the steamers on which they traveled. Uncle John "wasn't obtrusive about his heart. You wouldn't have known he had one." But he nevertheless regarded his heart as so extraordinary that he left it to science. The "joke of the matter" was that when he died at eighty-four, just five days before Florence died, it was discovered that he didn't have heart trouble. The diagnosis had been wrong. "It had certainly jumped or squeaked or something just sufficiently to take in the doctors, but it appears that that was because of an odd formation of the lungs."

The situation of Florence and Jimmy, who were unwittingly thrown together by Uncle John, will only later gradually reveal its irony to us, but given the intricate pattern of Ford's system of parallels, the story of Uncle John's illness yields an immediate irony. For suppose that Florence also had no heart trouble, and suppose that it was all deception, that again the doctors had been deceived.

Florence's duplicity, her feigned heart trouble, and the moral laxity that made it necessary in her eyes (Florence fears that Dowell will be able to recognize that she is not a virgin) are only gradually revealed to the reader through the course of Parts One and Two. Thus, for example, in Chapter V of Part One, Dowell speaks of the problem of taking care of heart patients. The context is the keeping of train schedules. Florence, he remarks, would rush with him to make connections. "But, once in the German Express, she would lean back, with one hand to her side and her eyes closed. Well, she was a good actress" (p. 48) [p. 52]. Less than a page later Dowell baldly remarks that there was nothing wrong with Edward Ashburnham's heart— and juxtaposition once more suggests that perhaps there is nothing the matter with Florence's heart either. Yet the reader has nothing more concrete to go by until Part Two, where gradually Ford parcels out relevant bits of information. Again the reader meets a maze of clues, and only slowly does the whole story emerge. Ford's technique in this particular instance is the technique behind the success of many of the incidents in *The Good Soldier*.

Part Two begins with an account of Dowell's courtship of Florence. Its method is to parody romantic love: the heroine is whisked off to a hiding place and locked in her room; there is an elopement by rope ladder; the marriage ceremony takes place at four in the morning. Now the Misses Hurlbird, introduced in Chapter II of Part One, begin to play their role more fully. During the courtship they object to Dowell's presence, and yet they will not reveal what it is specifically they object to. They can only hint at it; "national manners," as Dowell puts it, prevents their disclosure. And they can "shudder" and "wail" over Dowell's statement that he and Florence are to live in Europe, but they cannot divulge the basis for their concern. So Dowell reasons for them: "That may have been partly because they regarded Europe as a sink of iniquity, where strange laxities prevailed" (p. 81) [p. 78]. But such an explanation is clearly inadequate, for, as Dowell himself says, their protest went to extraordinary lengths.

They even, almost, said that marriage was a sacrament; but neither Miss Florence nor Miss Emily could quite bring themselves to utter the word. And they almost brought themselves to say that Florence's early life had been characterized by flirtations—something of that sort. I know I ended the interview by saying:

"I don't care. If Florence has robbed a bank I am going to marry her and take her to Europe."

And at that Miss Emily wailed and fainted. But Miss Florence, in spite of the state of her sister, threw herself on my neck and cried out:

"Don't do it, John. Don't do it. You're a good young man," and she added, whilst I was getting out of the room to send Florence to her aunt's rescue:

"We ought to tell you more. But she's our dear sister's child."

Florence, I remember, received me with a chalk-pale face and the exclamation:

"Have those old cats been saying anything against me?"

[pp. 81-82] (p. 79)

The inference is obvious (as is the understatement of "flirtations"). But why are the sisters so concerned about Europe, and what lies behind this scene? Similarly, a few pages later we have Uncle John's sermon to Dowell after the wedding breakfast.

Old Hurlbird took the opportunity to read me a full-blooded lecture, in the style of an American oration, as to the perils for young American girlhood lurking in the European jungle. He said that Paris was full of snakes in the grass, of which he had had bitter experience.

[p. 86] (p. 82)

Is this merely the puritanical mind of a New Englander reacting to the evils of Europe and the allures of Paris? Or is there something more concrete that he is alluding to? A reader coming to this section of the novel for the first time would be hard pressed to answer, as he would be to explain the aunts' reactions; and yet he already has a series of clues to provide him with a solution, for there is clearly something in the past which they feel should prevent Dowell from marrying Florence, and somehow Europe is connected with it.

Early in the chapter Florence divulges to Dowell that she wants a husband wealthy enough to procure an estate near Fordingbridge, from which her family originally came in 1688; her dream is to be an English lady. A glimpse of English home life nurtured her desire.

She had spent, it seemed, two months in Great Britain—seven weeks in touring from Stratford to Strathpeffer, and one as paying guest in an old English family near Ledbury, an impoverished, but still stately family, called Bagshawe. They were to have spent two months more in that tranquil bosom, but inopportune events, apparently in her Uncle's business, had caused their rather hurried return to Stamford. The young man called Jimmy had remained in Europe to perfect his knowledge of that continent. He certainly did: he was most useful to us afterwards.   [pp. 79-80] (p. 77)

So far no inference can be drawn. The pointed relevance of this to the scene with the aunts and to Uncle John's lecture is apt to escape the inattentive reader, especially if he has been put off by Ford's deliberate indirections. It is not so much that the reader doesn't see as that he has to read on a few pages more to realize that once again Ford's art of selection is operating and that everything is connected.

Just before Uncle John's speech about "the perils for young American girlhood lurking in the European jungle," we are given a partial revelation in the midst of another revelation; we now have it openly stated that Florence did not have heart trouble. Dowell tries to reconstruct how she arrived at her decision to play the role of a heart patient, and he wonders how she could have been so cruel.

Still, I believe there was some remorse on my account, too. Leonora told me that Florence said there was—for Leonora knew all about it, and once went so far as to ask her how she could do a thing so infamous. She excused herself on the score of an overmastering passion. Well, I always say that an overmastering passion is a good excuse for straight actions—she might have bolted with the fellow, before or after she married me. And if they had not got enough money to get along with, they might have cut their throats, or sponged on her family, though, of course, Florence wanted such a lot that it would have suited her very badly to have for a husband a clerk in a drygoods store, which was what old Hurlbird would have made of that fellow. He hated him. No, I do not think there is much excuse for Florence.
                                                    [p. 85] (pp. 81-82)

As Dowell comments about the courtship, he "had, no doubt, eye-openers enough" (p. 86) [p. 82], and no doubt now we have too. In the course of the paragraph it develops that the "fellow" could only be Jimmy. The reasons for the concern of the Misses Hurlbird over Dowell and Florence's "European career" and for Uncle John's lecture are now clearer. But a complete disclosure of the significance of Europe doesn't come until the night Florence commits suicide, when the Englishman Bagshawe tells Dowell that at Ledbury he saw Florence coming out of Jimmy's bedroom at five in the morning. Long before this, however, we have deduced the essential connection, partially from the tone, partially from the information that Jimmy was in Paris with the two in the year immediately after their marriage, but largely from an additional clue Dowell drops. In describing Jimmy to the reader, he remarks: "I understand that he had been slim and dark and very graceful at the time of her first disgrace" (p. 88) [p. 85]. Ford's rhetoric of narrative is such that long before the reader possesses the precise knowledge of an event he has for all practical purposes been over the ground again and again.

The early events involving Florence and Jimmy and then Dowell, if given in chronological sequence, would read as follows: On the 4th of August, 1899, her birthday, Florence Hurlbird set off with her Uncle on a trip around the world. They were accompanied by a young man named Jimmy whose function it was to look after the uncle. During the summer of 1900 they spent a week of their stay in England with the Bagshawe family. On the 4th of August, while staying with this family, Florence became the mistress of Jimmy. They were almost immediately discovered. The trip ended and they returned to America. Sometime in the ensuing year John Dowell met Florence at the Stuyvesant's apartment on Fourteenth Street in New York. He courted her and married her on the 4th of August, 1901. They immediately set sail for Europe. On their Atlantic crossing there was a storm at sea which weakened Florence's heart. She was carried off the ship at Le Havre with a doctor's warning that even a channel crossing to England might prove fatal. The marriage remained unconsummated.

In Europe they settled in Paris. Jimmy was also in Paris and he resumed his relationship with Florence. Dowell knew nothing of their affair, and he had no idea that Florence did not really have heart trouble. Shortly afterward, the Dowells began to go to Nauheim in season for Florence's health. . . .

THREE

The Good Novelist

The story is the thing, and the story and the story,
and . . . there is nothing else that matters in the
world.

The novel proper begins in Chapter III with the first meeting
between the two couples in the dining room at Nauheim in
August, 1904. It is twilight. Dowell, who is alone, is seated at his
table, waiting for Florence. Ashburnham enters the room, and
Dowell, from his vantage point, studies him.

It is always something of an ordeal for newcomers to enter a
dining room filled with regular inhabitants. Ashburnham, however,
takes it in his stride. He "bore it like an Englishman and a
gentleman" (p. 25) [p. 32], revealing nothing of his feelings.
Dowell knows who Ashburnham is because one of the little habits
by which Dowell kills the idle hours of his day is to check the
police reports that guests fill out when they arrive.

As Dowell watches, the head waiter leads Ashburnham to a
table which is not a particularly desirable one. Up to this point
Ashburnham's face has, "in the wonderful English fashion,"
revealed nothing, but now the idea that the fading sunlight falling
across the table makes this seating arrangement undesirable seems
to occur to him, as it has to Dowell a moment earlier. Something
in his face must reveal this, though the narrator does not say
what. Instead he leaves Ashburnham (where he is to remain for
some pages) indecisively standing beside the table recently vacated
by the Grenfalls of Falls River, N.J., and goes on to describe
the composed face that remains in his memory.

There was in it neither joy nor despair; neither hope nor fear; neither boredom nor satisfaction. He seemed to perceive no soul in that crowded room; he might have been walking in a jungle. I never came across such a perfect expression before and I never shall again. It was insolence and not insolence; it was modesty and not modesty.

[p. 25] (p. 32)

This leads the narrator to the outer features of Ashburnham: fair, wavy hair, blond moustache, pink face; his smoking jacket padded to give him the air of the slightest possible stoop. He talked only of "martingales, Chiffney bits, boots; where you got the best soap, the best brandy, the name of the chap who rode a plater down the Khyber cliffs; the spreading power of number-three shot before a charge of number four powder." Once, though, he did tell Dowell where in England to buy his special shade of blue tie cheaper than in America, and once he gave him a wise lead on the stock market. And that—until a month before the telling of this story—was all Dowell knew of Edward Ashburnham. Ashburnham's main occupation seemed to Dowell, whenever he stepped into his room, to be the opening or closing of one of the innumerable leather cases he traveled with.

Dowell has moved in his reflections from the scene in the dining room forward in time to the period of years in which he associated with Ashburnham. Now Ford's already established control of time and space allows him to shift the focus of presentness once more, to the time of Dowell's writing of this account. The tone changes; irony enters the narrator's voice as he remembers how he was deceived. Ashburnham engaged in affairs with a number of women. Dowell is unable to understand what it was they all saw in Edward. How did he attract them? What did he find to talk to them about? For that matter, what did he say to them when they were under the scrutiny of Leonora and himself:

Ah, well, suddenly, as if by a flash of inspiration, I know. For all good soldiers are sentimentalists—all good soldiers of that type. Their profession, for one thing, is full of the big words—"courage," "loyalty," "honor," "constancy." And I have given a wrong impression of Edward Ashburnham if I have made you think that literally never in the course of nine years of intimacy did he discuss what he would have called "the graver things." Even before his final outburst to me, at times, very late at night, say, he has blurted out something that gave an insight into the sentimental view of the cosmos that was his. He

would say how much the society of a good woman could do towards
redeeming you, and he would say that constancy was the finest of
the virtues. He said it very stiffly, of course, but still as if the statement admitted of no doubt.   [pp. 26-27] (p. 34)

"Constancy! Isn't that the queer thought," Dowell remarks. "And
yet I must add that poor dear Edward was a great reader—he
would pass hours lost in novels of a sentimental type—novels
in which typewriter girls married marquises and governesses earls.
And in his books, as a rule, the course of true love ran as smooth
as buttered honey."
     Like Emma Bovary, Ashburnham has acquired his ideas of love
from reading romantic and sentimental literature. Like Emma,
he believes in the Romantic illusion. He acts from his belief, in
his particular case, from "his intense, optimistic belief that the
woman he was making love to at the moment was the one he
was destined, at last, to be eternally constant to" (pp. 27-28)
[p. 34]. By his actions Ashburnham brings upon himself and
those around him disaster and tragedy. Indeed, it is even possible to say that, like Flaubert's heroine, he corrupts those who
love him "from beyond the grave."
     But Ford, unlike a Flaubert, is not prepared to say that all
the ideals behind Ashburnham's love and all the romantic experiences he has encountered have been in their nature illusory.
Instead he deliberately complicates Ashburnham's life by his final
experience as viewed through Dowell's eyes. Once again, the
tense of memory shifts, this time to "the very end of things,
when the poor girl was on her way to that fatal Brindisi and he
was trying to persuade himself and me that he had never really
cared for her." Dowell "was quite astonished to observe how
literary and how just his expressions were. He talked like quite
a good book—a book not in the least cheaply sentimental."
Ashburnham was able to talk to him this way, Dowell reasons,
because he regarded him not so much as a man as "a woman or
a solicitor."

Anyhow, it burst out of him on that horrible night. And then, next
morning, he took me over to the Assizes and I saw how, in a perfectly calm and business-like way he set to work to secure a verdict
of not guilty for a poor girl, the daughter of one of his tenants who

had been accused of murdering her baby. He spent two hundred pounds on her defense. . . . Well, that was Edward Ashburnham.

[p. 28] (p. 35)

The portrait of Edward Ashburnham is finished—except that Dowell has forgotten his eyes. "They were as blue as the sides of a certain type of box of matches" and "perfectly honest, perfectly straightforward, perfectly, perfectly stupid." (As in *Madame Bovary*, the color blue, with its romantic connotation, suffuses the descriptive detail of the novel: all the characters have blue eyes; there is the blue sea, Dowell's blue tie, Florence's dress of blue figured silk, Leonora's "blue tailor made," and so on.) Dowell's ironic tone once more suggests a shift in the significance of events. With those eyes, he remarks, Ashburnham was able to catch the gaze of every woman in a room "as dexterously as a conjuror pockets billiard balls."

By degrees the narrator is returning to the dining room we left some pages earlier. We go back to the physical description of Edward with which time originally shifted; then we are in the room: "and there he was, standing by the table." Now the reason for delaying a description of Ashburnham's eyes becomes apparent. Florence enters the room beside Leonora. In Edward's eyes Dowell saw the pride of possession. Then their gaze became "perhaps more direct, harder if possible—hardy too. It was a measuring look; a challenging look." We do not know what the cause is, and the narrator does not explain. Instead he draws an analogy. The gaze is one such as he saw in Edward's eyes once when he was playing polo and saw a long chance to make a goal. Dowell heard him say to himself on that occasion: "Might just be done." And of course he did it.

Well, it was just that look I noticed in his eyes: "It might," I seem even now to hear him muttering to himself, "just be done."

I looked round over my shoulder and saw, tall, smiling brilliantly, and buoyant—Leonora. And, little and fair, and as radiant as the track of sunlight along the sea—my wife.

That poor wretch! To think that he was at that moment in a perfect devil of a fix, and there he was, saying at the back of his mind: "It might just be done." It was like a chap in the middle of the eruption of a volcano, saying that he might just manage to bolt into

tumult and set fire to a haystack. Madness? Predestination? Who the
devil knows?   [pp. 29-30] (p. 36)

This is all we are given—but the clue is enough. There seems
no doubt that Edward's gaze is directed at Florence, even though
the narrator doesn't say so, and that what Dowell sees now,
reconstructing the scene, is that at that moment, with that
oeillade, Edward Ashburnham must have been deciding to make
Florence his mistress.

Why Leonora and Florence enter the dining room together we
are not told. We aren't even quite sure that they are together—
and to understand the scene completely we have to wait some
thirty pages, when Ford divulges that the two women enter arm
in arm immediately after an incident in the hotel corridor with
Maisie Maidan, a young innocent, as her name suggests, genuinely
ill with heart trouble, whom the infatuated Edward has brought
from Burma to Nauheim. Florence had come round a screen in
the hotel corridor to find the gold key that hung from Leonora's
wrist caught in Mrs. Maidan's hair. Leonora had just slapped
Mrs. Maidan for coming out of Edward's room, falsely led to
conclude that she had passed the last two hours with him. Edward,
however, had not been there, and Mrs. Maidan had merely entered to return a scissors case. Leonora has made a dreadful mistake, as she quickly realizes. She has also unwittingly revealed
herself to Florence, and it is for this reason that she decides to
keep Florence near her until she can dispel the impression the
incident may have created. Thus the two women enter the dining
room together. Florence offers to share their table with the Ashburnhams, and Leonora says, "in quite a loud voice and from
quite a distance: 'Don't stop by that stuffy old table, Teddy. Come
and sit by these nice people!'" (p. 30) [p. 37]. And so, as
Florence remarks, the round table has begun.

The action of the novel begins, then, in Chapter III with a
man contemplating a woman as a possible mistress. This is juxtaposed, in Chapter IV, to the woman making a conquest of the
man, which occurs on the 4th of August, 1904, during one of the
couples' cultural side-trips to M——. Dowell always liked such
excursions, undertaken as part of the "cure," for he felt relaxed
and off-duty from his job as nurse to Florence while she went

about educating Ashburnham, explaining such matters as "how Ludwig the Courageous wanted to have three wives at once—in which he differed from Henry VIII, who wanted them one after the other, and this caused a good deal of trouble" (p. 39) [p. 44]: a cultural situation that will reveal its ironies to us in the course of the excursion. On this particular day, on their train ride to the castle of St. Elizabeth of Hungary, Dowell felt pleasure in simply enjoying the countryside. One rural sight particularly amused him. A brown cow hitched its horns under the stomach of a black and white animal and threw it right into the middle of a narrow stream. Dowell bursts out laughing but no one notices. Florence is busy imparting information about Ludwig the Courageous, the others are busy listening to Florence. Yet the attentive reader will appreciate the significance of the one cow displacing the other; for the situation is analogous to the event that is shortly to take place in the Prussian castle.

There, in a room that may once have served Martin Luther as a bedroom, the couples examine a pencil draft of the Protest in a large glass case. Florence becomes excited.

"And there," she exclaimed with an accent of gaiety, of triumph, of audacity. She was pointing at a piece of paper like the half-sheet of a letter with some faint pencil scrawls that might have been a jotting of the amounts we were spending during the day. And I was extremely happy at her gaiety, in her triumph, in her audacity.

[p. 44] (p. 48)

Looking up into Captain Ashburnham's eyes, Florence says: "It's because of that piece of paper that you're honest, sober, industrious, provident, and clean-lived." Otherwise, she goes on, he would be "like the Irish or the Italians or the Poles, but particularly the Irish. . . ." Florence lays one finger upon Captain Ashburnham's wrist. Dowell senses "something treacherous, something frightful, something evil in the day." But he can't define it. He was horribly frightened, he remembers, and then he discovered that the pain in his left wrist was caused by Leonora's clutching it. Leonora rushes out of the room, down the winding staircase, out of the castle, and onto a terrace. Dowell follows her. Below, she asks Dowell if he sees what is happening. He replies that he doesn't.

"Don't you see," she said, with a really horrible bitterness, with a really horrible lamentation in her voice, "Don't you see that that's the cause of the whole miserable affair; of the whole sorrow of the world? And of the eternal damnation of you and me and them. . . ."

[p. 45] (p. 49)

In Ford's narrator, Leonora's words produce only bafflement. A minute ago upstairs he had temporarily thought "that she must be a madly jealous woman—jealous of Florence and Captain Ashburnham, of all people in the world!" (p. 45) [p. 49]. Now, on the terrace, frightened and amazed, he loses track of Leonora's words, and thinks only of bringing her medical assistance. But then Leonora takes hold herself. " 'Don't you know,' she said, in her clear hard voice, 'don't you know that I'm an Irish Catholic?' " (p. 46) [p. 50].

Leonora's words of proffered explanation, which suggest that she has taken offense over the religious content of Florence's talk, give Dowell "the greatest relief" that he has ever been given in his life. "They told me, I think, almost more than I have ever gathered at any one moment—about myself" (p. 46) [p. 50]. For Leonora's explanation allows Dowell to believe that he has not seen what he has seen, to forget the incident, in effect, and to go on with the relationship with the Ashburnhams, which is what he wants most in life at this time. "I do not believe that I could have gone on any more without them. I was getting too tired" (p. 67) [pp. 66-67]. He also believes, though the reader may remain doubtful, that if Leonora had said that she was jealous of Florence, he would "have turned upon Florence with the maddest kind of rage." "Mere silly jibes at the Irish and at the Catholics," on the other hand, "could be apologized out of existence." Dowell has had his moment of awareness—and dismissed it, concealing the meaning of events from himself, much as Victorian society concealed from itself the sexual derelictions that occurred before its eyes.

If Ford's narrator, for both personal and social reasons, conceals what he has seen in the incident that day at M——, Ford's reader has witnessed an event the meaning of which he cannot possibly conceal from himself. Indeed, Ford has heightened the significance of the event by its historical setting: the castle "where the Reformer and his friends met for the first time under the protection of the gentleman that had three wives at once and formed an alliance with the gentleman that had six wives, one after the other" (p. 43) [p. 47]. The suggested parallel between Ludwig the Courageous and Edward Ashburnham is unmistakable (in a parenthesis, after his description of the castle, Dowell adds: "I'm not really interested in these facts but they have a bearing on my story"), as is the deliberate ambiguity behind Leonora's words ("Don't you see that that's the cause of the whole miserable affair; of the whole sorrow of the world?"), which suggests that the sexual laxities of Edward and Florence are the result of the disintegration of a uniform cultural and religious tradition. It is doubtful that this was Ford's own view. Although he was a Catholic, his imagination in the last half of the novel adds complexity and depth and qualification to this sexual-cultural-religious pattern.

Around the scene with Leonora, outside the castle, Ford builds the last two chapters of the first part of the novel. The fifth chapter opens and closes with the scene, the sixth commences with it. To see the artifice of these chapters, into which Ford places the thread of psychologically controlled revelation, fusing and dissolving the relative pastness and presentness of events, it is necessary to gain an overall perspective of the novel's progression of effects.

Chapter III has shown Edward taking the measure of Florence as a possible sexual conquest. Chapter IV has given its complement, the woman making a bid for the man. So far we have merely the beginning of another adulterous affair, both participants willing, with the woman bluntly throwing it up in the face of the wife, while the husband of the woman refuses to believe what he sees. But next we learn, in Chapter V, that Edward was already carrying on another liaison with a woman, Mrs. Maidan, and we learn that Leonora has tolerated, even contributed to it, because she has viewed it as the least of possible evils. It also develops that Edward has had a series of affairs. It is no normal marriage bed that Florence has disturbed.

But, like an oceanographer, we have only begun to plunge beneath the surface and take a sounding; we have yet to penetrate the murky recesses of our aqueous world. For Florence to have an affair with Edward she must remove her rival for his affec-

tion. The fifth chapter describes the process by which Florence
supplants Mrs. Maidan, or, really, only conveys a sense of it,
though Ford's rhetoric of narrative is so masterful that the effect
is as if he had given a line-by-line exposition of Florence's
intrigues and Edward's sallies in her direction. Instead, Ford
makes the reader draw his own conclusion. The only concrete
instance he gives may well be merely an illustrative example
created by Dowell in the course of an explanation to the reader:
Mrs. Maidan is described as soaking "her noonday pillow with
tears whilst Florence, below the window, talked to Captain Ashburnham about the Constitution of the United States" (p. 52)
[p. 54]. We also learn that it was on the same day as the couples'
trip to M—— that "poor Mrs. Maidan died. We found her dead
when we got back—pretty awful, when you come to figure out
what it all means . . ." (p. 67) [p. 66]. But we do not yet know
what it all does mean, though it now seems clear that death is a
party to the affair—and, foretold, though not explained, we have
yet the death of Florence herself to look forward to. And beyond
that there is the fact that the pattern is to repeat itself once
more with horrifying consequences.

The sixth chapter selects a time when Florence has become in
fact Edward's mistress, which occurs one week after the death
of Mrs. Maidan. Following an early morning scene between the
two women, in which Leonora accuses Florence of murdering
Mrs. Maidan, we are given more details of Maisie Maidan's death:
"What had happened on the day of our jaunt to the ancient city
of M—— had been this" (p. 73) [p. 71]. We learn that Mrs.
Maidan had overheard a conversation between Edward and
Florence (just as Florence later overhears one between Edward
and Nancy) and that with this she had realized her position,
including the ignominious fact that Leonora, with mixed motives,
had paid her passage. She packs to leave Nauheim and to return
to her husband in India. In the excitement her heart fails. Leonora
discovers the body, grotesquely fallen into her trunk, which "had
closed upon her like the jaws of a gigantic alligator" (pp. 75-76)
[p. 73]. She also discovers the note Mrs. Maidan was planning
to leave behind. This she hides from Edward, who, imagining
that Mrs. Maidan's death "had been the most natural thing in
the world. . . . soon got over it. Indeed, it was the one affair of

his about which he never felt much remorse" (p. 76) [p. 74]. Thus ends the first part of *The Good Soldier*.

In dipping beneath the surface, in moving behind the calm facade of Nauheim, with its unbroken routine of baths and meals and rest periods, its concerts by the Kur orchestra, its trips to places of historical interest, we have discovered that nothing is as it seems in this world of social convention: we have a wife of the one party who will do nothing to stop the affair and a husband of the other party who refuses to see. And we have the reverse, their partners, both conscious of the duplicities they are practising, both inhabiting the spurious climate of the sick, neither physically ill, both morally corrupt. Finally, we have an encroaching pattern of involvement—and its complement, a pattern of revelation—in which one simple liaison becomes the commanding center of a universe.

In broadest outline the four parts of *The Good Soldier* are organized around two major triangles: Florence, Edward, and Leonora in the first two parts; Nancy, Edward, and Leonora in Parts Three and Four. Now, to consider only Parts One and Two. Before the couples meet at Nauheim we have, in sum, two triangles also. In Part One, it would be Mrs. Maidan, Edward, and Leonora. Part Two presents its complement. It begins by focusing on Dowell and Florence. Their courtship and marriage, the ocean voyage which produced Florence's "heart," Florence's early affair with Jimmy, and their life in Paris with Jimmy are diagrammed. Thus a similar triangle: Jimmy, Florence, and Dowell. And just as in Part One Florence supplanted Mrs. Maidan, so Part Two contains a similar substitution. Edward enters the Dowells' Paris life and supplants Jimmy. Gross structure, then, reveals a carefully modulated balance between parts.

One very obvious problem which Ford's handling of time solves in the first two parts of the novel is the nine years' intimacy. Once the affair had commenced, nothing else of consequence happened in those nine years; still, Ford has to create the effect of the passage of time, and his method is such a sure one that he confidently refrains from elaborating any event which occurred during that interval. Most of the events occur in prior time or in the first month of the intimacy between the couples. For the

rest, the dislocation of time produces a fifty-page interval between
the inception of the affair that day at M——— and its close nine
years later with Florence's suicide. In addition, Ford gives the
reader three pages of telescoping (pp. 98-100) [pp. 92-94] in
which there are references to the narrator's diaries and a pin-point-
ing of a few entries in 1905 and 1906. That is all—and yet the
dislocation of chronology has been so effective that Ford can
calmly state a psychological truth, sure that his audience will be
convinced of the passage of time: "The death of Mrs. Maidan
occurred on the 4th of August 1904. And then nothing happened
until the 4th of August 1913" (p. 77) [p. 75].

To prevent the reader's being confused by the shimmering
haze that the time-shift creates, Ford parcels out his time lapses
between the occurrences of one repetitive date. Thus, on the 4th
of August, 1874, Florence was born. On the 4th of August,
1899, she set out on the trip around the world with her uncle
and Jimmy. On the same date in 1900 she was discovered
coming out of Jimmy's room. On the 4th of August, 1901, she
married Dowell and they started on the sea voyage that caused
her "heart." On the same date in 1904 she made her bid for
Edward, and Maisie Maidan died. Finally, on the 4th of August,
1913, she overhears Edward talking to Nancy Rufford (who
has now grown to young womanhood) in a way she regards as
that of a lover. Overcome, she commits suicide, though it appears as if her death were the result of a heart attack. Just before
this occurs she is seen by the Englishman Bagshawe in the lobby
of the hotel. Bagshawe is trying to make Dowell's acquaintance,
and without knowing that Dowell is Florence's husband, he dis-
closes Florence's sexual indiscretion with Jimmy. A summary of
this kind opens Part Two—except that Ford elusively withholds
from the reader the significance of the 4th of August, 1900, and
the same date in 1913 until he can reveal both at once. Thus
the beginning and the end of Florence's illicit sexual life are
juxtaposed.

In one of her more aberrant moments in *I Have This To Say*[1]
Violet Hunt tells of discovering the manuscript of *The Good
Soldier* in a dust bin, its pages shredded into a hundred fragments,
which she then had to piece together before the manuscript
could be sent to the publisher John Lane. A hostile critic might

suppose that this incident is responsible for the disrupted chronology of the novel. Such a conclusion would of course be wrong, for the finely wrought structure of the novel hinges on Ford's use of a fragmented time-scheme. Yet there are a series of discrepancies in Ford's use of time which should be cleared up, or, where that is impossible, at least noted, for in a novel of broken time segments the touchstones to chronological sequence are important. In the sequence concerning the elopement of Dowell and Florence, for example, it is impossible to know exactly what happened over the four-day span, as it is even to be sure what happened on each day. The interview with the aunts and Dowell's discovery in the evening that Florence is gone occur on the 1st of August. On the 2nd Dowell goes to New York to procure passage, but whether it is on the 2nd or 3rd of August that he tracks down Florence and has his interview with the uncle it is impossible to say. A minor point, but there are other confusions in *The Good Soldier* that are more important.

The most important discrepancy in Ford's use of time is the date of August 4, 1904. The third chapter of Part One opens with August of that year, and the time seems to refer to the meeting of the two couples. But, then, after the confusion in Dowell's mind about dating the trip to M—— ("I can't remember," Dowell remarks [p. 37 (pp. 42-43)], "whether it was in our first year of acquaintance. . . . but it must have been in the first or second year"), he is able to date the trip with certainty, because it occurred on the same day as Mrs. Maidan's death (p. 67) [p. 67], which he then tells us occurred on the 4th of August (p. 77) [p. 75]. Thus the meeting of the two couples and the trip to M—— and Mrs. Maidan's suicide would all have to have occurred in a space of four days. This can't be, however, since we have already been told (p. 51) [p. 53] that Mrs. Maidan died after the first month of their acquaintance. Further confusion comes when Dowell identifies the 4th of August as the day on which the couples met (p. 98) [p. 91]. What has happened is that Ford has used one date for two separate events.

A minor series of errors follows in the wake of this: the Ashburnhams were to be with Colonel Hervey in Linlithgowshire for the month of September commencing with either the 11th or the 18th (p. 55) [p. 57], and yet Dowell's diary reveals that

Edward was in Paris with them until the 21st of that month
(p. 98) [p. 92]; Florence tired of Jimmy and took over
Edward in 1903 (p. 90) [p. 85], which would be a year before
the couples met; Edward was twenty-seven at the time of the
Kilsyte case (p. 157) [p. 140], but the affair of La Dolciquita
occurred in 1895 (p. 56) [p. 58] when he would have been
merely twenty-four—and the Kilsyte case occurred before the
incident at Monte Carlo (the discrepancy here might be accounted for by the fact that in the section of the novel printed
in Wyndham Lewis's Vorticist magazine *Blast* Edward's age in
1904 was thirty-six, which would have made him twenty-seven
in 1895). There are other minor discrepancies in time, but it
should be pointed out that with the exception of August 4,
1904, the discrepancies cause surprisingly little trouble to the
reader.

What saves the sequence is Ford's expert use of psychological
probability, the fewness of important events around which the
novel centers, and the use of one repetitive date, August 4th,
on which, during various years, significant events occur. Ford
never baffles the reader's sense of chronology deliberately, though
a great deal of ingenuity could be put into deciphering the "nine
years and six months less four days" (p. 7) [p. 18] that Dowell
speaks of.

Ford's sense of time, reflected in his constant use of the time-
shift, is almost wholly an artistic rather than a philosophical
concern. Ford is no Bergsonian. He is concerned, as in a sense
all writers are, with the transience of man's life, with the structure of values man erects in his hope of warding off change.
Beyond this—and the structure of *The Good Soldier* would seem
to support the point—Ford seems to be saying that life is a long
series of connecting mirrors before which we move, from panel
to panel, never able to see the image behind us and never seeing
the image of the next frame. The exclusive present is all we
have, and that is specious. No event is the same twice; even our
memory of an event is different each time. And yet the continuity
of human experience is precisely that it does repeat itself (for
Ford, of course, ironically). Thus the whole pattern of Edward
Ashburnham's life, and indeed the pattern of the novel, has been
a preparation for this final love affair.

FOUR

The Master Craftsman

O Age gone lax! O stunted followers,
That mask at passions and desire desires,
Behold me shrivelled, and your mock of mocks;
And yet I mock you by the mighty fires
That burnt me to this ash.

Ezra Pound "PIERE VIDAL OLD"

"The girl," as Edward always called her, serves in the last half of *The Good Solder* as catalyst. And with an ironic twist, the introduction of genuine innocence and genuine love (juxtaposed to Florence's deceits and her self-seeking and Edward's earlier lusts) produces a *progression d'effet* of horror for which the sequence we have been following is mere preparation. The first action of the plot Nancy engages in sounds the dominant note: she is at least partly responsible for the suicide of Florence. At Leonora's instigation, on the night of August 4, 1913, Florence follows Edward and Nancy to the concert at the Nauheim Casino. She finds them seated outside in the dark on a public bench. The Casino orchestra is playing the Rakóczy march in the background. Florence is dressed in black for the death of a relative. Peeping from behind a tree trunk, she hears Edward declare his love to the girl. She rushes back to the hotel, where in the lobby she sees Bagshawe talking to her husband. She surmises that he is about to reveal the incident with Jimmy in Bagshawe's manor house years before. Upstairs in her room Florence commits suicide.

The development of a triangular relationship among Nancy, Edward, and Leonora, which the death of Florence helps create, and the horror that it produces ironically mirror what has gone before. The Romeo-and-Juliet theme, parodied in Dowell's courtship, now takes on the serious and tragic note of unrequited love, with Leonora playing the sharp-tongued nurse. (It goes further than this, of course; Leonora turns pander to offer a virgin sacrifice to her own love of Edward.) Other echoes occur: as Edward innocently kissed a servant girl in a railway carriage years before (the "Kilsyte case"), and as Dowell, innocently experiencing his one minute of passion at the beginning of his elopement, embraced Florence, so Nancy in all purity kisses Edward on the forehead. It is an inauspicious beginning. For in the next few pages we are confronted with a symbol of detumescence as Edward kneels before his bed in prayer (pp. 133-134) [pp. 121-122]. And while the earlier affairs led to lust, deceit, adultery, and suicide, true love now leads to Nancy's self-immolation, her "worse than death" (p. 121) [p. 112], and Edward's self-abnegation and suicide.

As Ford reaches the midpoint of his novel with the death of Florence, he is faced with the delicate problem of shifting the focus of events from Florence, who has been a major participant in Parts One and Two, to Nancy, who, growing up in a convent during this time, has been barely mentioned in the narrative thus far. There is real danger that the death of Florence will produce a falling-off of attention—such as occurs in *Wuthering Heights,* for example, after the death of Catherine Earnshaw in Chapter XVIII—and that the novel will seem to split into two parts, with two separate stories. As we know from Ford's germinal account of the Nancy story years before in *The Spirit of the People,* it was originally separate and complete in itself. Ford's imagination has woven it into a larger pattern which includes the events at Nauheim. It is his rhetoric of narrative that must now unite the whole of these events into a single psychological progression.

In Dowell's mind, of course, Ford has been anticipating this moment since he first alluded to Nancy and Edward and their tragic situation in the very first chapter of the novel. Throughout the first half of the novel he has also subtly suggested and foreshadowed events yet to come. One of the major reasons for Ford's rearrangement of chronology has been to achieve this unity of circumstance and event. But the actual moment of joining the two narrative strands still presents him with a unique artistic problem. At this critical juncture Ford brings all his skill to bear upon the narrative structure. In the first place, he makes the pages surrounding the death of Florence among the swiftest moving in the novel. The reader is given no opportunity to question or to doubt events. More important, Ford arranges circumstances so that Dowell mistakenly believes Florence's death was merely accidental, brought on by a heart attack—and while Dowell continues to believe this until many months later, in fact until after the death of Edward, the reader has to wait only a few pages to reach this point in time and Dowell's final revelation concerning Florence and Edward. Ford abridges time. He manipulates the tenses of memory so that Dowell's mind jumps forward to a November evening at Branshaw Manor. He and Leonora are seated in Leonora's study waiting for tea. Edward has been dead about a week (a month before the narrator is writing this), and Dowell is discussing with Leonora the length of his stay. Leonora says: "Oh, stop here for ever and ever if you can. You couldn't be more of a brother to me, or more of a counsellor, or more of a support. You are all the consolation I have in the world. And isn't it odd to think that if your wife hadn't been my husband's mistress, you would probably never have been here at all?" (p. 104) [p. 98]. "That," Dowell remarks, "was how I got the news—full in the face like that." But Dowell, as we have come to expect of him, feels no emotion. Things merely become clearer as unexplained pieces of the past fit together.

She looked across the lawn and said, as far as I can remember:
"Edward has been dead only ten days and yet there are rabbits on the lawn."
I understand that rabbits do a great deal of harm to the short grass in England. And then she turned round to me and said without any adornment at all, for I remember her exact words:
"I think it was stupid of Florence to commit suicide."
[p. 105] (pp. 98-99)

Thus Dowell learns the truth about Florence's death through the ironic juxtaposition of the deaths of the two major participants in the first half of the novel, both suicides; through a juxtaposition that is produced in Leonora's mind by the association of the sexually fecund and destructive rabbits with Florence. But this irony of the rabbits plays across the entire pattern of the novel. There is yet another meaning to be wrung from Leonora's words, for the childless Leonora is to marry Rodney Bayham, "who is rather like a rabbit" (p. 238) [p. 205], and she is to become pregnant by him. This is the "Mr. Rodney Bayham, who will keep a separate establishment secretly, in Portsmouth, and make occasional trips to Buda-Pesth" (p. 240) [p. 207]. "Yes, society must go on; it must breed, like rabbits" (p. 254) [p. 219].

One effect of this short but revealing scene with Leonora, which all but concludes the story of Florence, is to create anticipation in the reader about the story of Edward and Nancy. It also locates Dowell firmly in the center of events in Part Four of the novel, for one of Ford's major problems is to justify Dowell's presence in the last half of the novel. He rather ineffectively justifies this through Dowell's interest in Nancy—but his desire to marry her, if not implausible, is at least not predictable from anything Dowell has revealed about himself in his narrative thus far. Hence Ford is careful not to overelaborate. "I don't know," Dowell remarks, "that analysis of my own psychology matters at all to this story. I should say that it didn't or, at any rate, that I had given enough of it" (p. 103) [p. 97]. Ford simply has Dowell, two hours after the death of Florence, and while still in a "cataleptic" state, blurt out to Leonora: "Now I can marry the girl." Dowell remarks that "it is as if one had a dual personality, the one I being entirely unconscious of the other." However willingly or unwillingly the reader may accept the dubious self-revelation and Dowell's explanation of a "dual personality," Ford is careful not to let the reader pause over it. His complex narrative is such that a reader is busy piecing together the crucial conversation with Leonora. Ford begins Part Three in the middle of their conversation, with Leonora's reply: "Of course you might marry her" (p. 103) [p. 97]. Dowell asks "whom," and Leonora replies, "the girl." It is only after two discursive paragraphs have intervened that we have Dowell's opening remarks: "Now I can marry the girl." This technique of beginning a conversation in the middle and then gradually reveal-

ing its circumstances and its earlier content was one Ford later
developed and made extensive use of in *Parade's End.*

The artifice of the narrator in the last half of *The Good Soldier,*
and particularly in the final pages, is not made so plausible as
it could be. Dowell was present at very few of these events, and
we do not have his eye-witness accounts to at least most of the
physical action, which we had in the first two parts of the novel.
Indeed, during his first two weeks at Branshaw Teleragh, after
being called there from America by telegrams from Edward and
Leonora, he saw nothing wrong at all: "those three presented to
the world the spectacle of being the best of good people. . . .
I can't remember, right up to the dinner, when Leonora read out
that telegram [from Nancy's father, stating that arrangements
were all made, and Nancy was to leave for India the next
morning]—not the tremor of an eyelash, not the shaking of a
hand. It was just a pleasant country house-party" (p. 246)
[pp. 211-212]. In fact, as Dowell goes on to point out, Leonora
keeps it up until eight days after Edward's funeral, when she first
reveals that Florence was Edward's mistress and that she died
by her own hand. Thus Dowell, reconstructing events, can only
present the accounts of Edward and Leonora, sometimes in their
words, sometimes in his own; and, as he has done before, he
often uses both participants to give insight into a scene. Again
he is careful to maintain the convention of objective reporting:

And that evening Edward spoke to me. [p. 202] (p. 176)

I don't know what it [the letter from Nancy's mother] contained.
I just averaged out its effect on Nancy. . . . [p. 211] (p. 183)

Leonora told me these things. [p. 214] (p. 186)

and to plead bafflement before the nature of the events:

I don't attach any particular importance to these generalizations of
mine. They may be right, they may be wrong; I am only an ageing
American with very little knowledge of life. You may take my generalizations or leave them. [p. 244] (p. 210)

I don't know whether, at this point, Nancy Rufford loved Edward
Ashburnham. I don't know whether she ever loved him . . . I don't
know. I know nothing. I am very tired. [p. 245] (pp. 210-211)

I don't know. I leave it to you.   [p 245] (p. 211)

I can't make out which of them was right. I leave it to you.
                                                    [p. 246] (p. 211)

But about the inner workings of Nancy's mind Dowell can know
next to nothing; it has to be all deduction. Dowell is careful here
to make no mention of how he obtained his information, and the
reader is kept so busy piecing together events that he has little
time to question the author's presentation.

Once Ford has justified Dowell's continued presence in the
novel, and once he has established the reality of the Nancy–
Edward situation—"over her he wore himself to rags and tatters
and death—in the effort to leave her alone" (p. 116) [p. 107]—
he alters the pace of his narrative and reverts in his method of
handling time to the straight flashback. He now goes back and
surveys the early lives of Edward and Leonora, their marriage,
their growing marital troubles, and the succession of women who
came between them. In effect, Ford offers his reader temporary
relief from the strain of following a complicated narrative pattern.
He is also slowly recharging his narrative, for the climax of the
Edward–Nancy situation cannot follow hard upon the climax
of the Edward–Florence situation and be effective. Ford fills the
psychological and chronological gap in the narrative at this point
with the story of Edward and Leonora.

The Ashburnhams had married young; she had been nineteen
and he twenty-two. It was largely a marriage arranged by their
families, though Leonora very soon felt for Edward a love of "the
deepest description." Edward, on the other hand, merely had
"the very greatest admiration" for Leonora. "He admired her
for her truthfulness, for her cleanness of mind, and the clean-
runness of her limbs, for her efficiency, for the fairness of her
skin, for the gold of her hair, for her religion, for her sense of
duty" (p. 140) [pp. 126-127]. But she lacked for him "the
touch of magnetism" which means love. "I suppose, really,"
Dowell remarks, "he did not love her because she was never
mournful; what really made him feel good in life was to comfort
somebody who would be darkly and mysteriously mournful."
Ashburnham's conception of romance is part of his Victorian
inheritance. As Esmé Wingfield-Stratford points out, in *Those*

Earnest Victorians, romance was "the very breath of the early Victorian culture," becoming rapidly "the fashion, almost a tyranny,"[1] and quickly accomodating itself "to the standards of the English-drawing room, or genteel parlour."

There was its temple, and the Young Lady was its high priestess. However hard-worked and practical they might be in reality, the dream life of Flora and Caroline was passed in a world of castles and abbeys peopled by polite men in armour and saintly ecclesiastics, and haunted by well-mannered spectres.[2]

And "nothing was so dear to the romantic heart as a refined melancholy. . . . Ladies showed their breeding by an occasional fainting fit or mild hysterical outburst." It is a Flora or a Caroline, "darkly and mysteriously mournful," that Ashburnham is nostalgically searching for.

For five or six years, however, the marriage between Leonora and Edward was a happy one, though their union did not produce any children. ("It will give you some idea of the extraordinary naïveté of Edward Ashburnham," Dowell remarks on page 147 [p. 132], "that, at the time of his marriage and for perhaps a couple of years after, he did not really know how children are produced. Neither did Leonora." Ashburnham achieved adulthood with "his virgin intelligence untouched in this world"; Leonora "had been handed over to him, like some patient mediaeval virgin." In his chapter entitled "The Cult of the Double Bed," the author of *Those Earnest Victorians* remarks that, while the purpose of Victorian marriage was clearly the production of children, as the double bed, "otherwise so obviously inconvenient, is a silent witness to,"[3] the Victorians "were careful to invest the marriage chamber with a taboo of absolute secrecy. . . . To provide a safety valve for masculine animal instincts, that were not allowed to exist save behind the portals of silence, an outer darkness was provided, peopled by beings whose very existence it would have been unrefined for Flora to have suspected, and into which Charles and Reginald faded away at discreet intervals."[4] Leonora was disturbed by their lack of offspring, and was inclined at times to view it as divine punishment for having married a non-Catholic. Edward, who was an Anglican, would not agree to raise as Catholic any future male children.

Gradually tension developed between Leonora and Edward. Leonora was one of seven daughters of a hard-pressed Irish landlord, and her husband's liberality in running his estate became a grievance to her. "Ironically enough, the first real trouble between them came from his desire to build a Roman Catholic chapel at Branshaw. He wanted to do it to honour Leonora, and he proposed to do it very expensively" (p. 142) [p. 128]. Leonora did not want the chapel; she could easily drive to the nearest Catholic church; and she paid little attention to Edward's emotional receptivity to Catholicism at the time. But it was Leonora's objection to Edward's generous treatment of tenants whose crops failed that first produced an outburst of anger on Edward's part.

You see, he was really a very simple soul—very simple. He imagined that no man can satisfactorily accomplish his life's work without loyal and whole-hearted co-operation of the woman he lived with. And he was beginning to perceive dimly that, whereas his own traditions were entirely collective, his wife was a sheer individualist. His own theory —the feudal theory of an overlord doing his best by his dependents, the dependents meanwhile doing their best for the overlord—this theory was entirely foreign to Leonora's nature. She came of a family of small Irish landlords—that hostile garrison of a plundered country. And she was thinking unceasingly of the children she wished to have.

[p. 146] (pp. 131-132)

More and more Leonora disapproves of Edward's handling of the estate; she tries to curb what she regards as excesses.

Into this strained situation, from which there seemed no relief, came the Kilsyte case. In a railway carriage Edward impulsively kissed a servant girl of nineteen who was crying. (Edward was traveling third class because of Leonora's economies.) The girl was crying because another servant girl had taken away her young man. Ashburnham's motive was to comfort the girl; he felt at least "half-fatherly." The girl reacted by screaming and pulling the emergency cord. There was a trial, in which Edward came off very well. The incident, however, had estranged him from Leonora, for during the trial "there came suddenly into his mind the recollection of the softness of the girl's body as he had pressed her to him. And from that moment, that girl appeared desirable to him—and Leonora completely unattractive" (pp. 156-157) [p. 140]. Ashburnham "began to indulge in daydreams in which he approached the nursemaid more tactfully and carried the matter much further." Dowell is careful to point out that Ashburnham was not "a pathological case." He had "all the virtues that are usually accounted English" (p. 151) [p. 135], and "was just a normal man and very much of a sentimentalist" (p. 152) [p. 136]. "The outline of Edward's life was an outline perfectly normal of the life of a hard-working, sentimental, and efficient professional man" (p. 152) [p. 136]. And yet, of course, "he wanted to be looked upon as a sort of Lohengrin."

At that time, he says, he went about deliberately looking for some woman who could help him. He found several—for there were quite a number of ladies in his set who were capable of agreeing with this handsome fellow that the duties of a feudal gentleman were feudal. He would have liked to pass his days talking to one or other of these ladies. But there was always an obstacle—if the lady were married there would be a husband who claimed the greater part of her time and attention. If on the other hand, it were an unmarried girl he could not see very much of her for fear of compromising her. At that date, you understand, he had not the least idea of seducing any one of these ladies. He wanted only moral support at the hands of some female, because he found men difficult to talk to about ideals. Indeed, I do not believe that he had, at any time, any idea of making anyone his mistress. That sounds queer; but I believe it is quite true as a statement of character. [p. 158] (p. 141)

Ironically, Ashburnham's idealism draws him into a series of adulterous liaisons, and ultimately leads him to suicide. The multiplicity of the design, however, merely illustrates the underlying singleness of Edward's ideals. It is Ashburnham's values that Ford is projecting, and it is these values that worry the technique of the novel, as well as the conscience of its protagonist.

After the Kilsyte incident, the Ashburnhams took a trip to Monte Carlo. There Edward became infatuated with the Spanish dancer, La Dolciquita. "He took her in the dark gardens and remembering suddenly the girl of the Kilsyte case, he kissed her. He kissed her passionately, violently, with a sudden explosion of the passion that had been bridled all his life" (p. 159) [p. 142]. He passed the night in her bed. But then La Dolciquita would have nothing more to do with him; the risk of losing the Grand Duke was too great—unless Ashburnham was willing to provide

an insurance policy. She would live with him for one month for
the equivalent of two years of money paid her by the Grand
Duke—in effect, for one hundred thousand dollars.

Edward went mad; his world stood on its head; the palms in front of
the blue sea danced grotesque dances. You see, he believed in the
virtue, tenderness, and moral support of women. He wanted more than
anything to argue with La Dolciquita; to retire with her to an island
and point out to her the damnation of her point of view and how
salvation can only be found in true love and the feudal system. She
had once been his mistress, he reflected, and, by all the moral laws,
she ought to have gone on being his mistress or at the very least his
sympathetic confidante. But her rooms were closed to him; she did
not appear in the hotel. Nothing: blank silence. To break that down he
had to have twenty thousand pounds. You have heard what happened.   [p. 161] (pp. 143-144)

Edward "spent a week of madness; he hungered; his eyes sank
in; he shuddered at Leonora's touch." And "he drank like a fish
after Leonora was in bed and he spread himself over the tables,
and this went on for a fortnight" (p. 163) [p. 144]. He gambled
heavily to make the sum he needed to possess La Dolciquita. In
a single night he lost forty thousand pounds. The next night
La Dolciquita appeared in his room and told him to come to her
the next day. She set a more modest price and they went off to
Antibes for a week. Meanwhile Leonora had heard of Edward's
gambling losses, and on the advice of a Mrs. Colonel Whelen
had gone off to England to consult her solicitor and her spiritual
adviser. When Edward returned to Monte Carlo from Antibes
and La Dolciquita, he found a telegram waiting for him from
Leonora. She asked him to return to London. There Leonora tried
to salvage what was left of their income. She forced Edward to
give her and her attorney the management of the estate and to
request a transfer to Burma where they could live more cheaply.
She intended to make back what Edward had lost at the gaming
tables.

The Ashburnhams were in India eight years. In Burma Edward
met Mrs. Basil, the wife of a fellow officer. She "was a nice
woman and very, very kind to him" (pp. 168-169) [p. 149],
Dowell remarks. "I suppose she was his mistress, but I never
heard it from Edward, of course. I seem to gather that they

carried it on in a high romantic fashion, very proper to both of them. . . ." Edward's affair with Mrs. Basil, with its Kiplingesque overtones, lasted until her husband was transferred. At about that time Major Basil extracted three hundred pounds from Edward; he continued to blackmail him regularly in the ensuing years. Shortly after this Ashburnham himself was transferred to another station, where he met Mrs. Maidan. The ease with which Edward attached his affections to the young woman made him "suspect that he was inconstant," which greatly upset him.

The affair with the Dolciquita he had sized up as a short attack of madness like hydrophobia. His relations with Mrs. Basil had not seemed to him to imply moral turpitude of a gross kind. The husband had been complaisant; they had really loved each other; his wife was very cruel to him and had long ceased to be a wife to him. He thought that Mrs. Basil had been a soul-mate, separated from him by an unkind fate—something sentimental of that sort.

[p. 173] (p. 153)

But even while writing long weekly letters to Mrs. Basil, he found himself infatuated with Maisie Maidan.

Ford's version of the erotic myth, as radical for 1915 as was Butler's version of Victorian family life for 1903, is today a commonplace of the contemporary novel, so much so that Ashburnham is easily recognizable as the precursor of the all too familiar protagonist who makes a religion of passion. Beside this later hero, however, Ashburnham stands like some archetypal figure, dwarfing him, making his performance appear almost ventriloquial. For a large part of the greatness of *The Good Soldier* lies in the versatility of the telling, in the breadth of Ford's exploration of the many faces of passion. One peripheral but insistent motif accompanying Ford's account of Edward's conduct is the tradition of courtly love: the ennobling love of a knight for a lady, with its four characteristics or "marks," as C. S. Lewis identifies them: Humility, Courtesy, Adultery, and the Religion of Love.[5] As James Trammell Cox points out in "Ford's 'Passion for Provence,'" "all of the essential features of the courtly lover are present in the portrait of Edward Ashburnham that Dowell draws: the identification of Edward with [the] knight errant of the romances; the ennoblement of love, with the exclusion of this ennoblement from the marriage relationship; the languishment and melancholy of the courtly lover; the service and the gifts and the valor; the constancy; the poetry; the secrecy and jealousy; and most important of all the religion of love."[6] The conventions of courtly love reverberate through the tales of Edward's earlier loves—La Dolciquita, Mrs. Basil, Mrs. Maidan, and, of course, Florence. And while used in these earlier instances for both ironic and farcical purposes, they will take on a tragic note in the final tale of Ashburnham's unrequited love for Nancy Rufford.

After eight years in India, the Ashburnhams were both somewhat physically ill from the climate. At this point Leonora, having restored the finances of their estate, suggested they return to England. On their way they would drop Mrs. Maidan at Nauheim. Edward asked Leonora if they could take her, and, as it turned out, Leonora had already arranged the matter with Charlie Maidan. Leonora thought that Edward would quickly lose interest in Mrs. Maidan, and she wanted to please him. She was still in love with him, and her main passion was to get him back. Indeed, she now turned over to him the management of the estate, the income of which was again five thousand pounds a year. "You have managed the job amazingly," he compliments her. "You are a wonderful woman" (p. 175) [p. 155]. And then, on shipboard, where he is happy attending the wants of the invalided Maisie Maidan, he impulsively remarks: "By Jove, you're the finest woman in the world. I wish we could be better friends" (p. 177) [p. 156].

Florence knocked all that on the head. . . .   [p. 181] (p. 160)

Before Ford turns to the Nancy–Edward story, in Part Four, he once more has Dowell reëxamine the meaning of events thus far in the novel, particularly Florence's responsibility for what happened. "Florence was a contaminating influence—she depressed and deteriorated Edward; she deteriorated, hopelessly, the miserable Leonora." For Florence was above all "an unstoppable talker. You could not stop her."

Edward and Leonora were at least proud and reserved people. Pride and reserve are not the only things in life; perhaps they are not even the best things. But if they happen to be your particular virtues you will go all to pieces if you let them go.   [p. 185] (pp. 162-163)

Florence talked. "That was what was terrible, because Florence forced Leonora herself to abandon her high reserve—Florence and the situation" (p. 192) [p. 168]. Leonora, we know, "had been drilled—in her tradition, in her upbringing—to keep her mouth shut" (p. 177) [p. 157]. And though there had been times, during Edward's earlier affairs, when in her marital agonies she had nearly yielded to the temptation of speaking, she had always managed to restrain herself. "You must postulate that what she desired above all things was to keep a shut mouth to the world, to Edward, and to the women that he loved."

In front of Dowell, of course, Leonora maintained a successful face. Indeed, even at the end, when called to Branshaw by telegrams, Dowell is unable to discern what, if anything, is wrong. Neither Edward nor Leonora talk to him "about anything other than the weather and the crops." He imagines that what has happened is that some undesirable young man has been attracted to Nancy and that Leonora wants Dowell "to come back and marry her out of harm's way." But this, he informs us, is not what had happened at all.

What had happened was just hell. Leonora had spoken to Nancy; Nancy had spoken to Edward; Edward had spoken to Leonora—and they had talked and talked. And talked. You have to imagine horrible pictures of gloom and half lights, and emotions running through silent nights—through whole nights. You have to imagine my beautiful Nancy appearing suddenly to Edward, rising up at the foot of his bed, with her long hair falling, like a split cone of shadow, in the glimmer of a night-light that burned beside him. You have to imagine her, a silent, no doubt agonized figure, like a spectre, suddenly offering herself to him—to save his reason! And you have to imagine his frantic refusal—and talk. And talk! My God! [p. 201] (p. 175)

Thus, as he has so frequently done in the past, Ford foreshadows the action to come. His "argument" in fact, is remarkably explicit, though of course the reader is drawn on by his desire for details. But what makes our knowledge of these events so painful is neither Dowell's naïveté, his illusory satisfactions, which by now we are accustomed to:

And yet, to me, living in the house, enveloped with the charm of the quiet and ordered living, with the silent, skilled servants whose mere

laying out of my dress clothes was like a caress—to me who was hourly
with them they appeared like tender, ordered, and devoted people,
smiling, absenting themselves at the proper intervals; driving me to
meets—just good people! How the devil—how the devil do they do it?
[pp. 201-202] (pp. 175-176)

Nor is it the disappearance of the public faces of Leonora and
Edward, as they break down and talk to Dowell. Nor is it ultimately the erotic metamorphosis of Edward, or the gradual
deepening of the farcically funny into the metaphysically tragic.
It is our awareness that the real source of the trouble is the
inadequacy of the values and conventions of the characters to
a changing and almost necessarily hypocritical society in which
they live. As Wingfield-Stratford remarks, "there was a grimness,
as of Hell itself, beneath the veneer of Victorian gentility."[7] It
is the Victorian aftermath in which Ford's characters are living.

What Ford does with his narrative structure after he has foreshadowed the climactic incident that occurs during Nancy's stay
at Branshaw (quoted above) is to develop the triangle situation
largely around a single night—the night on which Ashburnham
announces that he has written Colonel Rufford that Nancy ought
to go to him in India—the 12th of November 1913. This is also
the night on which Nancy receives a letter from her mother and
Leonora insists that Nancy should belong to Edward. Ford
frames the events of this night, however, around another night
later in time, the night before Nancy is to leave for Brindisi. The
three of them, together with Dowell, are seated at dinner. A
telegram arrives from Nancy's father. Arrangements are such that
she is to leave the next day. That night Edward talks to Dowell.

Ford then goes backward in time, to early in the fall when
the three returned from Nauheim to Branshaw. Leonora breaks
down, has headaches, and is nursed by Nancy. In her free time
Nancy accompanies Edward to local meets. A specific situation
gives her her first clue as to how things really stand between
Edward and Leonora. Edward generously gives a young fellow
named Selmes, whose father has lost his money, a horse worth
thirty or forty pounds. Over this there is an interchange between
Leonora and Nancy, with the young girl admiring Edward's conduct. "I wish to God," Leonora says to the girl, "that he was your
husband, and not mine. We shall be ruined. We shall be ruined.

Am I *never* to have a chance" (pp. 208-209) [p. 181]. Then, one evening two weeks later, Edward announces at dinner that he has written Colonel Rufford. Leonora, whose secret wish is now to torment Edward with the girl's presence, strongly objects to the girl's leaving. Nancy, taken aback, puts her hand over her heart and cries out: "Oh, my sweet Saviour, help me!" (p. 211) [p. 183]. Edward says nothing.

That night Nancy opens a letter from her mother (whom she has assumed is dead; to the world of polite society, of course, the runaway Mrs. Rufford is beyond the pale, and hence as good as dead). Leonora has failed to prevent this letter from reaching the girl, as she has prevented others, because for the first time in nine years she has gone into Edward's room—for the purpose of proposing that he divorce her. He doesn't answer her. Leonora then goes to the girl's room. Nancy says that she has heard from her mother and that she must go to her in Glasgow; she is in want and starving (which of course is not the case; she is well taken care of by a man rather ironically named White). Leonora insists that Nancy must stay at Branshaw. Edward is dying because of his love for her. "I know it," the girl replies. "And I am dying for love of him."

"You can't let that man go on to ruin for want of you. You must belong to him."
The girl, she said, smiled at her with a queer, faraway smile—as if she were a thousand years old, as if Leonora were a tiny child.
"I knew you would come to that," she said, very slowly. "But we are not worth it—Edward and I." [p. 216] (pp. 187-188)

Nancy's words, as remembered by Leonora, end Chapter II. Then follows a chapter that goes back into Nancy's world, reconstructing not only her feelings about Edward but handling with an extraordinary adroitness her coming to awareness about sexual matters and the meaning of adultery. This is largely done through her reading in the newspapers and then discussing with Leonora the divorce proceedings of a couple named Brand whom they know. Chapter IV returns again to the scene in the girl's bedroom, with Nancy discovering, as Leonora talks to her, that she loves Edward. ("For that fact suddenly slipped into place and became real for her. . . .")

The effect of breaking the scene of the night of November 12th into two parts and interjecting Nancy's self-discoveries is to make all the events of Nancy's past converge on this moment of crisis. The introduction of Nancy's parents into the story at this point, and the resulting complex of tensions, brings Nancy's early environment once more before our eyes. It also emphasizes her role as pawn and crowds into the scene one more sordid image of the present situation. (How much better at this point is Nancy's foster mother, Leonora, than her real mother?) Then the moment is over. Edward takes command and straightens out the situation involving Nancy's mother. Leonora and Nancy, suddenly realizing a sense of identity with each other, spend the night together huddled in each other's arms, talking and talking. "And all through the night Edward could hear their voices through the wall" (p. 232) [p. 200]. The next morning he telegraphs Dowell, and the business of Mrs. Rufford is settled by a telegram from White, the man with whom she has been living. He is taking Mrs. Rufford to Italy.

The complexity of Ford's narrative in these pages is such that not surprisingly he finds it desirable to have Dowell pause and summarize events thus far.

I have been casting back again; but I cannot help it. It is so difficult to keep all these people going. I tell you about Leonora and bring her up to date; then about Edward, who has fallen behind. And then the girl gets hopelessly left behind. I wish I could put it down in diary form. Thus: On the 1st of September they returned from Nauheim. Leonora at once took to her bed. By the 1st of October they were all going to meets together. Nancy had already observed very fully that Edward was strange in his manner. About the 6th of that month Edward gave the horse to young Selmes, and Nancy had cause to believe that her aunt did not love her uncle. On the 20th she read the account of the divorce case, which is reported in the papers of the 18th and the two following days. On the 23rd she had the conversation with her aunt in the hall—about marriage in general and about her own possible marriage. Her aunt's coming into her bedroom did not occur until the 12th of November. . . . [p. 222] (pp. 192-193)

Thus, Dowell remarks, Nancy had three weeks for introspection. During that time she learned the nature of romantic love. Nancy Rufford is the one symbol of innocence in the novel. She wor-

ships Edward in an adolescent way, admiring both the comic
opera soldier in him and the genuine heroics that made him
jump repeatedly off a troop ship to rescue soldiers who had
plunged into the ocean because of the unbearable heat. Nancy
also loves Leonora. And she sees their married life as idyllic, in
contrast with the misery the marriage of her parents has produced.
The present idyll and the misery of the past conspire to make the
naïve and convent trained Nancy intensely susceptible to romantic
ideas.

Ford compresses Nancy's developing awareness of romance
largely within three short pages.

She began thinking above love, she who had never before considered
it as anything other than a rather humorous, rather nonsensical matter. She remembered chance passages in chance books—things that
had not really affected her at all at the time. She remembered someone's love for the Princess Badrulbadour; she remembered to have
heard that love was a flame, a thirst, a withering up of the vitals—
though she did not know what the vitals were. She had a vague recollection that love was said to render a hopeless lover's eyes hopeless;
she remembered a character in a book who was said to have taken
to drink through love; she remembered that lover's existences were
said to be punctuated with heavy sighs.   [p. 223] (p. 193)

Once, at dusk, alone in the hall at Branshaw, she played the
little cottage piano. "A silly, lilting, wavering tune came from
before her in the dusk—a tune in which major notes with their
cheerful insistence wavered and melted into minor sounds, as
beneath a bridge the high lights on dark waters melt and waver
and disappear into black depths." The tune went with Herrick's
words: "Thou art to all lost loves the best, / The only true plant
found." Suddenly Nancy finds herself crying, "all light, all sweetness, had gone out of her life. Unhappiness; unhappiness; unhappiness were all around her."

She remembered that Edward's eyes were hopeless; she was certain
that he was drinking too much; at times he sighed deeply. He appeared as a man who was burning with inward flame; drying up in
the soul with thirst; withering up in the vitals. Then, the torturing
conviction came to her—the conviction that had visited her again
and again—that Edward must love someone other than Leonora.
With her little, pedagogic sectarianism she remembered that Cath-

olics do not do this thing. But Edward was a Protestant. Then Edward loved somebody. . .

  And, after that thought, her eyes grew hopeless; she sighed as the
old St. Bernard beside her did.   [p. 224] (p. 194)

At meals she drank too much wine. She would grow gay, but
then the feeling would fade. "She felt like a person who is burning up with an inward flame; desiccating at the soul with thirst;
withering up in the vitals." Then, once when Edward has gone
out to a meeting of the National Reserve Committee, she tries
whiskey.

  Flame then really seemed to fill her body; her legs swelled; her
face grew feverish. She dragged her tall height up to her room and
lay in the dark. The bed reeled beneath her; she gave way to the
thought that she was in Edward's arms; that he was kissing her on
her face, that burned; on her shoulders, that burned, and on her
neck, that was on fire.   [p. 225] (pp. 194-195)

Deceptively she imagines that the anguish she feels at Edward's
love of another is sympathy for Leonora. Later she learns that
she herself loves him, and later yet, one night in early December,
after Leonora has talked and talked to her, disclosing Edward's
past indiscretions, while all the while convincing the girl that
she must belong to him, she will offer herself to Edward, though
not because of her love of him.

And she looked at him with her straight eyes of an unflinching cruelty and she said: "I am ready to belong to you—to save your life."
  He answered: "I don't want it; I don't want it; I don't want it."
                                            [p. 242] (p. 208)

Cruelty can only be compounded by cruelty in the events to follow. For the agonizing thing for the reader is that there is yet
more to come—even though Ford seemingly has exhausted all
grammatical tenses and all modalities of irony by which to
narrate events in relation to each other.

  What Ford does as he approaches the fifth and sixth chapters,
which in effect form the coda to the novel, with Nancy offering
herself to Edward, her removal to India, her telegram, and
Edwards' suicide, is to remove his narrator further in time from
events. Dowell remarks: "I am writing this, now, I should say,

a full eighteen months after the words that end my last chapter"
(p. 233) [p. 201]. Once more Ford foreshadows events to come.

The end was perfectly plain to each of them—it was perfectly
manifest at this stage that, if she did not, in Leonora's phrase, "belong to Edward," Edward must die, the girl must lose her reason
because Edward died—and that after a time Leonora, who was the
coldest and strongest of the three, would console herself by marrying
Rodney Bayham and have a quiet, comfortable, good time. That end,
on that night, whilst Leonora sat in the girl's bedroom and Edward
telephoned down below—that end was plainly manifest. The girl,
plainly, was half-mad already; Edward was half dead; only Leonora,
active, persistent, instinct with her cold passion of energy, was "doing
things." What then should they have done? It worked out in the
extinction of two very splendid personalities—for Edward and the girl
were splendid personalities, in order that a third personality, more
normal, should have, after a long period of trouble, a quiet, comfortable, good time. [p. 233] (p. 201)

Thus when we come to the end of the novel, to the two last
events, the trip to the station to see the girl off and Edward's
suicide, we come to the scenes in full knowledge of what is to
happen because of them. We have really been there before—at
least for all purposes but the final telling. We have come as close
to moving beneath the social facade as Ford is able to take us:
to discovering as completely satisfying an explanation of what has
happened as is possible in this world; while his characters, in their
attempts to reach satisfaction, have all fallen by the wayside.

Not one of us has got what he really wanted. Leonora wanted
Edward, and she got Rodney Bayham, a pleasant enough sort of
sheep. Florence wanted Branshaw, and it is I who have bought it
from Leonora. I didn't really want it; what I wanted mostly was to
cease being a nurse-attendant. Edward wanted Nancy Rufford and I
have got her. Only she is mad. It is a queer and fantastic world. Why
can't people have what they want? The things were all there to content
everybody; yet everybody has the wrong thing. Perhaps you can make
head or tail of it; it is beyond me. [p. 237] (p. 204)

But if Dowell, after all this, still cannot reconcile himself to
what has happened, at least Edward Ashburnham, "the good
soldier," in his effort to be true to his code, has had the privilege
of coming within sight of his goal, of realizing his "mad passion

to find an ultimately satisfying woman," and of refusing the sacrifice of Nancy.

Ultimately the meaning behind Ashburnham's tragically unsuccessful search for an experience that fulfills his romantic idealism lies less in the complex circumstances of Ford's narrative than in the cultural forces that motivated it. Ford's unique vantage point between two centuries allows him to see Ashburnham's final romantic experience as the experience that marks the end of an age. But history does not suddenly end or cultural forces cease to be. Ford's revelations in depth concerning the sexual conscience of nineteenth-century England also reveal the broad outline of our cultural inheritance, particularly the twentieth century's growing sense of the disparity between romance and reality, inner and outer worlds, ideals and factual experience: dualisms all related to the central dualism of mind and body.

It is not very surprising a generation later to find Ford, under the name of Braddocks, as a figure in *The Sun Also Rises,* Hemingway's version of "Romance In Our Time." In the same book Robert Cohn, who upholds the values of romantic love, has been reading W. H. Hudson, one of Ford's favorite authors.

That sounds like an innocent occupation, but Cohn had read and reread "The Purple Land." "The Purple Land" is a very sinister book if read too late in life. It recounts splendid imaginary amorous adventures of a perfect English gentleman in an intensely romantic land, the scenery of which is very well described. For a man to take it at thirty-four as a guide-book to what life holds is about as safe as it would be for a man of the same age to enter Wall Street direct from a French convent with a complete set of the more practical Alger books.[8]

Hemingway's narrator, Jake Barnes, also has something of the same virus in his system, as he comes more fully to realize in the course of the novel's events. His own predicament is complicated by a wound acquired during the war which has made the sexual act impossible. But Jake is nevertheless haunted by his own private romantic dream of a life with Brett Ashley, with whom he is in love. Early in the book he deliberately takes a Parisian prostitute named Georgette to dinner, then presents her to the crowd at Braddocks' table as the girl he is engaged to. Later that evening Brett asks him why he took up with Georgette. He replies: "I don't know, I just brought her." "You're getting damned romantic," she says. "No, bored," is Jake's answer.[9] His less than candid reply is the mark of how difficult it is even for him, with his heightened awareness, to kill the hopeless romanticism within himself, to be a "good soldier" by Hemingway's standards and to live with "grace under pressure." In a startlingly imaginative way Ford's *Good Soldier* foreshadows cultural tragedies yet to come.

APPRENTICESHIP

FIVE

The "Impressionist Novel"

> Whether the beginnings of things notable
> Have in them anything worth noting.
> Whether an acorn's worth the thinking of
> Or eagle's egg suggests the sweep of wings in
>   the clear blue,
> Is just an idle question.
>   "BEGINNINGS: FOR ROSSETTI'S FIRST PAINTING"

In Douglas Goachu's "interview" with Ezra Pound in *Nimbus* in 1956, imaginatively constructed from literary remarks Pound had made in the past in his essays and published letters, Pound is made to comment: "Only the other day I was reading, or reading *at,* a novel of Fordie's published around 1910 which has merit, but which must be incredible, or incomprehensible, to your generation, or at any rate the next."[1] Perhaps, as Pound says, Ford's early novels would be "incredible" and "incomprehensible" to the general reader—if they were read by him at all. Heroines who play the violin. Heroes who carry dachshunds under their arms. Distant social reforms. Forgotten art movements. Most of Ford's early novels of contemporary life recall a civilization that, existing only yesterday, has vanished almost as completely as the Inca's. They appear curious in subject matter and quaint in outlook. They date in a way that Ford's own *Good Soldier,* which deals basically with the same defunct society, does not.

The interest these early novels hold for us today lies largely in what they reveal about Ford's development as a novelist. No writer sits down at forty and writes a masterpiece like *The Good Soldier* without having learned a great deal about his craft. On the other hand, Ford's claim, in the Dedicatory Letter to the novel, that before *The Good Soldier* he had never really tried to put into any novel all that he knew about writing, seems at least in part disingenuous, particularly in the light of his early novels. Hence one of the questions most worth asking about Ford's early career as a novelist is: Why didn't he write *The Good Soldier,* or a novel of comparable stature, before the age of forty?

If we were to take Ford's word at face value, the reasons for his slow maturation lay in his unusual childhood and the attendant faddisms of his youth. "I came out of the hothouse atmosphere of Pre-Raphaelism where I was being trained for a genius," he remarked in *Memories and Impressions.* "I regarded that training with a rather cold distaste."[2] Ford's own explanation has hung on, useful to biographer and critic alike.

Ford's youthful achievements as a writer, which he treats in his reminiscences as more or less accidental occurrences, obviously owe something to his association with his grandfather and the brilliant artistic and cultural milieu of Fitzroy Square. It seems natural that he should want to be an artist of some kind. On the other hand, his choice of writing, instead of composing or painting, may, as he says, have been accidental, founded on the discovery that he had an amazing facility with words. In any case, a personal need to prove his worth, to demonstrate his own "genius" in the midst of so many "geniuses," seems to have been present, and may later have led to the habit of mind which made a constant outpouring of books necessary. Ford's social idealism, his antagonism to modern industrialized society, and his interest in mediaevalism and Morris socialism, all reflected in the subject matter and themes of his novels, clearly stem from his childhood among the Pre-Raphaelites. So also does the conduct of his early adulthood. He might well have been thinking of himself and his young adult years spent rusticating in the country, in part as a devotee of William Morris, when he wrote that "it was a singularly unhealthy frame of mind which caused a number of young men, totally unfitted, to waste only too many good years of their lives in posing as romantic agriculturists."[3] "Though it is very well to live with love in a cottage in your young years when the world is a funny place, and the washing-up of dishes such a humorous incident as makes of life a picnic, the writer who passes his life at this game will be in the end but a poor creature, whether as a man or a writer."⁴ In retrospect, Ford felt that both his years of sedentary country life and his childhood, spent in the rarified atmosphere of Pre-Raphaelitism, had made the profession of novelist more difficult for him. For one thing, they complicated the problem of finding a suitable subject matter to write about. With perhaps Conrad immediately in mind, he remarks that he had come to agree with writers such as W. E. Henley who believed that the writer should be a "man of action" before he begins to write. "I doubt," Ford concludes, "whether any writer has ever been thoroughly satisfactory unless he has once had some sort of normal existence. No greater calamity could befall one than to be trained as a genius."⁵

As appropriate as it seems and as useful as it is to the biographer and critic, there is something about the idea of being trained for genius which is deceptive. For one thing, it suggests something more specific in the way of education than Ford ever enjoyed. More important, while it explains the derivation of Ford's attitudes toward art and life, and while it offers reasons for his vast literary endeavors, particularly for the hasty composition and failures of imagination in his early novels, it fails to draw attention to the sheer talent that made such a flow of novels possible. It also confuses talent with genius.

Ford was a vastly original genius whose talent for years ironically prevented him from writing the great and original novels he should have written. It was Ford's talent that attracted Conrad and drew him into an alliance with Ford. It was Ford's talent that made possible his facile imitations of Henry James and prolonged his apprenticeship. It is talent, not genius, that Ford exhibits in his early novels. Ford once remarked that "great writers, or strong personalities, when they have passed their impressionable years, are no longer subject to influences. They develop along lines of their own geniuses."⁶ Ford's own "impressionable years" lasted much longer than they would have had he been less talented. This is part of the story his early novels have to tell. The other part is a story of artistic growth and development which ultimately made possible the achievements of *The Good Soldier* and *Parade's End*.

Ford's first novel, *The Shifting of the Fire,* saw print in 1892, the year its author turned nineteen. It is not a bad novel. It is not a very good one either. But it is not unreadable, and for a nineteen-year-old author the performance is more than creditable. The plot of *The Shifting of the Fire* is melodramatic: a sacrificing heroine marries a villainous, rouge-using sexagenarian, named Kasker-Ryves, in the hope that he will shortly die and she can use his money to rescue a ruined sweetheart. The die-hard husband discovers her plan and takes revenge through calculated acts of mental cruelty. Around this plot a series of minor plots revolve. An American cousin attempts to marry the hero and thus thwart a possible happy ending. The villain's son makes an early reformation, disposes of his own fortune for a socialistic ideal, and departs with his bride for New Zealand and a happy life. There is the discovery that Little Maud (!) is the daughter of Kasker-Ryves by a wife he deserted on his climb upward. Finally, of course, Kasker-Ryves confesses his sins, repents, and dies. Yet the novel is not quite over: there is the last minute complication that the heroine may have poisoned Kasker-Ryves. Then, after her innocence is established, the happy ending follows as one might expect.

The plot of *The Shifting of the Fire* and the majority of its characters derive from the conventions of Victorian fiction. More contemporary is the heroine, Edith Ryland, whose desire to be a concert violinist brings her into conflict with her cotton-broker father from Manchester, allowing the young Ford to overtly handle the theme of commerce versus art, a theme that frequently appears in Ford's later works, though in more subtle form. There are other suggestions of the later Ford in this first novel, such as the triangle situation between two women and a man, here left undeveloped, and the theme of frustrated passion; but in general there is very little to seize upon as suggesting the direction Ford's novels would later take.

What seems original about *The Shifting of the Fire* today is the young author's attempt at technical innovation, which obviously owes something to the theater of his day. Portions of the novel are constructed in the manner of a well-made play. The inner selves of the major figures are presented in soliloquies:

"Yes, I do think I'm really pretty—at least by this light I seem quite beautiful—but it may be the light that does it, and I suppose I am apt to look at myself with an indulgent eye, and only from the side of my face which looks best."

[p. 2]

while stage directions are substituted for passages of narrative and scenes are manipulated as if viewed from a theater loge:

The box she kept at the bottom of a great clothes press, and this was the first time she had opened it since her marriage, and she could not resist lingering over its contents once again. There was the necklace he had given her, and the bracelets, and the gold ring—she could not help kissing it. (*Mr. Ryves was very restless that night, and he wanted his wife to get up and read to him. His step was very noiseless when he wished, and he had a knack of opening a door without making the least noise in the world.*) Edith was kneeling on the floor, with her back to the door, leaning over the box. There was one thing Clement had given her that she valued more highly than any other thing in this world—a little bottle with a great poison label—this she seized and kissed a hundred times. (*Mr. Ryves had another knack, that of closing a door very, very gently, almost inaudibly.*)

[pp. 202-203]

But more important for the reader of the later Ford than this early interest in technique is the language of *The Shifting of the Fire,* which is just as Victorian as its melodramatic plot and its gallery of nineteenth-century types.

The novel begins with a piece of description, a scene-setting which opens the curtain on a darkened stage.

Without the house the wind was blusteringly bringing down the few leaves that remained on the trees skirting the north side of the park, and occasionally beating in a solid mass against the sides and windows of the house, or playing with the undulating shrieks round the chimney-pots. The air was filled with a mighty rustling that drowned the distant rumble of traffic, never ceasing in this our city. Without the house the air was grey with twilight, and hazy yellow high up around the street lamps. The year was reluctantly tottering through its last sixth of life, and the boisterous winds shrieked in derision at its decline. But within the house calm was on everything, even the sound of the wind without hardly made itself heard, and certainly did not drown the tick of the great old Dutch-cased clock in the passage. In the drawing-room all was darkness and quiet save where the coals cast a glow onto the red tilework of the open fireplace. A young girl standing before the fire with her elbows on her hands, was gazing at the dim reflection of her face, lit up by the red fire below, in the great glass over the mantelpiece. . . .

This is what we commonly call "poetic prose," and we recognize it by its heavy-handedness: the too-easy alliterative pattern, the exaggerative words and phrases, the too frequent personification, the rhetorical accent of "this our city" and its forced caesura. The wind, we notice, is not only blustering and boisterous; it also bleats, plays, rustles, and shrieks. Compare this passage with part of a poem by Ford, with the same subject matter.

> All within is warm,
>   Here without it's very cold,
>   Now the year is grown so old
> And the dead leaves swarm.[7]

The difference in style is striking. Ford's poetic manner is more natural than artificial, more modern than *fin de siècle*. His descriptive prose, on the other hand, is composed of derivative language, unnatural and fabricated, with a derivative cadence. It is a literary language.

In the preface to the 1913 edition of his *Collected Poems*, an older Ford makes a distinction about literary influences which applies to the novelist as well as the poet. In this instance he is concerned with diction, with the poet's selection of language. He criticizes Tennyson and Morris and the poets of the nineties— "Dowson, Johnson, Davidson, and the rest"—because they wrote "in derivative language": "It is not their choice of subject [to which he objects], it is their imitative handling of matter, of words, it is their derivative attitude. . . ."[8] He goes on to contrast, in a rough way, "the late Victorian writers" [Tennyson and Morris are in his mind] who "imitated Malory and the Laxdaela Saga and commented on them," and the poets of his own day [De la Mare and Yeats] who "record their emotions at receiving the experience of the emotions of the former writers." The latter attitude, Ford says, "is critical rather than imitative."

The distinction Ford is making revolves around the way a writer learns his craft from the resources at his disposal. "Reading," Ford comments, "is an excellent thing." It is, in fact, the primary source of a writer's education, but, he goes on, reading "is an experience that one should go through not in order to acquire imitative faculties, but in order to find—oneself."[9] To draw upon another writer's (or another era's) style, manner, tone, and diction to define one's own style is different from slavish imitation.

It is not hard to see the reading of the bookish young Ford getting into his first novel. The setting of the scene with which the novel opens, for example, has its counterpart largely in Dickens.

> Not only is the day waning, but the year. The low sun is fiery and yet cold behind the monastery ruin, and the Virginia creeper on the Cathedral wall has showered half its deep-red leaves down on the pavement. There has been rain this afternoon, and a wintry shudder goes among the little pools on the cracked, uneven flag-stones, and through the giant elm-trees as they shed a gust of tears. Some of these leaves, in a timid rush, seek sanctuary within the low arched Cathedral door. . . .[10]

Yet, to be more precise, it is not in this case merely a single author that Ford is imitating. It is the voice of an era. Here, for example, is a passage from a later scene in *The Shifting of the Fire.*

> The earth hugged itself under its covering, and trees took strange forms in the misty middle distance—nor was there man, beast, nor bird abroad to testify that aught would ever come to life again, and in truth there was little to tell that anything had ever lived save the forms of dead songbirds that here and there lined the hedges. Then must the traveller on the road, perforce, adopt a swift pace from very strength of the cold, neither heed in his hustle the slippery places of the road, but passing, with whatever luck God vouchsafe him, over all alike; and bad it is for him if he be not warmly clad from tip of toe to end of nose.   [p. 120]

And here is one from *The Mill on the Floss:*

> Snow lay on the croft and river-bank in undulations softer than the limbs of infancy; it lay with the neatliest furnished border on every sloping roof, making the dark-red gables stand out with a new depth of color; it weighed heavily on the laurels and fir trees till it fell from them with a shuddering sound; it clothed the rough turnip-field with

whiteness, and made the sheep look like dark blotches; the gates were all blocked up with the sloping drifts, and here and there a disregarded four-footed beast stood as if petrified "in unrecumbent sadness". . . . But old Christmas smiled as he laid this cruel-seeming spell on the outdoor world, for he meant to light up the home with new brightness. . . .[11]

The parallels are striking. It is almost as if Ford were consciously imitating the early George Eliot (and as if, for that matter, George Eliot were imitating Dickens). Yet there is a difference between the two passages which is readily apparent. The passage by Ford is weak, for the vigor and grace of the original are absent. Indeed, the vagueness of Ford's winter scene is striking. In place of real snow, real trees, real birds—a real landscape— there is a "misty middle distance" filled with spectral trees and the corpses of dead songbirds. There is hardly any concreteness in the landscape. Instead we have something akin to generalization—of situation (the conditions of rural winter), of action (a walk through a snow-filled countryside), and of imagery (snow-covered trees, dead songbirds)—to which only a general and imprecise emotional response is expected. Nor does the conversation that follows, between the hero, Clement Hollebone, and his walking companion, Lord Tatton, alleviate the vagueness of the scene.

"I say, Holly, old boy," said his lordship suddenly, "did you ever read anything by Daudet the Frenchman, doncher know?"

"Why, yes, I've read the immortal Tartarin's adventures," Hollebone replied.

"No, I don't mean those," said his lordship; "they're funny. As a general rule one's apt to read French novels when one wants something a little fishy, or at least I used to, you know. I don't do it since —since I knew her. But, you know, lately I've been tryin' to read some books, and so I went to a feller who I knew knew all about 'em and asked him to lend me some 'at it'd do a chap good to read, and among 'em was one by Daudet. *Lettres de mon Moulin,* I think he called 'em, and in 'em was a short story that this landscape here, with the snow and stars, reminded me of, 'cos it's like a picture of the birth of Christ. . . ."   [pp. 120-121]

Both the imprecision of response and the lack of concrete detail in Ford's winter scene stem from the nature of his imitation. He is trying to reproduce the voice of an era by duplicating its effect. Hence he does not for a moment see his landscape as real; he is interested only in rough verbal equivalents that will produce an appropriate tone. It is for this reason that the posturing author intrudes.

Neither cares he [the traveler] much to converse with his fellow, lest in turning his head to one side he uncover an ear that is sheltered warmly by the collar of his coat, but he keeps his face as steadfastly fixed whitherward he goes, and gets in anticipation what joy he can from the warm fireside that awaits him at his journey's end. [p. 120]

The moralizing of the intruding author is meant to give authenticity to the winter scene; but the voice rings hollow, the words lack conviction, in part because Ford has failed to see that what lent authenticity to such passages of description as the one we have quoted from *The Mill on the Floss* was the keen eye of the observer taking in the landscape detail by detail. A second reason is historical.

Mid-Victorian prose, especially that of Dickens, was written to be read aloud. Dickens naturally had his ear tuned first to the Victorian hearth, where the patriarch read the latest Monthly Part to the assembled family, then to the lecture platform, where he himself read to the crowds who jammed the auditoriums to hear him. He expected to be listened to, and his effects are in part designed exactly for such circumstances. By the time of *The Shifting of the Fire* the convention is dead, and the same theatrical quality that was perfectly natural in Dickens becomes in the early Ford mere fustian. Yet Ford, who passionately desired to write as well as he and a few others talked, had to find for himself something very similar to the Mid-Victorian voice before he could develop the flexible style of *The Good Soldier* and *Parade's End*.

In the years following *The Shifting of the Fire* Ford turned to the continent for models. While collaborating with Conrad on *The Inheritors* (1901) and *Romance* (1904), he fell under the spell of Flaubert. "Buried deep in rural greennesses," their evenings spent before the fire at Pent Farm, the collaborators discussed the craft of the author of *Madame Bovary*. Because Flaubertian realism was based on significant things, details, concrete particulars, they made a tenet of "selection" and cultivated *le mot juste*. They made experiments, together and separately, in points of style and cadence, searching for a nonliterary language. They "used to ask each other how, exactly, such an effect of light and shade should be reproduced in very simple words."[12] Their desire was "to achieve a style—the habit of a style—so simple that you would notice it no more than you notice the unostentatious covering of the South Downs. The turf had to be there, or the earth would not be green."[13] They concluded that a passage of good style begins with a fresh, usual word, and continues with fresh, usual words to the end; "there was nothing more to it."[14]

Conrad and Ford's "greatest admiration for a stylist in any language was given to W. H. Hudson of whom Conrad said that his writing was like the grass that the good God made to grow and when it was there you could not tell how it came."[15] Occasionally they "became enthusiastic" over a phrase of Stephen Crane's, such as "the waves were barbarous and abrupt."[16] Ford also admired Crane's remark about the prose style of Robert Louis Stevenson. According to Crane, when Stevenson wrote, "With interjected finger he delayed the action of the time piece," he put back the clock of English fiction 150 years.[17] But aside from their enthusiasm for Hudson and Crane, and other writers who occasionally met their high standards, "it was Flaubert, Flaubert, Flaubert all the way."[18]

What Flaubert gave to the world was not merely one book—not five or six; it was a whole habit of mind that is changing the face of the globe. For communication between man and man is the most important, the most beneficent of human gifts—and just and true communication can only be achieved by an appallingly serious study of Language. . . . And do not believe that any literary quality, of whatever nature, can be achieved without this seriousness. Read, if Flaubert is too serious for you, the *cochonneries* of Maupassant—for God knows I am no kill-joy—and you will find just Flaubert's economy and appropriateness of words, achieved only after the same seriousness in their study. You won't, that is to say, find a phrase that is over-written; you will not find one that is slipshod.[19]

Not surprisingly, Ford and Conrad's "chief masters in style were Flaubert and Maupassant: Flaubert in the greater degree, Maupassant in the less."[20] The passage in prose, however, that Ford always took as a "working model" occurs in Maupassant's *"La Reine Hortense."*

Maupassant is introducing one of his characters, who is possibly gross, commercial, overbearing, insolent; who eats, possibly, too much greasy food; who wears commonplace clothes—a gentleman about whom you might write volumes if you wanted to give the facts of his existence. But all that de Maupassant finds it necessary to say is: "C'était un monsieur à favoris rouges qui entrait toujours le premier." . . . He was a gentleman with red whiskers who always went first through a door.[21]

If Flaubertian realism had its lesson in style—good prose succeeds by "a succession of tiny, unobservable surprises";[22] "the proof of prose is in the percentage of right words. Not the precious word: not even the startlingly real word"[23]—it was also the wellspring of Ford and Conrad's concern with technique. Because Flaubertian realism was impersonal, impartial, objective, they banned themselves from the pages of their books. They made it a tenet that the author should suppress himself, as Flaubert had done. There was to be no intrusive author breaking in to dispel the "illusion of reality," as happened frequently in Thackeray, for example, whose interruptions Ford found particularly objectionable. In Ford's eyes, Thackeray, with his uneasiness over point of view, had performed illusion-shattering acrobatics before his readers. Ford's point can be illustrated from *The Newcomes.*

That a biographer should profess to know everything which passes, even in a confidential talk in a first class carriage between two lovers, seems perfectly absurd; not that grave historians do not pretend to the same wonderful degree of knowledge—reporting meetings the most occult of conspirators; private interviews between monarchs and their ministers, even the secret thoughts and motives of those personages, which possibly the persons themselves did not know. All for which the present writer will pledge his known characters for veracity is that on a certain day certain parties had a conversation, of which the upshot was so and so.[24]

Ford also found objectionable the author's moralizing, his taking sides, as Thackeray did frequently. As Ford's imaginary reader in *The March of Literature* puts it, having supposedly come across such a passage in Thackeray: "Hullo! I really thought this was something real I was looking at. But here's that wearying old W. M. T. bucking in, broken nose and all. . . . So that it's really only a silly novel."[25] Flaubertian realism, on the other hand, demanded authorial reticence. "It was Flaubert," Ford remarks in *The English Novel,* "who shiningly preached the doctrine of the novelist as a Creator who should have a Creator's aloofness, rendering the world as he sees it, uttering no comments, falsifying no issues. . . ."[26]

Flaubertian realism was not the only source of Ford and Conrad's literary theories, however; there was also "impressionism," which, as Ford remarks, "struck London in a sort of literary folkwave in the early nineties."[27] Its influence on Ford and Conrad can be seen in their theory that "the general effect of a novel must be the general effect that life makes on mankind."

A novel must therefore not be a narration, a report. Life does not say to you: In 1914 my next-door neighbour, Mr. Slack, erected a greenhouse and painted it with Cox's green aluminum paint. . . . If you think about the matter you will remember, in various unordered pictures, how one day Mr. Slack appeared in his garden and contemplated the wall of his house. You will then try to remember the year of the occurrence and you will fix it as August, 1914, because having had the foresight to bear the municipal stock of the City of Liège you were able to afford a first-class season ticket for the first time in your life.[28]

Life, they argued, does not narrate; it makes *impressions* on our brain. The novel should imitate life. More specifically, it should be psychologically real, not merely an imitation of experience but of the process of experiencing. The impressionists in painting had sought a manner of representation that more nearly approached the physical process of seeing. The images that the eye observes, they discovered, are of a bewildering variety and irregularity; colors are often violently juxtaposed. Thus they broke down color into its constituent hues, creating on their canvases a juxtaposition of colors which merged and produced an effect of vividness upon the spectator's retina. Ford and Conrad sought an analogous manner of representation in fiction. For the painter's eye, they substituted memory, seeking to achieve a form that more nearly approached the psychological process of re-

membering ("The object of the novelist is to keep the reader
entirely oblivious of the fact that he is reading a book. This of
course is not possible to the bitter end. . . ."[29]); ultimately they
found it, as the story of Mr. Slack's greenhouse illustrates, in
the convention of time rearranged by a narrator.

Like the impressionist painters, then, Ford and Conrad based
their theory of the novel on a concept of reality in which what is
"real" depends upon "the psychology of the patron," that is, the
viewer or reader.[30] Furthermore, whether painter or writer, "the
impressionist gives you, as a rule, the fruits of his own observation
and the fruits of his own observation alone."[31] (In his essay "The
Art of Fiction" Henry James had said that "a novel is in its
broadest definition a personal, a direct impression of life: that,
to begin with, constitutes its value, which is greater or lesser
according to the intensity of the impression."[32]) Ford illustrates
his point by a quotation from Tennyson.

> And bats went round in fragrant skies
> And wheeled or lit the filmy shapes
> That haunt the dusk, with ermine capes
> And wooly breasts and beady eyes.

"Now that is no doubt very good natural history," Ford remarks,
"but it is certainly not Impressionism, since no one watching a
bat at dusk could see the ermine, the wool or the beadiness of
the eyes."[33] The realism of the impressionist writer, according
to Ford, emphasizes the seen and the felt.

Like the impressionists in painting also, Ford and Conrad saw
experience as fragmentary, discontinuous, of the moment. "Impressionism," Ford said, "is a thing altogether momentary."[34]
Its aim is to capture "the record of the impression of a moment."[35]
"My task," Conrad said in the Preface to *The Nigger of the
Narcissus,* is "to make you hear, to make you feel—it is before
all, to make you *see.*"

> To snatch in a moment of courage, from the remorseless rush of
> time, a passing phase of life, is only the beginning of the task. The
> task approached in tenderness and faith is to hold up unquestioningly,
> without choice and without fear, the rescued fragment before all eyes
> in the light of a sincere mood. It is to show its vibration, its color, its
> form; and through its movement, its form, its color, reveal the sub-

stance of its truth—disclose its aspiring secret: the stress and passion within the core of each convincing moment.[36]

For Ford and Conrad, as for the impressionist painters, the emphasis on the moment produced a chain of consequences revealed not merely in their elaborate efforts to achieve subtle effects of changing light and movement (Conrad's terminology, one notices, is borrowed from the language of painting) but also in the attempt to capture the complex rhythm of modern life and, in so doing, to deal with what today we call the existential dilemma.

For both Ford and Conrad the connective links between "rescued fragments" of experience were as important as the fragmented experiences themselves, were indeed part of the experiences, since without connections of some sort events remained isolated, unrelated, and meaningless in the wider context of life. Hence they relied heavily on juxtaposition, as had the impressionist painters, to achieve their effects and patterns. Image was juxtaposed to image, event to event, scene to scene, conversation to conversation.

. . . The juxtaposition of the composed renderings of two or more unexaggerated actions or situations may be used to establish, like the juxtaposition of vital word to vital word, a sort of frictional current of electric life that will extraordinarily galvanize the work of art in which the device is employed. . . . Or let us use the still more easy image of two men shouting in a field. While each shouts separately each can only be heard at a distance of an eighth of a mile, whilst if both shout simultaneously their range of hearing will be extended by a hundred-odd yards. The point cannot be sufficiently laboured, since the whole fabric of modern art depends on it.[37]

Ford's description of juxtaposition, it should be pointed out, is inadequate to describe the remarkable effects he achieved by his daring use of it.

The technical device that made such juxtaposition possible was the time-shift. Like juxtaposition, which in its broadest sense is the basis of *all* art, the shifting of time is not new to literature. One has only to think of the *Oedipus Rex* of Sophocles and recall the messenger, who, once on stage, moves time backward to recount past events. Basically what Ford and Conrad did achieve by their technique of the time-shift was to eliminate such cumbersome devices as the messenger. In other words, they were doing away with the old apparatus behind the time-shift. Like the impressionist painters, they felt that previous techniques got in the way of portraying modern life. An instance from the history of impressionism illustrates the point. Manet's painting *Olympia* portrayed a nude courtesan reclining on a couch and attended by a Negress. Manet's nineteenth-century audience was outraged, not because of the nudity of his courtesan, but because his nude was frankly a naked woman. Previous painters had painted their nudes as coy, seductive, and so on. Ford strove for a realism similar to Manet's. His handling of passion and its related themes was impossible, as we shall shortly see, under the older conventions of novel writing. It is not that Ford is realistic and earlier writers unrealistic, we should add; Ford, like Manet, simply practiced a new realism.

In his use of technical devices, Ford actually most closely resembles the post-impressionist painter Georges Seurat, who developed the technique of pointillism, or divisionism, as he preferred to call it; in effect Ford broke up time the way Seurat broke up light. "The function of the time-shift," as Hugh Kenner has pointed out, "was to do away with plot—plot in the sense of linear sequence."[38] The climactic arrangement of physical events lost its significance to the psychological ordering not so much of events as of their meanings. In place of the chronological development of incidents, Ford and Conrad substituted a progression of psychologically controlled revelations (*progression d'effet*), so that as a story progresses it is "carried forward faster and faster with more and more intensity." The "New Form" of the novel became

the rendering of an Affair: of one embroilment, one set of embarrassments, one human coil, one psychological progression. From this the Novel got its Unity. . . . The whole novel was to be an exhaustion of aspects, was to proceed to one culmination, to reveal once and for all, in the last sentence, or the penultimate; in the last phrase, or the one before it—the psychological significance of the whole.[39]

(It should be pointed out that Ford's requirement that the "New Form" possess a final revelation "in the last sentence, or the penultimate," is satisfied by only *The Good Soldier,* and perhaps *Some Do Not . . .*; the description does not fit any other novel by Ford, and none at all by Conrad.)

If the narrative technique of Ford and Conrad is based on a profound revolution in human psychology—in our conception of the way man views and has knowledge of reality—it is also based on an equally profound revolution in morals, in the way man views his fellow man and judges his conduct. An author no longer took sides, made pronouncements, or judged his characters; he remained aloof. "The main and perhaps most passionate tenet of impressionism was the suppression of the author from the pages of his book. He must not comment; he must not narrate; he must present his impressions of his imaginary affairs as if he had been present at them."[40] Also, novels no longer necessarily ended with finality.

To the theory of Aloofness added itself, by a very natural process, the other theory that the story of a novel should be the history of an Affair and not the invention of a tale in which a central character with an attendant female should be followed through a certain space of time until the book comes to a happy end on a note of matrimony or to an unhappy end—represented by death. That latter—the normal practice of the earlier novelist and still the normal expedient of the novel of commerce or escape—is . . . designed to satisfy a very natural human desire for finality.

Normal humanity, deprived of the possibility of viewing either lives or life, makes naturally for a pessimism that demands relief either in the drugs of the happy ending or in the anodynes of superstition— one habit being as fatal to the human intelligence as the other. But there is no need to entertain the belief that life is sad anymore than there is any benefit to be derived from the contemplation of fictitious and banal joys.[41]

Ford's point needs stressing. All narrative structures carry with them—have, in effect, built into them—not merely assumptions about what constitutes the real (to take an obvious example, the stream of consciousness novel) but also attitudes toward the individual and society, and values by which conduct and action are judged. Dickens' rhetoric of narrative, for example, carried with it a middle-class sentimentality which only in his late novels, such as *Hard Times,* could he escape, and then only barely, through the mechanism of plot. Furthermore, his use of melodrama, pathos, and humor reflected conventional Victorian morality—even while he was attacking English institutions in such novels as *Bleak House* and *Little Dorrit.* The outcome of a Dickens novel is predictable. "You always know beforehand," Ford remarks in *The March of Literature,* "what Dickens will do with the fraudulent lawyer on whose machinations hang the fate of a score of his characters."[42] Vice is punished, virtue rewarded, and the hero and heroine live happily ever after.

The unsatisfactoriness of this kind of narrative structure (based, for one thing, on the convention of serial publication in which each Monthly Part had to end with what Ford calls a "strong situation") for the kinds of meaning Ford and Conrad wished to convey in their novels is obvious: in their view, it falsifies life. But there is a more subtle point here, as a glance at *The Good Soldier* reveals. For suppose *The Good Soldier* were told in the Dickensian mode. Would there be any doubt that Captain Ashburnham would emerge as a villain? Or that moral injunctions would indiscriminately be leveled at all the guilty parties, unless they reformed? Or, for that matter, that the novel would end happily? Ford's narrative technique in *The Good Soldier* is another matter. As much as anything, it is designed so that Ford can convey something like the following in terms of meanings: in spite of the wrecked marriage between Dowell and Florence, in spite of the wrecked marriage between Edward and Leonora, in spite of Maisie Maidan's death and Florence's suicide, in spite of Edward's suicide and Nancy's insanity—in spite of all these things, Edward Ashburnham's passion was not only the "real thing" but the central power of the novel. Perhaps it is no wonder that Ford did not achieve a marriage between form and content until he was forty. As late as *A Call* (1910), he was to write, in an "Epistolary Epilogue," a mock Dickensian ending to his novel, partially in disgust at his own inability to communicate his meaning to the reader with the new techniques he was trying to use.

In one of Dickens' novels, Ford felt, he had escaped from a predominantly moralistic view, and this was *Great Expectations,* which, like *Vanity Fair,* Ford viewed as a great novel: "They are not . . . works founded on any conventional scheme of ethics and they propound no conventional solutions of evils; they are simple records, that from time to time attain to the height of renderings, of life transfused by the light of their writers' temperaments as modified by their vicissitudes."[43] In Ford's eyes *Great Expectations* was "a muted book," with all "the usual qualities" of Dickens modified. It was a product "of a passionate world-weariness with humanity and humanity's contrivances."[44] On the basis of this book Dickens qualified, "in the quite technical sense," as a realist.[45] "Realism" Ford defined as "a frame of mind reinforced by the new literary technique of impressionism, with an increased attention to the quality of words, which gave to its product a singular vividness."

The frame of mind of realism was founded on a basis of relatively gentle cynicism or, as in the case of Flaubert, of disillusionment. For essentially, Flaubert was an optimist—a believer in perfectibility who was disappointed that humanity, with all the opportunities it had had, had never got any farther on the road to sanity, reasonable behaviour and altruism. But it was possible to belong to his school without being cynical at all: thus the young James regarded the world with eyes merely of wonder; Gautier with rather joyful curiosity; Turgenev with a tremendous benevolence together with a really constructive passion for bettering Russia. Thus the real *trait-d'union* between all these authors and modernity in general was the technical one which this writer prefers to call impressionism.[46]

If Ford and Conrad felt a natural kinship with Flaubert, as well as with Turgenev and James, nevertheless their artistic problems were not Flaubert's. It was initially because of Flaubertian realism that they banned themselves from the pages of their books, suppressing the author as Flaubert had done. And here they ran into difficulty, for neither Conrad nor Ford was temperamentally suited to suppressing himself, though for different reasons. Conrad, perhaps in part because of his Polish inheritance, needed the security of personal reference to conceal his essential foreignness from his English audience. He also needed philosophic distance from his subjects. On the one hand, he needed an authoritative, lofty platform from which to view events; on the other, he needed the license of a commentator to put himself on the inside of events when he needed to be not foreigner but insider. Both of these poses he found in his master mariner, Marlow.

Like Conrad, Ford was also in a sense a foreigner. Son of a German emigré, and grandson of a Pre-Raphaelite painter, he was twice removed from the mainstream of English society. His problem was no easier than the deracinated Conrad's, no less critical than the expatriate Henry James's. None of the three could write of English manners with the ease, say, of E. M. Forster. James needed point of view and centers of consciousness; Conrad needed Marlow and an inversive method. Ford turned to the time-shift, and, later, the stream of consciousness, at least in part to figure and justify in his art his personal disinvolvement from the society that is its subject matter. Like Conrad, he eventually found his persona, first in Dowell, the narrator of *The Good Soldier,* and later in Christopher Tietjens, his mythopoeic hero. But he did not come upon these or comparable figures early in his career, as Conrad did with Marlow. One has to remind oneself that *all* of Ford's statements that deal directly with the technique of novel writing were set down after *The Good Soldier,* and many of them after *Parade's End.* That is, Ford was looking back in retrospect, in the light of his own achievements. This does not mean that he did not share with Conrad in the early years of the century the fully developed theories he talks of, in his Conrad volume, particularly, and in *Thus to Revisit.* It is more plausible to assume that he was in possession of them and simply did not know how to put them to use. (*The Inheritors,* one should point out, makes use of a first-person narrator.) But this is only a part of the story. More precisely, Ford fell under the spell of Henry James, and hence he sought another alternative solution to his artistic problems than the one chosen by Conrad.

Ford's characteristic tone was that of well-informed gossip. (In his volumes of reminiscence he often sounds surprisingly like the Thackeray of the passage we quoted earlier from *The Newcomes,* though of course Ford's style is less mannered.) Gossip of any kind hinges on being in the know, on having inside information to retail, whether about the literary and artistic great (of whom Ford wrote so often in his volumes of memoirs), or about the sexual life of Captain Ashburnham. Flaubertian realism, with its

emphasis on the impersonal and the impartial, with its tenet of
author suppression, left Ford outside, staring at things, at appearances, instead of penetrating to what lay underneath, reality.
Hence Ford turned to the sources nearest at hand, searching for
a model that would enable him to capture an insider's view without violating the Flaubertian canon.

The natural vehicle of gossip is dialogue. It is not surprising
then that for a long time Ford believed such inside information
could best be given to the reader by dialogue, nor is it very surprising that he turned to the novels of Henry James for model
conversations. Unfortunately Ford's attitude was imitative, not
critical, and the results were curiously affected conversations with a
hollow Jamesian ring, such as in *The Benefactor* (1905), his
second independent novel.

> Clara said: "I was so miserable. I'm so tired of it all. If only I
> could get away."
> She half pointed a long, sensitive, white hand toward the sea.
> "Beyond the horizon?" George asked sympathetically.
> "Beyond—beyond all horizons," she assented. She added: "If only
> you knew."   [p. 190]

But Ford's early heroes never allow themselves to know—until it
is too late, until the novel is over. They make their discoveries
on the very last page, not before, at which point only an un-
satisfactory course of action is left for them to follow. Thus
George Moffat, the hero of *The Benefactor,* renounces Clara
Brede, the heroine, who has been hoping that George, although
married and unable to obtain a divorce from his wife, will ask
her to go off with him (a sacrifice of respectability which she has
decided to make). But George, who feels responsible for the
relapse of Clara's father, the Reverend Brede, into insanity, cannot bear the additional responsibility of Clara's life. Even the
implausible, last-minute financial success of George's novel,
Wilderspin, written at Clara's urging, which rescues him from
bankruptcy, changes nothing. George goes off alone, perhaps to
live the rest of his life in a small Italian pension, bringing the
curtain down with a Jamesian finale.

The trouble behind Ford's use of Jamesian dialogue, in which
everything is implied, not stated, is that in his hands the cere-

monial nature of such conversations becomes inhibiting; any truly dramatic or realistic or revealing word may be a breach in propriety or decorum—unless you merely talk around the subject.

"Ah, yes, beyond the horizon," George said musingly, with his eyes on the juncture of sky and sand and sea. "My dear young lady, the question is—and it's the same for every one of us—what we should find there." It was, after all, George's manner rather than his matter that was so eminently soothing.   [p. 216]

With that last sentence the author betrays not only his character's, but also his own, inability to broach the matter. The small talk is to remain small talk. Jamesian dialogue will not serve Ford as microcosm. His characters cannot directly confront each other, and the dialogue fails to convey what Ford's story should be telling.

The Benefactor is only in part a "Jamesian pastiche," to use the phrase Ford applied to several of his novels. Its plot line stems directly from Turgenev's *Nest of Gentlefolk,* and the story of George, whose Scottish wife will not divorce him, was apparently modeled on Ruskin's life.[47] In addition, there are literary echoes of Jane Austen and Oliver Goldsmith in both the landscape and the characters, and of Thomas Hardy in the mob of villagers. Reverend Brede's two daughters, Clara and Dora, seems to have had literary models: the one in Meredith's heroine, the other in Dora Spenlow. It seems plausible that the surname "Brede" was used because Stephen Crane lived nearby at "Brede Place" during Ford's years in the country. More important in terms of Ford's later career is the tale of unrequited passion between an older man and a younger woman, and the use of a double figure, George's brother Gregory.

The major plot of *The Benefactor* concerns George's "meddling" in the life of the Brede family. He is responsible for Reverend Brede's resolve to reënter the pulpit, and he is instrumental in the marriage of Dora Brede to Thwaite, the editor of an art magazine, *The Salon.* But the proposed therapy does not help Mr. Brede, whose mental instability was produced by the guilt he felt over his wife's death; and in the strain of preaching he tumbles from his pulpit with a stroke. The marriage of Thwaite and Dora also turns out unhappily; once again George, patron and benefactor of writers and artists, has been taken in by a "deserving" writer. In George, with his kindness and goodness, his world-weariness, his idealism and his "meddling," we have the prototype of the Fordian hero. In time this figure will evolve into the hero of *Parade's End,* Christopher Tietjens.

It is in *The Benefactor* that Ford first developed one of his major techniques for handling time: he begins a scene, setting locale and time, then shifts backward in time to various earlier events, and finally concludes by returning to the scene with which he began. This method, which he used in all his later novels, particularly the Tietjens books, depends on the scene-in-the-present serving as an envelope, or frame, to encompass and round off the flashbacks. In *The Good Soldier* and the Tietjens novels, the method is used in conjunction with the time-shift; as it is used in *The Benefactor* and the Katherine Howard trilogy it is much more closely aligned to the flashback both in its obviousness and in its formality.

Slightly over halfway through the novel, in the third section, Clara Brede and George Moffat go for a walk on the beach. During the walk a number of shifts in time occur. Ford's method in each instance is to signal the change by also shifting from omniscient narrative to the point of view of either George or Clara. Additional framework for the shifts is produced by the use of typographical and formal devices (chapters and breaks within chapters). There are also parallel shifts; that is, the same event is viewed first by George, then by Clara. The whole thirty-page section comes to a close when Mr. Brede, who is following George and Clara, catches up with them.

Schema: Section 3, "The Blackening Pearls"

Chap. III; p. 187   1.   The conversation between George and Clara. They are walking on the beach, Mr. Brede in the distance pursuing them. Dora and Thwaite have been recently married, at the most four days before this walk. There has been a three-month break in time since the last chapter.

Break in space; p. 193   2.   A telescoping of George's time from the last chapter (three months previously) to the night before the wedding. Then a conversation between George and Thwaite, seen through George's eyes. Thwaite, Bohemian author of *Love*

Poems of Sidonia, is concerned with his new-found responsibility, a middle-class wife-to-be. Specifically, he is worried about a proper and inexpensive place to stay with Dora on their honeymoon in Paris. Ironically, George is at this time plagued with money problems of his own far more serious than those of Thwaite, who makes pointed reference to George's never having to worry about money.

Chap. IV; p. 202   3. The wedding breakfast. Done briefly, partly to introduce the South American cousin Carew, but mainly to give Clara's feelings about her relatives. Transition is through the mind of Clara, who is conscience-stricken because she has kept Dora's dowry from her to help George, if necessary. Thwaite owes George money, and Clara rightly suspects that Thwaite, if given the dowry, would not use it to pay George back.

No break. Simple transition through Clara; p. 206   4. The night before the wedding. George has given Dora and Thwaite his collection of his painter-father's sketches for his most famous portraits. The nature of the wedding gift makes Clara realize that George is bankrupt. Clara reveals to Dora that she is in love with George.

Chap. V; p. 212   5. The night before the walk between George and Clara. Carew, the South American cousin from La Plata, seeks George's advice about asking Clara to marry him. George, of course, is irritated and becomes conscious that he wants no one but himself to have Clara.

Break in space; p. 214   6. "Next morning George walked with Clara Brede along the sand." The scene comes to a close when, on page 218, "Mr. Brede, remotely suggesting a shortness of breath, obtruded suddenly between them."

Some things become apparent from this paradigm. For one thing, in each scene, with the exception of the wedding breakfast, the structuring device is a conversation between two people which ends in a revelation for one of them. The ordering of the scenes is quasi-climactic; the center of importance is not the wedding breakfast but George, then Clara, then George *and* Clara. When the scene again reverts to present time the dialogue between George and Clara, which closely echoes the words and phrases of their earlier talk as they walked on the beach, carries with it an additional meaning. For all of this, the series of time-shifts is far from a complete success. The reader's attention, for one thing, is divided between the framing device (the walk on the beach) and the shifts. There is no irony intended by the sequence of the night before the wedding, the wedding breakfast, and again the night before the wedding. The major effect is one of suspense. On the other hand, the effectiveness of the frame is largely dissipated by the two lengthy pseudo-Jamesian conversa-tions. What Ford achieves in the long run is not the fluidity of life but the fixity of the photographer's bath. Each shift is formally signaled by chapter and subdivision. Each requires setting and dialogue. Each one, in other words, requires a plot of its own. In the long run this method is uneconomical.

SIX

Tietjens in Disguise

"He's an incredible ass. . . ."
AN ENGLISH GIRL

It took Ford over twenty years of writing to find his true subject matter and the individual techniques he needed to handle it. During those laborious twenty years he fell under the varying influences of Turgenev, Flaubert, Conrad, and James. It was not Conrad but James who played the largest role in the development of his art. What Ford learned in collaborating with Conrad was his own—nothing borrowed, nothing imitative. But James presented him with the linked temptations of easily borrowable or easily accessible themes and techniques and style.

On re-reading this morning, after an interval of perhaps twenty-five years, *The American,* I find that I have introduced, almost exactly as he stands in that book, one of Mr. James' characters into one of my own novels, written five years ago. You see, I first read *The American* during a period of my boyhood passed very largely in Paris, and very largely in exactly the same society as that in which Newman himself moved. And having read the book at the same time I really, twenty years after, thought that Valentin de Bellegarde was a young man that I had met somewhere. . . . Yes, indeed, I thought Valentin was one of my own connections whom I had liked very much. And so I considered myself perfectly justified in lifting his figure, with such adornments and changes as should suit my own purpose, into one of my own novels.[1]

Ford's somewhat belated self-revelation and his less than successful attempt at self-justification are an index of the complex story of his indebtedness to James.

If Count Carlo Canzano, who is modeled on Valentin de Bellegarde, carries some of the authenticity of the Jamesian world into *An English Girl* (1907), it is not because Ford knew the same social world as James (which of course he did not), or because Ford himself had met Canzano on occasion during afternoons-at-home (as he is claiming here), but because Canzano is a thoroughgoing imitation of James.

A trip to America which Ford and his wife took in 1906 was the immediate occasion that suggested *An English Girl*. Ostensibly the novel deals with the "international theme" in the same way as "Lady Barberina" and *Portrait of a Lady*: it plays upon the moral and cultural antinomies of two civilizations as, in this case, "an English girl" becomes involved in the American scene. Actually, the heroine, Eleanor Greville, shares the stage with a hero, the American Don Collar Kelleg, and the novel is more *his* than hers. For into a typical Jamesian situation Ford introduces his own particular heroic fantasy: the deracinated young hero, out of joint with his time, filled with aesthetic idealism and social purpose, but helpless to act. That fantasy is merely a shorthand cipher of Ford's own problem as an artist.

Don and Eleanor are engaged to be married. They have met while studying art under Whistler in a Paris atelier. As the novel opens, they have just learned of the death of Don's father, an American businessman who made his fortune through juggling stocks and manipulating holding companies. Overnight Don becomes "the richest man in the world," and the position of the couple changes. They can no longer look forward to the simple, retired life of the English family of means. Don assumes "a portentous identity" in the eyes of the world.

A voice behind her back uttered:
"Oh, I suppose he's come down to see if he won't buy the cathedral."
And another:
"Oh, he *couldn't* do that, could he? Doesn't it belong to the State or something."   [p. 7]

To Don the inheritance becomes a burden. Society must be repaid for the wrongs committed by his father in amassing such a fortune. " 'Heaven knows,' he said, 'it is not power that's given me. It's a burden; it's a duty' " (p. 13).

The upshot is a trip to America. Don and Eleanor—accompanied by her father, her aunt, and her cousin Augustus, who is in love with her—travel to the new world to see how Don can best spend the money to benefit society. The central portion of the novel is concerned with the sea voyage and American types met on shipboard. Ford deals with his Americans in almost vitriolic fashion, singling out eccentricities and fastening upon unpleasant traits; but the Dickensian streak is not strong enough to make them very interesting. They are merely repellent. America itself is handled in a similar fashion, with a loose, rambling, impressionistic collage of detail. In sum, America too is unpleasant, and long before the climactic news that Don can do absolutely nothing with his money, since it is securely tied to Kelleg Enterprises by his father's will, the hero has sickened of his native country. His reaction to Coney Island during a ferryboat ride is violent. "I'll suppress the whole thing!" (p. 265). And Broadway at night, seen from his hotel window—"the jingle and cries of blazing, contagious, jostling Broadway"—fares no better. " 'It's all hopelessly material,' he muttered aloud. 'There's nothing that isn't blatant, vulgar, hideous' " (p. 284).

Don is helpless before the modern world. Eleanor braves him: "Dear boy! If you want William Morris effects and floppy gowns this isn't surely the place to come to for them" (p. 263). Her allusion is an accurate index to the purlieus of Don's mind.

Ford's culture-conscious aesthete—believer in a rural, pseudo-medieval, aristocratic world—is metaphorically bound helpless to the mast of a ferryboat plying between Manhattan and Staten Island. Ulysses hears the sirens, but their voices are not those of beautiful maidens of the sea. They are the ubiquitous cries of the machinery of an industrial world. Instead of seduction, repulsion follows, for Don, who is committed to social progress, cannot stand what he hears and sees.

Eleanor's father—an eccentric book-reviewer who at meals stands through the first course—delineates Don's problem, which is a mirror of his own.

Don is acting precisely as I've acted all my life. He hates modern circumstances. I don't say that he wants what *I* want. He doesn't. He isn't for the Tory Party right or wrong. But he *is* for Aestheticism right or wrong. He *does*, really, want the American people to go in

for certain European virtues—for Poetry and the Higher Thought
and Rational Dress.   [p. 268]

But it is Eleanor's cousin Augustus who has the final word in the
portrait of Don: "He's the tamest sort of cat. He's an incredible
ass . . ." (p. 80). (The ellipsis is Ford's.)

Don Collar Kelleg, the "incredible ass," is clearly a younger
version of Ford's famous hero—he is Christopher Tietjens without brain or backbone. Entombed in a mausoleum of novelistic
conventions that appear as quaint today as the daguerreotype, he
has only to be exhumed to reveal the outlines of Ford's generic
hero. He is "excellent and gentle" (p. 50); he is the "noblest and
best man you've ever seen" (p. 51); he has "a remarkably developed moral sense" (p. 58); he is "unreasonably kind" (p. 58).

Ford's gauche vanity? Hardly, though the author is clearly involved with his hero. But there is more here than that. What we
see is a writer whose devotion to society, to mankind, is nothing
short of reckless. So much so that for years his hero simply
appears to be "an incredible ass." And the author himself?

He was a longish, leanish, fairish young Englishman, not unamena-
ble, on certain sides, to classification—as for instance by being a gentleman, by being rather specifically one of the educated, one of the generally sound and generally pleasant; yet, though to that degree neither
extraordinary nor abnormal, he would have failed to play straight
into an observer's hands. He was young for the House of Commons,
he was loose for the army. He was refined, as might have been said,
for the city, and quite apart from the cut of his cloth, he was scepti-
cal, it might have been felt, for the church. On the other hand he
was credulous for diplomacy, or perhaps even for science, while he
was perhaps at the same time too much in his mere senses for poetry,
and yet too little in them for art. You would have got fairly near
him by making out in his eyes the potential recognition of ideas; but
you would have quite fallen away again on the question of the ideas
themselves. The difficulty with Densher was that he looked vague
without looking weak—idle without looking empty.[2]

The vagueness that James so unerringly seized upon in Ford
when he modeled Densher after him is the same vagueness that
can be felt surrounding Ford's early heroes. They inhabit a
vacuum of ill-defined social purpose and moral goodness.

"He's much too kind," Eleanor said, and Mr. Greville uttered the solitary word:

"Precisely!"

"And that means," he pursued triumphantly, "that he hasn't any kind of system in his morality." He turned definitely upon Don. "You can't get through life like that!" he said seriously and with an air of shaking his head ever so minutely.

"You mean," Don said, "that Eleanor will never know where to have me?"   [p. 58]

A silly conversation about a silly man. But move fifteen years forward. Remove the pseudo-Jamesian tone; transform a hysterical Don and a stuffy Eleanor into an enraged Sylvia and a set-upon Christopher; interject real conflict into the endless dialectical analyses. For Sylvia does not at all *know where to have* Christopher.

"You want to know why I hate my husband. I'll tell you; it's because of his simple, sheer immorality. I don't mean his actions; his views! Every speech he utters about everything makes me—I swear it makes me—in spite of myself, want to stick a knife into him, and I can't prove he's wrong, not ever, about the simplest thing.   [p. 39]

In reality, it is the humanity, the morality, of Christopher's views which bothers her. "He'll profess that murderers ought to be preserved in order to breed because they're bold fellows, and innocent children executed because they're sick" (p. 40). And "he's so formal he can't do without all the conventions and so truthful he can't use half of them" (p. 32). "But what does he want?" asks Perowne, with whom Sylvia has been having an affair. " 'He wants,' Sylvia said, 'to play the part of Jesus Christ' " (p. 379).

There is something of the same fool about Christopher as there is about Don, and the premise underlying their conduct is one that Ford, the child of Pre-Raphaelitism, never stopped believing. Eleanor's father says at one point in the novel: "The man's a poet: that's what the trouble is" (p. 235). And at the end of the novel, Canzano writes to her: "My dear, Don is a genius." But poet-geniuses do not inhabit the world of real men— at least not without making fools of themselves. The castles of thought in which the Aesthetic Movement dwelt proved this. And yet the world of real men is the lifeline of the novel. Jettison this world and you write make-believe. You live in fairyland.

There is nothing in *An English Girl* to justify calling Don either a "poet" or a "genius." His conduct is simply ludicrous. Christopher is a more baffling case, and hence far more real. With his abilities he should have been "Lord Chancellor or Chancellor of the Exchequer" (p. 432). Sylvia says to him: "What could you not have risen to with your gifts, and your influence . . . and your integrity." And Macmaster, Tietjens' friend and coworker in the Office of Statistics, sees the same brilliance in him: "He had no doubt that Tietjens was the most brilliant man in England of that day, so that nothing could give him more anguish than the thought that Tietjens might not make a brilliant and rapid career towards some illustrious position in the public services" (p. 48). Christopher disappoints each of them, but it is not for lack of talent. Ford distributes the blame more subtly.

There is one crucial difference between Don Collar Kelleg and Christopher Tietjens. Both are out of joint with society and their time, but Tietjens is sure of his ground, Don is not.

> "What you ought to do," Mr. Greville said, "is to find yourself."
> He hadn't got to bother about trains of thought, but about what he wanted. And Mr. Greville hazarded the further speech:
> "If a man is determined to inflict himself on his time it is his duty first to consider what *he is!* For what is criminal is to wobble once you have begun. A man has to define what his ideal is and then to make for it."
> "Ah," Don said, "that is what people have been telling me all my life. . . ."   [p. 127]

Christopher Tietjens. Both are out of joint with society and their sieges him, but he will never desert his beliefs. Don is unable to discover what he should believe. He does wobble. He deserts America, then reverses himself and deserts Eleanor for America at the end of the novel. Thus the story leaves off where it should begin. And it is for Christopher, many years later, to go on slowly and painfully to discover both his role in an alien world and ways to cope with a society devoid of meaning.

Thus when it is no longer Ford's hero who is baffled by society, but *society* that is baffled by the hero, Christopher Tietjens emerges, larger than life—a generic portrait—neither incredible nor an ass; and the qualities that before made Ford's hero ludicrous and pathetic will in *Parade's End* make him human, and perhaps even more than human.

If Ford had to sever the umbilical cord that linked him to the Aesthetic Movement to obtain maturity in his art, he also had to free himself from the Jamesian vision. This overmastering vision of the world obscured Ford's personal subjects from him for years; the Jamesian world was neither the England Ford knew, the England of Edward Ashburnham and Tietjens, nor the America he had visited in 1906, the America of Florence and Dowell and the Misses Hurlbird. Ford's token handling of the "international theme" in *An English Girl* demonstrates how unfordian the subject matter really is, for it is only in a closing letter from Canzano to Eleanor, after the action of the novel is over, that the theme is finally asserted.

You are cowardly—all you English are cowardly: you are afraid of your own emotions: you are afraid that if you become passionate you will lose dignity. That's why you insist on maintaining your frigid exteriors.
[p. 307]

Remove the Jamesian overlay here, and what remains is something very close to the matter of *The Good Soldier* and *Parade's End*. The emotions, passion, hover underneath the Jamesian veneer, which conceals and disguises even from the author what his proper subject matter is. For it is there—in the story of Eleanor and her cousin Augustus, who is in love with her.

"Oggie dear," she said softly, "oughtn't a man—a man of our class —to be less a slave of his passions?"
[p. 180]

But Ford will not let his cardboard characters enter the real world.

"Oh, you intolerable woman!" he brought out like a curse: "one is or one isn't. Do you suppose I *want* to love you? I'd give my eyesight and my hearing and my taste and my touch not to care for you. Do you suppose I am 'indulging' in something? Why, you talk like a temperance reformer telling a sot to abstain from drink. I'm not drinking, am I? I don't get any pleasure out of it."

"Well, Oggie dear," she said, "I'm not blaming you. I asked you a question. I don't know how men are made. I thought you ought to be able to find distractions."
[p. 180]

Eleanor's empty words have swallowed the latent plot. Further
talk only dissipates the conflict, while the surprise appearance
of Oggie's mother on the scene proves to be not a complication
but an irrelevancy.

"I don't see what's to be done," she said. She sat still, rather depressed, looking at the paste buckles on her shoes that, in the moonlight, shot direful rays at her eyes as the boat swayed a little. "I'm
sorry for you. But I can't mend anything."
"Yes, I know you're sorry," he said, "you've been very decent to
me."
An odd, draped, white object poked itself from the hatchway beside
them, and in the pale stillness had a ghostly semblance of pricking up
fantastic ears.
Augustus's voice hissed out:
"I see you mother. Come and listen if you want to listen. But, by
God, you're driving me to suicide. It's as much murder as if you
put arsenic in my toast." He was shaking violently in his dancing
slippers, his face grew even bluer in tinge. And accompanied by a
deep exasperation from Augustus the figure turned its face below
the level of the deck. His mother had gone to find Don. [pp. 180-181]

That is all Ford can make of it. Along with Aunt Emmeline's
footsteps this particular plot strand disappears into the night, for
although Augustus talks of suicide, no one, least of all the reader,
takes him seriously. Nor is Don ever allowed to learn of Oggie's
love. Ford, perhaps unconsciously, has avoided conflict by allowing Aunt Emmeline, instead of Don, to overhear the two.

Now consider the same subject matter, the same basic scene,
eight years later in *The Good Soldier*, told this time by a narrator.
Dowell is reconstructing in his mind what must have happened
on the night his wife Florence overheard Edward Ashburnham,
her lover, declare his love for another. Dowell himself was not
present. Indeed, he wasn't even aware that his wife had been
unfaithful to him until after her suicide. Thus he is only now
piecing out the events of the evening on which Florence learned
that Ashburnham had forsaken her for his ward, Nancy Rufford.
It was immediately after this that Florence committed suicide.

"It was a very black night." Florence was dressed all in black,
because she was in mourning for a deceased cousin. "The girl
[Nancy] was dressed in cream-coloured muslin, and must have

glimmered under the tall trees of the dark park like a phosphorescent fish in a cupboard. You couldn't have a better beacon" (p. 109). The Casino orchestra was playing the Rakóczy march. Florence came creeping over the short grass behind the public bench on which the two sat.

Anyhow, there you have the picture: the immensely tall trees, elms most of them, towering and feathering away up into the black mistiness that trees seem to gather about them at night; the silhouettes of those two upon the seat; the beams of light coming from the Casino, the woman all in black peeping with fear behind the tree-trunk. It is melodrama; but I can't help it. [p. 110] (p. 103)

Now this, we are sure, is very great art, even before we know why we think as we do. To put it simply, it has the ring of truth—and yet, if one thinks about it for a moment, this second scene is more unbelievable than its counterpart in *An English Girl*. "It is melodrama. . . ." Why, then, does it seem so believable?

In the first place, Ford has shifted the level at which he is approaching his subject matter. In *An English Girl* Eleanor and Oggie are simply too well-behaved to act improperly. They are mannequins with Jamesian sensibilities inhabiting a world composed of empty verbal formulae. In *The Good Soldier* the same politeness rules the world of Nauheim, yet hidden underneath the surface, and exposed only gradually, are lechery, adultery, feigned illness, blackmail, suicide, and insanity. That is, the suppressed ugliness of *An English Girl* breaks through the surface. (The correspondences between the two scenes, of course, are not one-to-one. Oggie's infatuation is the archetype of Ashburnham's incurable love of Nancy; Don is in the position of Dowell, the deceived narrator; Aunt Emmeline's role is that of Florence; and Eleanor's position, in this scene at least, is comparable to Nancy's.)

The point is that the outward show of manners is no longer equated with reality. In addition, double-lives means double-plot, and the disparity between the two lives of each of the characters, between the appearance and the reality, is heightened by turning the second series of events into melodrama.

The melodrama is believable because of a shift of attitude on the part of the author. An ironic tone has entered the story through the voice of the narrator; and because of his disbelief, his doubt that what has happened could really have happened, Dowell makes us accept the scene as a representation of the real world.

And that miserable woman must have got it in the face, good and strong. It must have been horrible for her. Horrible! Well, I suppose she deserved all that she got.   [p. 110] (pp. 102-103)

Dowell's doubt of the significance of it all insures credibility. And, one might add, so does the plot-structure, the dislocated time-sequence. We know of Florence's suicide before we learn its cause. Thus our attention is held by the acts of reconstruction which the narrator performs as he gradually discovers the true meaning of the events of the past nine years.

In *An English Girl* there is no such emergence of meaning, for in Ford's hand the Jamesian dialectic does not create tension and complexity. Instead of tautness, there is gush; instead of involvement, simplification. In James, on the other hand, it spells conflict; indeed, it often becomes the center of conflict, the fire over which James's characters are set to roast on moral spits.

Just as Ford had erroneously assumed that James's world could be his, so too he made the false assumption that his method could be. He sensed, quite rightly, that James was incapable of telling a story straight. And he himself suffered from the same disease. Whatever the reason in James's case, and perhaps that will always remain a mystery, Ford's was simply that he could not bear conflict. In his personal life, he was known to become torturously involved in a situation, rendering it unbearable, because he could not face things directly and resolve them. In his early novels there is a marked absence of real conflict. It goes skittering off the page with Aunt Emmeline. Hence the appeal of the Jamesian dialectic. It rendered complexity; it created tensions: it appeared to be the source of conflict in James's novels. It was not, of course. The substance of conflict stems from the nature of man coming into collision with the conventions of society. This Ford was to learn; indeed, it became his major theme in both *The Good Soldier* and *Parade's End*. One reason Ford was eventually to develop the time-shift was to cope with his inadequacy to handle conflict; *it* became his dialectical tool, the means for probing beneath the surface of society.

*   *   *

Just how much Ford had learned from Henry James can be seen
in the opening paragraph of his novel of 1910, *A Call*. It is a
more Jamesian beginning to a novel than any James ever wrote.

It was once said of Mr. Robert Grimshaw: "That chap is like a
seal"—and the simile was a singularly just one. He was like a seal
who is thrusting his head and shoulders out of the water, and, with
large, dark eyes and sensitive nostrils, is on the watch. All that could
be known of him seemed to be known; all that could be known of
the rest of the world he moved in he seemed to know. He carried
about him usually, in a crook of his arm, a polished light brown
dachshund that had very large feet, and eyes as large, as brown, and
as luminous, as those of his master. Upon the occasion of Pauline
Lucas's marriage to Dudley Leicester the dog was not upon his arm,
but he carried it into the drawing-room of the many ladies who wel-
comed him to afternoon tea. Apparently it had no attractions save
its clear and beautiful colour, its excellent if very grotesque shape,
and its complete docility. He called upon a lady at tea-time, and,
with the same motion that let him down into his chair, he would set
the dog upon the floor between his legs. There it would remain, as
motionless and as erect as a fire-dog, until it was offered a piece of
buttered tea-cake, which it would accept, or until its master gave it a
minute and hardly audible permission to rove about. Then it would
rove. The grotesque large-little feet paddled set wide upon the carpet,
the long ears flapped to the ground. But, above all, the pointed and
sensitive nose would investigate with minute attention, but with an
infinite gentleness, every object within its reach in the room, from the
line of the skirting-board to the legs of the piano and the flounced
skirts of the ladies sitting near the tea-tables. Robert Grimshaw would
observe these investigations with an indulgent approval; and, indeed,
someone else said—and perhaps with more justness—that Mr. Grimshaw resembled most nearly his own dog Peter.   [pp. 3-4]

James might grope and stumble for twenty pages on the foot-
paths of Waterbath with Fleda and Mrs. Gereth while setting in
motion what Ford once called his "romance of English grab";[3]
Ford walks into the drawing-room of Mrs. Tressilian beside Robert
Grimshaw, who, like Henry James, was the owner of a dachshund,
with all the ease of a man who knows perfectly well what he is
about.

The suavity of Ford's prose—no other word seems accurate—

is an index of how accomplished he is in the Jamesian manner. From

It was once said of Mr. Robert Grimshaw: "That chap is like a seal" —and the simile was a singularly just one.

to the light reversal and periodic close of

. . . and, indeed, someone else once said—and perhaps with more justness—that Mr. Grimshaw resembled most nearly his own dog Peter.

we seem to be listening to the authentic hum of tea-time gossip. Robert Grimshaw has been defined in terms of the world that circumscribes his actions.

This is no mean feat, for gossip is seldom merely true or false. More often, it has varying degrees of accuracy. "That chap is like a seal"; he is in part exactly that—in the part of him one segment of society sees. There is justness in the description. But, long before the author announces that, with more accuracy, he is like his dachshund Peter, we have made the discovery for ourselves. Indeed, we've been steered there by the author. The pivotal sentence—"all that could be known of him seemed to be known; all that could be known of the rest of the world he moved in he seemed to know"—operates, like much good prose, by negation; by the assurance that all *is not* known about Robert Grimshaw that can be known and that he *does not* understand all of the world he moves in. Moreover, it is clear that the lengthy description of the dog Peter is not mere whimsy. Hence the reversal—that Grimshaw most nearly resembles his dog Peter—does not jolt us. It flows into our consciousness with the insinuating ease of good gossip.

For a moment, here at the beginning of *A Call,* we are almost in the world of *The Good Soldier.* Ford seems to promise to move behind the drawing-room facade, with its tea-service and cakes, and to expose what lies beneath the hum. *A Call* is subtitled "the tale of two passions"; *The Good Soldier,* "a tale of passion." In the latter, once we dip below the politeness and formalities, the orderly routine, of the spa at Nauheim, we discover seething passion. The passion of *A Call* is a very tame affair, for the Jamesian manner prevents Ford from telling the story he wants to tell, and the novel collapses into a series of gestures and postures and preposterous conversations revolving about Robert Grimshaw's desire for two women.

"One wants Katya," Grimshaw said—"one wants Katya. She is vigour, she is life, she is action, she is companionship. One wants her, if you like, because she is chivalry itself, and so she's obstinate; but, if one can't have Katya, one wants. . . ."

He paused and looked at the dachshund that, when he paused, paused and looked back at him.

"That's what one wants," he continued. "One wants tenderness, fidelity, pretty grace, quaintness, and, above all, worship. Katya could give me companionship; but wouldn't Pauline have given me worship?"   [pp. 14-15]

Fifteen pages after that magnificent opening paragraph the Jamesian manner has become unconscious parody.

It is not merely the inordinate awkwardness of the first person singular indefinite pronoun in English, or the careless repetition of *she is* this and that and the other, or the inappropriate use of a dachshund to sum up the most desirable feminine qualities, that produces the false note of the passage; it is the embarrassment of the author as he attempts to render in passionate speech what the story itself should be implying. The Jamesian method is incapable, except by suggestion and nuance, of dealing with a sexual theme, and this Ford was to learn. It is not surprising, then, that in *The Good Soldier,* as Ford himself pointed out, there is "hardly any direct speech at all, and probably none that is more than a couple of lines in length."[4]

Like George Moffet of *The Benefactor,* Robert Grimshaw is a "meddling fool," Ford's typical gentleman of honor who ruins his own life and the lives of the people he cares about. He is torn between two women, Pauline Lucas (perhaps modeled on Turgenev's Pauline Lucca), and Katya Lascarides, his cousin. Katya is Greek, Robert is half-Greek. Robert had been raised, along with Katya and her sister, in the English home of the girls' parents. Katya and Robert were engaged to be married, but then the parents died, and the engagement was broken off. Katya refused to marry. Instead she made another proposal to Robert—that they live together without benefit of clergy. Her motive: upon her mother's death it had been disclosed that her parents had never wed. There had been no Greek priest in England at the time, and later the ceremony had seemed unnecessary. "I think," Katya remarks of her mother, "she regarded marriage—the formality of marriage, the vows, as a desecration. Don't you see she wanted to be my father's chattel, and to trust him absolutely —to trust, to trust! Isn't that the perfect relationship?" (p. 122). Katya desires a similar relationship with Grimshaw.

The novelty of Katya's proposal, of course, prevents the sexual theme from becoming real. Robert's repeated refusals are to be expected of Ford's gentleman of honor. Katya breaks down, spends time at a hydropathic establishment on the continent, and finally studies nervous disorders in Philadelphia, where she becomes a skilled psychologist. Meanwhile, Robert has fallen in love with Pauline but still feels honor-bound to Katya. In order to remain near Pauline, and to have reason for access to her company, he marries her off to his best friend, Dudley Leicester, a totally vacuous young English gentleman whom he hopes, partially through marriage to Pauline, to make into a responsible member of the ruling class—a good landlord to his tenant farmers, an M.P., a minor cabinet minister. Some months after Pauline has married Dudley, Katya changes her mind about marriage. According to Katya's sister, she has intended to marry him all along, but has meant first to have him "humbled and submissive, and tied utterly hand and foot" (p. 260). Pauline says to Robert: "You love me, and you have ruined our lives" (p. 275).

It is with two minor characters, Dudley Leicester and his old flame, Etta Stackpole (whose married name, Lady Hudson, is equally Jamesian), that the sexual theme in *A Call* breaks through the mosaic of nuances. Dudley is placed in a similar situation to Grimshaw's: he is caught in a sexual triangle created by Etta Stackpole. Unfortunately, Ford again avoids real conflict. He makes Dudley such an utter fool that he can only be totally innocent, and the plot takes a melodramatic turn.

While Pauline is out of town, attending upon her dying mother, Dudley goes to dinner at the Phyllis Trevors'. His dinner companion is Etta Stackpole, who traps him into seeing her home, then entices him into the house for further talk. Once inside, the phone rings (the "call" of the novel's title) and, in their haste to prevent the servants from awakening, Dudley answers it in the guise of the butler. The caller asks: "Is this 4,259 Mayfair?" Dudley says "yes," and the male voice then asks if he is speaking to Dudley Leicester. Startled, Dudley again replies "yes," and there is a click at the other end.

The incident of the phone call is traumatic for the hypochondriacal Dudley, who really loves Pauline. In his worry lest she will somehow learn of the incident he goes into a state of shock and has a nervous breakdown. He accosts strangers with the question of whether they are the mysterious caller of that fateful night. He even attacks his hatter.

"Are you the chap who rang up 4,259 Mayfair?"

"Sir! sir!" the little man cried out. Dudley Leicester shook him and shook him: a white band-box fell from the counter and rolled almost into the street.

"Are you? Are you?" Dudley Leicester cried out incessantly.

And when the little man screamed: "No! no!" Leicester seized the rounded smoothing-iron and raised it to the height of his arm so that it struck the brown, smoked ceiling. The little man ducked beneath the counter, his agonized eyes gazing upwards.

But at Grimshaw's cool, firm grasp upon his wrists, Leicester sank together. He passed his hand so tightly down his face that the colour left it, to return in a swift flush.

"I've got cobwebs all over my face," he muttered, "beastly, beastly cobwebs."   [p. 138]

There are two mysteries in *A Call*: one is the cause of Dudley's breakdown, about which the characters in the novel seem unnecessarily obtuse; the second is the identity of the mysterious caller, which Ford unnecessarily withholds from the reader for some two hundred pages. It takes Katya to discover the source of Dudley's trouble, and thus to commence his cure, and Robert finally reveals the source, long after there has ceased to be any real mystery about it. "It was I that rang up 4,259 Mayfair" (p. 278). Unobserved, he had passed Dudley and Etta on the street, and suspecting Dudley of philandering, he had phoned Etta Stackpole's upon returning home. Thus it is his one act of snooping that produces the story-line of the novel, slim as it is.

"I want to know," Grimshaw says to Etta Stackpole later, "what happened on the night he saw you home."

"I didn't think," she said expressionlessly, "that you could play the cad as well as the private detective."
Robert Grimshaw uttered sharply the one word, "Rot!"
"Well, it's a cad's question, and you must have played the private detective to know he saw me home."   [p. 175]

No English gentleman would interrogate Etta Stackpole as Robert Grimshaw does (and in any case the Ford of *A Call* would not let him question her if anything had happened). The explanation Grimshaw himself offers for his conduct stems from his racial background.

"I suppose," Robert Grimshaw said speculatively, "it's because I'm really Greek. My name's English, and my training's been English, and I look it, and smell it, and talk it, and dress the part; but underneath I should think I'm really a Dago. . . . Belonging to a clan makes you have what no Englishman has—a sense of responsibility. I can't bear to see chaps of my class—of my clan and my country—going wrong. I'm not preaching; it's my private preference. I can't bear it because I can't bear it. I don't say that you ought to feel like me. That's your business."
"My word!" Etta Stackpole said. . . .   [p. 163]

Inconsequential as this passage is, this is Ford searching for an observation post, for a position from which he can comment upon the actions of his characters. Here, for example, is Pauline serving the same function as Grimshaw.

"Tragedies! Yes, in our day and in our class we don't allow ourselves easy things like daggers and poison-bowls. It's all more difficult. It's all more difficult because it goes on and on. We think we've made it easier because we've slackened old ties. You're in and out of the house all day long, and I can go around with you everywhere. But just because we've slackened the old ties, just because marriage is a weaker thing than it used to be—in our day and in our class"—she repeated the words with deep bitterness and looked unflinchingly into his eyes—"we've strengthened so immensely the other kind of ties. If you'd been married to Miss Lascarides you'd probably not have been faithful to her. As it is, just because your honour's involved you find yourself tied to her as no monk ever was by his vow." [p. 274]

The false note is unmistakable. Pauline is saying what the story should be implying. But listen to Dowell in *The Good Soldier*:

> I call this the Saddest Story rather than "The Ashburnham Tragedy," just because it is so sad, just because there was no current to draw things along to a swift and inevitable end. There is about this story none of the elevation that accompanies tragedy; there is about it no nemesis, no destiny. Here were two noble people—for I am convinced that both Edward and Leonora had noble natures—here, then, were two noble natures, drifting down life, like fireships afloat on a lagoon and causing miseries, heartaches, agony of the mind, and death. And they themselves steadily deteriorated? And why? For what purpose? To point what lesson? It is all a darkness.
>
> [p. 164] (p. 146)

The authenticity of Dowell's voice comes in part from the traditional security of a narrator's license to comment, in part from the narrative structure of *The Good Soldier,* which takes the "strain" off the style. In *A Call* we see Ford rather agitatedly trying to find a commentator among his characters, while the narrative structure is marred by the obvious omission of the story it should be telling.

One index of the submerged Fordian plot lies in the character of Etta Stackpole, who speaks with the authentic, though somewhat hysterical, cadences of Sylvia Tietjens.

> "I've always wanted men about me, and I mean to have them. You never heard me say a good word for a woman, and I never did say one. I shouldn't even of your wife. But I am Etta Stackpole, I tell you. The world has got to give me what I want, for it can't get on without me. Your women might try to down me, but your men wouldn't allow it." [p. 66]

But for all her talk, Etta's sexual indiscretions are merely composed of flirting with Bugle, the farrier's son, and Moddle, the third footman. This Dickensian note reveals Ford's inability to handle the sexual theme overtly.

Nevertheless in *A Call* the Fordian themes that run through *The Good Soldier* and *Parade's End* emerge more fully than in his earlier novels. The characteristic affair of Ford's later fiction is also present: one psychological progression involving two women and a man. In Robert Grimshaw and Dudley Leicester we see Ford's concern with the English gentleman and the break-down of the traditions of the ruling class. At one point in the novel Grimshaw speculates about Dudley and his class.

Englishmen haven't any sense of responsibility. Perhaps it's bad for them to have it aroused in them. They can work; they can fight; they can do things; but it's for themselves alone. They're individualists. But there is a class that's got the sense of duty to the whole. They've got a rudimentary sense of it—a tradition, at least, if not a sense. And Leicester comes out of that class. But the tradition's dying out.

[p. 118]

The loss of that tradition is the subject matter of *Parade's End.*

A measure of the failure of the narrative technique of *A Call* can be seen in the admissions Ford makes in the "Epistolary Epilogue" and in the mock Dickensian ending he writes to the novel in this author's coda.

It was a summer evening four years later when, upon the sands of one of our most fashionable watering-places, a happy family group, consisting of a buxom mother and several charming children, might have been observed to disport itself. Who can this charming matron be, and who these lovely children, designated respectively Robert, Dudley, Katya, and Ellida?

And who is this tall and robust gentleman who, wearing across the chest of his white cricketing flannel the broad blue ribbon of His Majesty's Minister for Foreign Affairs, bearing in one hand negligent-ly the *Times* of the day before yesterday and in the other a pastoral rake, approaches from the hayfields, and, with an indulgent smile, surveys the happy group?   [p. 295]

Ford goes on indiscriminately to parcel out happy endings: Etta Hudson is converted to Catholicism and practices acts of piety at the end of her life; Jervis, Dudley's butler, remains a faithful servant by his master's side; Saunders, Robert's "man," retires to the country and on his savings opens a rose-clad hostelry on the road to Brighton; and Mr. Held, the Christian Scientist, takes orders, and, through the influence of Dudley, becomes chaplain to the British Embassy at St. Petersburg. There is never a hint or suspicion, of course, that Robert and Katya are any-thing but happily married.

"Thus, my dear ———," Ford addresses a nameless critic,

"you would have me end this book, after I have taken a great deal of trouble to end it otherwise" (p. 297).

The foxes have holes, the birds of the air have nests, and you, together with the great majority of British readers, insist upon having a happy ending, or, if not a happy ending, at least some sort of an ending. . . . You go to books to be taken out of yourself, I to be shown where I stand. For me, as for you, a book must have a beginning and an end. But whereas for you the end is something arbitrarily final, such as the ring of wedding-bells, a funeral service, or the taking of a public-house, for me—since to me a novel is the history of an "affair"—finality is only found at what seems to be the end of that "affair." There is nothing in life that is final. So that even "affairs" never really have an end as far as the lives of the actors are concerned. Thus, although Dudley Leicester was, as I have tried to indicate, cured almost immediately by the methods of Katya Lascarides, it would be absurd to imagine that the effects of his short breakdown would not influence the whole of his afterlife.   [pp. 298-299]

While the conventional fictional formulae of his day obviously did not satisfy the realism that Ford chose to practice, his lengthy self-defense suggests that in *A Call* he knew he had not succeeded in creating an appropriate narrative to convey his meaning. He admits, for example, that after serial publication in the *English Review* he had added "explicit passages of conversation" (some six pages in all) because "all the moderately quick minded, moderately sane persons who had read the book in its original form" failed to understand what to him "appeared plain as a pikestaff—namely that Robert Grimshaw was extremely in love with Pauline Leicester, and that, in the first place, by marrying her to Dudley Leicester, and, in the second by succumbing to a disagreeable personality [Katya], he was committing the final folly of this particular affair" (p. 302). In his own defense Ford remarks that he had failed to make such comments as this in the novel proper because of his belief that "for the author to intrude himself between his characters and his readers is to destroy to that extent all of the illusion of his work" (pp. 301-302). In *A Call* the Flaubertian requirement of author suppression still dominates Ford's realism.

What is clear in retrospect, looking over the whole of Ford's career, seems not to have been at all clear to him for a good number of years. From very near the beginning, his basic subject matter was a triangle situation involving two women and a man caught in a psychological net of their own making. Flaubertian realism would seem ideally suited for such a subject matter. Yet Ford's basic mode of thought was reminiscence, and his basic tone was that of intimate and informed talk. Flaubertian realism was impersonal and objective; Ford's whole bent was personal and partial. For a long time Ford apparently thought he could reconcile the two through Jamesian talk, while the real answer lay in another direction—first in Dowell, the narrator of *The Good Soldier,* and later in Christopher Tietjens, the hero of *Parade's End.*

With the introduction of Dowell and Tietjens, both somewhat Dickensian characters, Ford returned to the English tradition. For Ford's prose, just as much as Dickens', is written as if to be listened to, and the same theatrical tone is there.

Permanence? Stability! I can't believe it's gone. I can't believe that that long, tranquil life, which was just stepping a minuet, vanished in four crashing days at the end of nine years and six weeks. . . . No, indeed, it can't be gone. You can't kill a minuet de la cour. You may shut up the music-book, close the harpsichord; in the cupboard and presses the rats may destroy the white satin favours. The mob may sack Versailles; the Trianon may fall but surely the minuet—the minuet itself is dancing itself away into the furthest stars, even as our minuet of the Hessian bathing places must be stepping itself still. . . .
And yet I swear by the sacred name of my creator that it was true. It was true sunshine; the true music; the true plash of the fountains from the mouth of stone dolphins.   [pp. 6-7] (pp. 17-18)

This, we recall, is Dowell talking to the reader, to the "sympathetic soul" he imagines opposite him. He is recalling the events of the last nine years, events he is only now beginning to understand. He refuses to believe that what has happened could really have happened, for he has been taken in. Surrounding him has been lechery, adultery, suicide, and insanity; there has been darkness where he has seen sweetness and light. The imagery of Dowell's speech is at once preposterous and appropriate. A minuet de la cour, the sack of Versailles, the fall of the Trianon, the "splash" of fountains from the mouth of stone dolphins: there are

images for registering the disparity between conventional appearance—what was thought to have been—and the reality of events—
what actually occurred. This is essentially different from the
realism of Flaubert, for the adequation of particulars to the
situation is governed, not by some concept of *le mot juste*
grounded in concrete detail, but by the mind of Dowell and the
tone of voice which reflects that mind. And it is this difference
that distinguishes Ford's "impressionism" from Flaubert's realism.

Exactly the same principles of construction are visible in the
interior monologues of Christopher Tietjens. Christopher and
Valentine Wannop, in *Some Do Not . . .*, the first of the four
Tietjens volumes, are walking through the fields to her mother's
house after their breakfast at the Duchemins', where they have
formally met for the first time.

> This, Tietjens thought, is England! A man and a maid walk through
> Kentish grass fields: the grass ripe for the scythe. The man honour-
> able, clean, upright; the maid virtuous, clean, vigorous; he of good
> birth; she of birth quite as good; each filled with a too good breakfast
> that each could capably digest. Each just come from an admirably
> appointed establishment: a table surrounded by the best people, their
> promenade sanctioned, as it were, by the Church—two clergy—the
> State, two Government officials; by mothers, friends, old maids.
>
> [p. 105]

Here both particulars and syntax are governed by the qualities of
Tietjens' mind. The catalog of genteel characteristics given in
balanced and parallel clauses; the semi-officious *mot juste* of "an
admirably appointed establishment"; and the neatly parallel but
inaccurate plurals of "mothers, friends, old maids": these are
reflectors of Christopher's orderly, discursive, encyclopedic mind.
As the scene continues, Christopher and Valentine focus their
attention on the landscape before them, and interspersed now with
Christopher's thoughts are parenthetical snatches of pedagogic
dialogue.

> Each knew the names of birds that piped and grasses that bowed:
> chaffinch, greenfinch, yellow-ammer (not, my dear, Hammer! *ammer*
> from the Middle High German for "finch"), garden warbler, Dartford
> warbler, pied wagtail, known as "dishwasher." (These charming local
> dialect names.) Marguerites over the grass, stretching in an infinite
> white blaze; grasses purple in a haze to the far distant hedgerow;

coltsfoot, wild white clover, sainfoin, Italian rye grass (all technical names that the best people must know: the best grass mixture for permanent pasture on the Wealden loam).   [p. 105]

This is characterization by voice and intonation: confident, educated (though his etymology is pedantry), knowledgeable (he would appear to be a landowner), and indefatigably curious of his surroundings. Christopher and Valentine are performing the gymnastic ritual of a nation given over to comfortable shoes and Constable landscapes. This is a generic portrait of the country gentleman and his lady. The irony, of course, is that Christopher is not a country squire and Valentine is hardly his lady. She is a suffragette being searched for by the police; he is a minor government official on the outs with both his superiors and his wife, who has deserted him. It will not be until the fourth volume of the Tietjens tetralogy that this double image of English society will come into single focus.

Ford finally became able to capture the authentic voices of Dowell and Tietjens, and, as a consequence, to portray, in *The Good Soldier,* the "ruin of one man's small cockleshell," and in *Parade's End,* the betrayal of an entire society. Ford needed Flaubert's high seriousness, his passionate concern with technique and objectivity, and his insistence on an adult subject matter. But he also needed the voice of the English tradition, the voice heard most strongly in Dickens. In *The March of Literature* Ford said that Dickens was "hopelessly inartistic," except in one quality of his art, "and that the almost sole essential quality."[5] Dickens was "a master stylist," he said.[6] And Ford Madox Ford became one by a process of development which we would call "critical rather than imitative."

"PARADE'S END"

SEVEN

Modern Chronicle

"Tracts against the Time," Mr. Brede chuckled,
"that's what's needed."

THE BENEFACTOR

In the Tietjens series Ford is writing both chronicle and psychological novel. The point needs to be stressed, for Ford is not the usual chronicler, and his methods are not those of such writers as Bennett and Galsworthy; yet his achievement includes that of the chronicler: he captures the wide canvas, the broad scope; a panoramic view of "the public events of a decade," as he once described his subject matter.[1] In *Parade's End* Ford imaginatively applies the major device of Jamesian fiction, the minute and scrupulous analysis of the fine points of personal conduct, developed largely through dialogue, to a larger action, ultimately to the collective actions of society.

Writing of Ford's achievement, Storm Jameson remarked in 1929 that he "has succeeded in creating a picture of the years between 1912 and 1926 which wipes out (as the flame from a furnace would wipe out the light of a candle) such a picture as that drawn by Mr. Galsworthy in *The White Monkey* and *The Silver Spoon*. No other work . . . has so imprisoned the restless and violent spirit of those years when the ground moved under our feet."[2] Nor has any novel or series of novels come along in the intervening years to displace *Parade's End* from its position of primacy. From our vantage point in time, it now seems likely that the Tietjens tetralogy will retain its unique position among novels dealing with the England of that period.

Ford's Christopher Tietjens enters the stream of history at the moment when he has become an "anachronism." He is the "last Tory," a romantic medievalist, feudal in outlook and social theory. His ideas can only seem absurd, his gestures of personal honor outmoded, in the eyes of a society that no longer understands, and refuses to recognize, his code of "some do not." Before the first of the four Tietjens volumes is over, his historical perspective will already have cost him dearly in personal mishaps and disasters. Official England will dismiss him, English society will cut him, disown him. For all his ties to country, government, ruling class, the land, Tietjens will emerge in *The Last Post,* the fourth novel in the series, as an outsider forced to practice the tactics of disengagement.

In Ford's hand Tietjens' personal history becomes the vehicle for an account of the changes wrought upon the Victorian-Edwardian world by the advent of the twentieth century and made climactic by the Great War: the gradual weakening of moral fibre among the governing classes, the decay of manners, the erosion of principles that manners once represented, the duplicities now cloaked by decorum. In sum, economic error, political malfeasance, social irresponsibility, cultural disintegration.

Some Do Not . . . opens with one of the most quoted and discussed passages in Ford.

The two young men—they were of the English public official class —sat in the perfectly appointed railway carriage. The leather straps to the windows were of virgin newness; the mirrors beneath the new luggage racks immaculate as if they had reflected very little; the bulging upholstery in its luxuriant, regulated curves was scarlet and yellow in an intricate, minute dragon pattern, the design of a geometrician in Cologne. The compartment smelt faintly, hygenically of admirable varnish; the train ran as smoothly—Tietjens remembered thinking—as British gilt-edged securities. It travelled fast; yet had it swayed or jolted over the rail joints, except at the curve before Tonbridge or over the points at Ashford where these eccentricities are expected and allowed for, Macmaster, Tietjens felt certain, would have written to the company. Perhaps he would even have written to the *Times.*   [p. 3]

This is the train, as Hugh Kenner has put it, that is to be "figuratively wrecked at Sarajevo."[3] It is not a train running from London to Rye, as its occupants think, but as Robie Macauley has remarked, in his introduction to *Parade's End,* "from the past into the future, and ahead of them on their one-way journey is a chaotic country of ripped battlefields and disordered towns" (p. vii). The leather straps will become worn and darkened by sweaty hands; the mirrors will become smoked, cracked, imperfectly reflecting khaki uniforms and widows' weeds; the upholstery will become soiled, frayed, its pattern indiscernible. The geometrician of Cologne will seek employment as an artillery observer in the Kaiser's army. The smell of "admirable varnish" will be replaced by the unpleasant odor of human bodies. Switches will be left open, derailments will occur. Timetables will be disrupted, some of them forever.

The Victorian-Edwardian world is to go smash in the coming war, but there is little evidence, at least on the surface, of either cultural deterioration or disintegration in the appointments of this hygenic railway carriage, or in the two young men occupying it. Macmaster and Tietjens have the solidarity of education and position: "Their class administered the world, not merely the newly created Imperial Department of Statistics under Sir Reginald Ingleby. If they saw policemen misbehave, railway porters lack civility, an insufficient number of street lamps, defects in public services or in foreign countries, they saw to it, either with nonchalant Balliol voices, or with letters to the *Times*. . . ." Yet there is a series of significant, even crucial differences, both of class and of temperament, between these two young men, and the fates that await them around the bend of history are ultimately to be quite different. The events of the weekend on which they are embarking, in their immaculately appointed railway carriage, on a train that runs as smoothly (Tietjens thinks) as British gilt-edged securities, will subtly convey that all is not quite as it should be in this Panglossian world.

Macmaster is Scotch by birth, the son of a very poor shipping clerk in an obscure harbor town. He is small, dark, a Whig in politics. Ambitious, deferential to his superiors, Macmaster worries over dress and deportment and the details of advancement. He hopes to draw attention to himself not merely by his work in the Imperial Department of Statistics but also by his literary endeavors. He has recently written a monograph on Dante Gabriel Rossetti, which he hopes will be well received in the drawing-rooms of Mrs. Cressy, the Hon. Mrs. Limoux, and Mrs. Delawnay,

purveyors of influence, and he is looking forward to the ritual
of correcting the proofs of his small book in the railway carriage
as they travel down to Rye. He has even bought a gold lead pencil
for the occasion. Tietjens is a Yorkshireman, a gentleman, the
younger son of Tietjens of Groby. He is huge, a "meal sack" of
a man, blond, careless of appearance, indolent in manner, brilliant
of mind but lacking in ambition. Unlike Macmaster, he has a
habit of treating Sir Reginald, for whom both young men work,
with condescension. "Sometimes Sir Reginald would say: 'You're
a perfect encyclopaedia of exact material knowledge, Tietjens,'
and Tietjens thought that that was his due, and he would accept
the tribute in silence" (p. 5). But Tietjens is neither as casual in
personal matters, nor as free from worry, as his outward calm
might suggest to persons such as Sir Reginald. He is estranged
from his wife Sylvia, who left him four months earlier to go off
with another man and now demands to be taken back. In the
course of the weekend he must decide the details of any arrangement he makes with Sylvia, though he has already made up his
mind to take her back.

The opening pages of *Some Do Not . . .*, which rapidly sketch
in the patterns and relations among the major figures, as well
as a good deal of the wider context on which the novel is built,
suggest that Ford has successfully solved the problem that to some
extent always baffled "the master" himself: the question of how
to begin a Jamesian novel. For forty or fifty pages James would
slowly worry into existence the complex situations and the
sophisticated milieus of his novels, while the reader often staggered
under the weight of Jamesian idiom, nuance, indirection. The
Fordian apparatus, which provides both personal and public
referents for events to follow, moves much more swiftly and
easily, and unlike *A Call,* which opened with equal adeptness,
there is no later collapse into a pseudo-Jamesian manner of
disquisition. Ford remains true to his personal idiom. Attitudes
are quickly translated into gestures, postures, actions, largely by
the device of the time-shift. From the situation in the railway
carriage, Ford turns rapidly backward in time, developing his
narrative thread through a series of short scenes: Tietjens asking
his mother for financial aid for Macmaster during his college years,
Tietjens conversing with his father about Sylvia's elopement,

Tietjens phoning his sister Effie about taking care of their child Tommie after Sylvia has left, Tietjens telling Macmaster about Sylvia's elopement to Brittany with a man named Perowne. Then we return to the morning of the trip down to Rye. It is breakfast-time, the scene is Macmaster's and Tietjens' rooms in Gray's Inn. Tietjens has just received a letter from Sylvia.

> Tietjens said:
> "Sylvia asked me to take her back."
> Macmaster said:
> "Have a little of this!"
> Tietjens was about to say: "No," automatically. He changed that to: "Yes. Perhaps. A liqueur glass."
> He noticed that the lip of the decanter agitated, tinkling on the glass. Macmaster must be trembling.
> Macmaster, with his back still turned, said:
> "Shall you take her back?"
> Tietjens answered:
> "I imagine so." The brandy warmed his chest in its descent. Macmaster said:
> "Better have another."
> Tietjens answered:
> "Yes. Thanks."
> Macmaster went on with his breakfast and his letters. So did Tietjens. Ferens came in, removed the bacon plates and set on the table a silver water-heated dish that contained poached eggs and haddock. A long time afterwards Tietjens said:
> "Yes, in principle I'm determined to. But I shall take three days to think out the details." [p. 8]

A minute verbal action, weighted with understatement and the nuances of gesture, dramatizes the impact of Sylvia's demands upon Tietjens.

Ford's fragmented narrative line allows him to realize in nine pages the expository material that a novelist working with more traditional methods would have needed sixty pages to convey. He has, furthermore, been able to juxtapose the beginning and end of a chain of events—Sylvia's leaving and her proposed return —so that all the particulars of the past are brought to bear upon the present crisis. But the device of juxtaposition is one that the reader of Ford is already widely familiar with, as he is with the device of beginning a scene in the middle. More outstanding here,

and one of the real technical achievements of *Parade's End,* is
the density of context Ford creates in his brief and illuminating
scenes. Thus Tietjens' colloquies, the Socratic dialogues in which
he engages and his meditations and self-catechisms, while involved with delicate problems of personal honor, create cultural,
political, and civic dimensions for his conduct. There is always
the suggestion of a social idealism behind his personal idealism,
of a code of conduct preposterous yet ideal. Thus, for example,
not only Tietjens' personal taciturnity ("As Tietjens saw the
world, you didn't 'talk.' Perhaps you didn't even think about how
you felt.") but its historical dimension is revealed in the scene
with his father in Macmaster's drawing-room in Gray's Inn. After
five minutes of silence there is a short interchange between the
two, beginning with

> "You will divorce?"
> Christopher had answered:
> "No! No one but a blackguard would ever submit a woman to the
> ordeal of divorce."   [p. 6]

and concluding with the father's

> "Your mother's very well." Then: "That motor-plough didn't an-
> swer," and then: "I shall be dining at the club."   [p. 7]

Christopher asks that Macmaster be put up for membership in
the club, and his father agrees to see to it. The scene comes to
an end with Tietjens meditating on his relationship with his father,
which he regards as "an almost perfect one. They were like two
men in the club—the *only* club; thinking so alike that there was
no need to talk" (p. 7).

Scenes such as the one above, repeated in varied fashion
throughout the novel, gradually create the design behind Tietjens'
moral life. Despite his reticence of speech, he is always, we soon
realize, on the verge of making the impossible statement, the impossible gesture: "No one but a blackguard would ever submit
a woman to the ordeal of divorce." No one, we ourselves quickly
add, would say such a thing in such a way but Tietjens. Ford's
knowledge that his moral fable constantly verges on the preposterous underlines and helps to create the ambiguous reality of the
fictional world in which Tietjens lives.

We know from what Ford has said of the genesis of *Parade's End* that he saw his major figure as a "character, in lasting tribulation—with a permanent shackle and ball on his leg. . . . A physical defect it could not be, for if I wrote about that character he would have to go into the trenches. It must be something of a moral order and something inscrutable. . . ."[4] By the nature of his subject, "the world as it culminated in the war," Ford felt that his main character had to be "of some strength of mind and composure. No one else could have supported at once the tremendous pressure of the war and private troubles of a very dire description." The outward features and a good number of the personal traits of Tietjens Ford modeled after Arthur Marwood, his associate on the *English Review*. Marwood was a "heavy Yorkshire squire" with "dark hair startlingly silver in places," "keen blue eyes," "florid complexion," "immense, expressive hands" and "great shapelessness." He had once said of himself, standing beside Conrad's small figure: "We're two ends of human creation: He's like a quivering ant and I'm an elephant built out of meal sacks!" Marwood was a brilliant mathematician, had an encyclopedic mind, and was possessed of "infinite benevolence, comprehensions, and knowledges." "He was physically very strong and very enduring. And he was, beneath the surface, extraordinarily passionate—with an abiding passion for the sort of truth that makes for intellectual accuracy in the public service." Marwood's career was cut short by tuberculosis and he died before the war ended.

It was Marwood who told Ford the anecdote (coincidentally, as it so happened, while they were riding in a railway carriage between Ashford and Rye) that became the basis for the situation between Christopher and Sylvia. A young man of "pretty good family" took up with a woman on a train between Calais and Paris. She later persuaded him that he had got her with child and he felt that he had to marry her. Then he found out that the child might just as well be another man's. "There was no real knowing. . . . It was the hardest luck I ever heard of. . . . She was as unfaithful to him as a street walker. . . ." Except for his inappropriate marriage, the young man would have had a career in the Foreign Office. Divorce, moreover, was out of the question. "He held that a decent man could never divorce a woman.

The woman on the other hand would not divorce him because she was a Roman Catholic." To this story of the young English-man Ford added the story of a wealthy American whose wife left him. A year or so later, he "conceived an overwhelming passion for another woman." The wife returned, however, and would not give him a divorce.

The wealthy American of Ford's anecdote becomes a suicide. Marwood's young Englishman disintegrates into an alcoholic. Tietjens, on the other hand, has the courage to withstand the social and psychological pressures which bear down upon him—but only at great personal cost.

According to Ford, his two women, Valentine Wannop and Sylvia Tietjens, also had real-life counterparts. Valentine was modeled on Dorothy Minto, "who had played in the *Silver Box* of Galsworthy and was also one of the principal actresses in a play about Suffragettes." Sylvia first came to Ford in the form of a vision in the train station in Amiens: "She was in a golden sheath-gown and her golden hair was done in bandeaux extraordinarily brilliant in the dimness."

Other resources more personal also suggest themselves. Mrs. Wannop, for example, would seem to have been modeled on Violet Hunt's mother, Mrs. Alfred Hunt, who was a successful novelist. Valentine's father, a famous professor of Latin with pronounced educational theories of his own, apparently had his origin in the father of a friend of Stella Bowen, Margaret Postgate, who later married G. D. H. Cole (see *Drawn from Life*, p. 52). Both Stella Bowen and Violet Hunt obviously contributed to Ford's conception of his two women, and a good deal of Ford himself went into the makeup of Christopher Tietjens. Indeed, one of the more annoying aspects of *Parade's End* for the reader not inclined to be lenient with Ford is that, having given Tietjens some of his own traits, he then shamelessly has his other characters compliment Tietjens for possessing these very traits. He also creates fantasies about certain details of his private life. Nevertheless Ford was a great enough artist to transform the raw materials of his sources into an imaginative whole, and Tietjens resembles his real self as little as he does the real Marwood.

Far more important for our understanding of *Parade's End* than the knowledge of Ford's partial identification of himself with his hero is the recognition that the book carries with it the force of a brilliant lie: a justification for the way of life Ford had chosen for himself, for the pattern of his career and the intricacies of his personal conduct.

It seems necessary to isolate the one truly important relation that the Tietjens books have to Ford's life, because Ford's personality and the details of his private affairs have so often been willfully read into the novels—at the cost of an objective account of the books themselves. Walter Allen, commenting on both *The Good Soldier* and *Parade's End,* remarks: "By pushing, as it were, his personal problem out of arm's reach and staging it in terms of characters other than himself and those closely associated with him, he depersonalized it, raised it to the level of the material of art."[5] "His own kind of truth," Stella Bowen remarks in *Drawn from Life,*

was something that he lived in his life, in his tremendous humanity, his taste for all things living and growing and modest and un-selfconscious, and his knowledge of the aches and pains of the human heart. It was not in any logical viewpoint, but the vivid and poignant images which he could create. . . . And Ford's images build up into a harmonious and authentic picture—the picture of his idea of the good life; a life of frugality, of modest individualism, of trustfulness and gaiety and goodwill, unregimented, local, unambitious but full of savour; . . . the kind of life that he found in Provence.[6]

If Ford created the world of *Parade's End* out of the resources of his own personal experience, the Tietjens legend nevertheless dominates and controls its autobiographical elements.

Tietjens, one should point out, demands not to be taken too seriously at the level of the merely human. For one thing, Ford represents a transition between Dickensian humor and modern self-irony which permits him on occasion to be sentimental and nostalgic, tolerating within himself a certain amount of wishful dreaming (Tietjens' "private ambition had always been for saintliness"; see p. 187). It is equally important that Tietjens is a mythic figure. Such fictional characters seldom have private lives of any consequence; it is their public roles, their mythic selves, not their private beings, that are important. But Christopher's private self *does* impinge on his public self, in fact largely *is* his public self; and this is what helps to generate in *Parade's End* the particular quality—at once facetious, whimsical, far-fetched, outrageous, improbable; and ultimately both plausible and real—that distinguishes the Fordian universe. Ford is writing a novel of sensibility; the function of sensibility is to combine personal insight with general perception. Tietjens' thoughts, feelings, and reactions constitute not only a gloss of corrupt social and moral pressures as they affect Tietjens, but a minute historical record of general significance.

In the railway carriage to Rye, Macmaster looks up from the proofs of his book about the Pre-Raphaelite poet-painter and remarks: "You can't say the man wasn't a poet!"

"Since," he quoted, "when we stand side by side

> Only hands may meet,
> Better half this weary world
> Lay between us, sweet!
> Better far tho' hearts may break
> Bid farewell for aye!
> Lest thy sad eyes, meeting mine,
> Tempt my soul away!"

"You can't," he continued, "say that that isn't poetry! Great poetry."

"I can't say," Tietjens answered contemptuously. "I don't read poetry except Byron. But it's a filthy picture. . . ."   [p. 16]

Tietjens' objection to the love poetry of Rossetti, with its overtones of the mystical and soulful, and its suppression of physical realities, becomes clearer a moment later.

He continued with sudden fury:
"Damn it. What's the sense of all these attempts to justify fornication? England's mad about it. Well, you've got your John Stuart Mill's and your George Eliot's for the high-class thing. Leave the furniture out! Or leave me out, at least. I tell you it revolts me to think of that obese, oily man who never took a bath, in a grease-spotted dressing-gown and the underclothes he's slept in, standing beside a five-shilling model with crimped hair, or some Mrs. W. Three Stars, gazing into a mirror that reflects their fetid selves and gilt sunfish and drop chan-

deliers and plates sickening with cold bacon fat and gurgling about
passion." [p. 17]
The seeming eccentricity of Tietjens' outraged response to the
shams, the pretense and hypocrisy, of the love making of Pre-
Raphaelite poets and their followers gains new dimension as he
goes on to reveal his own personal code, with its emphasis on
integrity of conduct.

"I stand for monogamy and chastity. And for no talking about it.
Of course if a man who's a man wants to have a woman he has her.
And again, no talking about it. He'd no doubt be in the end better,
and better off, if he didn't. Just as it would probably be better for
him if he didn't have the second glass of whiskey and soda. . . ."
"You call that monogamy and chastity!" Macmaster interjected.
"I do," Tietjens answered. "And it probably is, at any rate it's
clean. What is loathsome is all your fumbling in placket-holes and
polysyllabic Justification by Love. You stand for lachrymose polyg-
amy. That's all right if you can get your club to change its rules."
"You're out of my depth," Macmaster said. "And being very disagreeable. You appear to be justifying promiscuity. I don't like it."
"I'm probably being disagreeble," Tietjens said. "Jeremiahs usually
are. But there ought to be a twenty years' close time for discussion of
sham sexual morality." [p. 18]

Clearly Tietjens is out of Macmaster's "depth." Indeed, the young
Scotsman has failed to understand him at all, except in one respect.
"I don't wonder," he remarks, "that Sylvia calls you immoral"
(p. 20). Society will join with Sylvia in condemning Tietjens.
Calumny after calumny will be heaped on his innocent head. But
ironically it is Macmaster, not Tietjens, who is to engage in a
Pre-Raphaelite love affair with all its poeticized shams and
dodges, and the duplicities of his private life are eventually to
carry over into his career in public affairs. He will supply the
government with faked statistics to justify its political immorality.
    In the railway carriage of the train to Rye, as Macmaster and
Tietjens engage in seemingly random small talk about Rossetti,
modern novelists, the lower classes, and the possibility of war,
the main theme of *Parade's End* begins to emerge. Tietjens gives
his own historical formulation, faintly preposterous, intensely
personal yet ultimately precise, of the relationship between public

and private events. Macmaster remarks that "war is impossible—at any rate with this country in it. . . . *We*—the circumspect—yes, the circumspect classes, will pilot the nation through the tight places."

"War, my good fellow," Tietjens said—the train was slowing down preparatorily to running into Ashford—"is inevitable, and with this country plumb centre in the middle of it. Simply because you fellows are such damn hypocrites. There's not a country in the world that trusts us. We're always, as it were, committing adultery—like your fellow—with the name of heaven on our lips."   [p. 20]

Sexual conduct is to become in *Parade's End* the single largest reflector of cultural disintegration, linking the present with the past in a pattern of historical causation and suggesting that the future has already been sabotaged.

Nowhere is the germ of the future more clearly seen than in the complex series of events, with their intricate cross references, both personal and political, that make up Tietjens, and Macmaster's weekend at Rye. As is perhaps obvious, there is simply no way of capturing everything involving the weekend, for the context constantly veers from the private to the public, from Tietjens' intensely personal problems to large questions dealing with national culture, with manners, morals, and social institutions. Ford's technical virtuosity is seldom more in evidence. Yet there is a way of seeing how Ford's rhetoric of narrative works in these hundred pages or so. For the large segments or chunks of dialogue, and indirect discourse, which are curiously terse and prolix at once, and which contain—hold in solution as it were—the incidents of the weekend, carry with them a ground bass which becomes increasingly pronounced as narrative-line and motif converge. It is this ground-tone that can be most easily traced.

The signs of the changing times are even visible in the most conservative of settings—the clubhouse of the golf course where the two young men are drinking tea with General Lord Edward Campion, Tietjens' godfather, and Paul Sandbach, a conservative M.P. and the husband of the General's sister, Lady Claudine. Sandbach comes from an industrial family in the Groby area, and there is no love lost between him and Tietjens. Sandbach is given to a "violent manner" (he has twice been suspended from

Parliament) and is symbolically lame. (So too is the general: "as a result of a slight but neglected motor accident. He had practically only one vanity, the belief that he was qualified to act as his own chauffeur, and since he was both inexpert and very careless, he met with frequent accidents" [pp. 55-56].) Sandbach's presence represents a general weakening of moral fiber among the governing classes, in part produced by the merger of *nouveaux riches* like Sandbach, whose money makes him desirable, and the traditional ruling classes.

Having in recent weeks seen Tietjens on the street with a girl of the lower classes, a bookmaker's secretary, Sandbach immediately assumes that the girl is Tietjens' mistress (whereas in reality Macmaster has been having an affair with the girl and Tietjens is trying to arrange for him to break off with her), and he wastes no time in informing General Campion of his conclusions. Not surprisingly, in the events of the day at the golf course, he will also assume that Valentine Wannop is Tietjens' mistress. She invades the links with a suffragette friend to harass a Liberal cabinet minister, the Rt. Hon. Edward Fenwick Waterhouse. Tietjens helps Valentine, and particularly her companion, who is not so athletic as Val, to escape their pursuers, two "city men," who are guests on the links, and a constable, there to protect the minister. One of the city men has already ripped the blouse of Valentine's companion, and the other is running after her, yelling: "Strip the bitch naked! . . . Ugh . . . Strip the bitch stark naked!" (p. 67). Tietjens brings him up short with: "You infernal swine. I'll knock your head off if you move!" And he trips the constable by throwing his golf bag at his legs. The girls make good their escape on a plank across a dyke, and then Valentine removes the plank and they are safe.

The attitudes of the various men toward the suffragettes are revelatory. Waterhouse, the cabinet minister, orders the caddies to stop pursuing the girls, whom he finds admirable. He also has Tietjens fix things with the constable (who has recognized Valentine and, reluctant to hurt her in any way, doesn't want to mention that he knows her) so that no charges are brought against Valentine. Campion is also relieved that Val made her escape. (He knows both her and her mother, and is aware that they are financially hard pressed; Lady Claudine brings them produce from her garden.) Sandbach, on the other hand, is infuriated and refuses to continue his golf match with Tietjens.

He said that Tietjens was the sort of fellow who was the ruin of England. He said he had a good mind to issue a warrant for the arrest of Tietjens—for obstructing the course of justice. Tietjens pointed out that Sandbach wasn't a borough magistrate and so couldn't. And Sandbach went off, dot and carry one, and began a furious row with the two city men who had retreated to a distance. He said they were the sort of men who were the ruin of England. They bleated like rams. . . .   [p. 69]

There has already been an incident in the clubhouse with the gauche city men, dressed in bright green coats and red knitted waistcoats and with florid faces. As they sat over their sloe gins and brandies, at the table next to Campion, Sandbach, Macmaster, and Tietjens, who were drinking their tea, the two men rudely listened to the conversation at the other table. They also carried on a lewd conversation about their own sexual feats: "The man with the oily hair said in a sickly voice that Gertie was hot stuff but not the one for Budapest with all the Gitana girls you were telling me of! Why, he'd kept Gertie for five years now. More like the real thing!" (p. 58). (Valentine's suffragette companion, one should point out, is ironically named Gertie.) The General, who is president of the club, finally feels compelled to suggest to the two men that "it isn't wise to discuss one's . . . eh . . . domestic circumstances . . . at . . . at mess, you know, or in a golf house. People might hear." Macmaster, silently taking the scene in, thinks to himself that, "for these Tories at least, this was really the end of the world. The last of England!" (p. 59).

On the golf course, after the suffragette incident, the two city men, like Sandbach, complain about Tietjens' conduct. Later the General relates to Tietjens that "they had objected to being called ruddy swine to their faces; they were going to the police. The General said that he told them himself, slowly and distinctly, that they *were* ruddy swine and that they would never get another ticket at the club after Monday. But till Monday, apparently, they had the right to be there and the club wouldn't want scenes." The General has to ask Tietjens to stay away until Monday.

Tietjens said that the fault lay with the times that permitted the

introduction of such social swipes as Sandbach. One acted perfectly
correctly and then a dirty little beggar like that put dirty little con-
structions on it and ran about and bleated. He added that he knew
Sandbach was the General's brother-in-law, but he couldn't help it.
That was the truth. . . . The General said: "I know, my boy: I
know. . . ." But one had to take society as one found it. Claudine had
to be provided for and Sandbach made a very good husband, careful,
sober, and on the right side in politics. A bit of a rip; but they couldn't
ask for everything! And Claudine was using all the influence she had
with the other side—which was not a little, women were so wonderful—to get him a diplomatic job in Turkey, so as to get him out of
the way of Mrs. Crundall! Mrs. Crundall was the leading Anti-Suffra-
gette of the little town. That was what made Sandbach so bitter against
Tietjens. He told Tietjens so that Tietjens might understand. [p. 76]

Sandbach's vindictiveness will take the form of urging some half
dozen of the young bloods who dine at Mountby that night to
go scouring the country lanes after dinner, mounted on motor
bikes and armed with loaded canes, in search of suffragettes
(p. 86).

As Tietjens, in the dressing room of the golf club that afternoon, and later, riding back to town in a fly, is called upon by
his godfather to justify himself—concerning Julia Mandelstein,
the bookmaker's secretary, and Valentine Wannop—the focus
slowly but irrevocably falls upon Sylvia and Tietjens' relationship with her. Once more the context of events becomes Tietjens'
personal problem over Sylvia. (He has already sent a telegram
to her in Germany agreeing to take her back, under certain conditions.) Ironically, the General is worried that Tietjens is
betraying Sylvia, even spending Sylvia's money on other women,
and that this is why Sylvia has separated from him. Campion
wants at least a plausible story to tell Lady Claudine; like Sandbach, he is convinced that both the bookmaker's secretary and
Valentine are Christopher's women. Thus Tietjens is once more
forced to consider his predicament and the stance he must take
toward society. He does not try to defend himself very much
to his godfather, though if he really tried, he feels, he could
make Campion believe him. But there is the attitude of society
in general to consider. And there is the child, who Tietjens isn't
even sure is his. "It was better for a boy to have a rip of a

father than a whore for mother!" (p. 77). And Tietjens, con-
sidering what has just happened, thinks to himself that "it was
natural for an unborn fellow like Sandbach to betray the solidarity
that should exist between men. And it was natural for a childless
woman like Lady Claudine Sandbach with a notoriously, a
flagrantly unfaithful husband to believe in the unfaithfulness
of the husbands of other women!" (p. 77). As the General goes
on talking, Tietjens barely listens, his mind still preoccupied
with the problem of his personal honor.

And all the other society women with unfaithful husbands. . . .
They must do their best to down and out a man. They would cut him
off their visiting lists! Let them. The barren harlots mated to faithless
eunuchs! . . . Suddenly he thought that he didn't know for certain
that he was the father of his child, and he groaned.
"Well, what have I said wrong now?" the General asked. "Surely
you don't maintain that pheasants do eat mangolds. . . ."
Tietjens proved his reputation for sanity with:
"No! I was just groaning at the thought of the Chancellor! That's
sound enough for you, isn't it?" But it gave him a nasty turn. He
hadn't been able to pigeon-hole and padlock his disagreeable reflections. He had been as good as talking to himself.   [p. 78]

The psychological pressures are beginning to be felt by Tietjens.
     Late evening finds Christopher, after dining with Waterhouse,
the cabinet minister, sitting in a smoking-jacket and playing pa-
tience in a garret-room. His mind is preoccupied with the conditions of his life with Sylvia.

He wanted to stop scandal if he could; he wanted them to live within
his income, he wanted to subtract the child from the influence of its
mother. These were all definite but difficult things. . . . Then one half
of his mind lost itself in the rearrangement of schedules, and on his
brilliant table his hands set queens and kings and checked their re-
currence.
     In that way the sudden entrance of Macmaster gave him a really
terrible physical shock. He nearly vomited; his brain reeled and the
room fell about. He drank a great quantity of whisky in front of Macmaster's eyes; but even at that he couldn't talk, and he dropped into
bed faintly aware of his friend's efforts to loosen his clothes. He had,
he knew, carried the suppression of thought in his conscious mind
so far that his unconscious self had taken command and had, for the
time, paralyzed both his mind and his body.   [pp. 79-80]

Before the events of the weekend are over the psychological pressure will have become so great that Tietjens will wonder whether he hasn't had a stroke.

Parade's End has sometimes been called an allegory of social decay,[7] but there is very little of the allegorizing tendency in Ford, and this is particularly true of the Tietjens novels, in which fact and symbol are continuous. (Coleridge in his lecture on *Don Quixote* remarks that "the symbolical cannot, perhaps, be better defined in distinction from the allegorical, than that it is always itself, a part of that, of the whole of which it is the representative."[8]) The importance of the events of the day comes not from any second level of significance but from the texture of cross references they supply. *Parade's End* is a realistic novel, but, as was also true of *The Good Soldier,* it presents a realism psychologically distorted.

Tietjens, it becomes clear as *Some Do Not . . .* proceeds, is a Dickensian figure with a Jamesian sensibility, and the world he inhabits, while peculiarly Fordian, has conscious overtones of the Dickensian—in its humor: " 'Well, what have I said wrong now?' the General asked. 'Surely you don't maintain that pheasants do eat mangolds. . . .' " In its major characters: Mrs. Wannop (who Tietjens says has "written the only novel worth reading since the eighteenth century"); General Campion, with his crochets and craggy thoughts; Christopher's brother Mark, who resembles in many ways a recurrent figure in Dickens' novels, "the Good Rich Man," as George Orwell called him; Christopher's father, who never smoked in the house but had twelve tobacco-filled pipes set among the hedges of his estate, and who was known to Mrs. Wannop as her "mascot, tea-tray"; Father Consett, the Irish priest; Lord Port Scatho, the banker; the mad clergyman, Breakfast Duchemin of Magdalen: and in innumerable minor characters, in both *Some Do Not . . .* and the subsequent volumes. The seemingly rambling plots of Ford's four novels also have a kinship with the plots of Dickens: in the way events crosscut all strata of society, and in the endless coincidences and complications attendant upon the simplest of actions. But Ford does not rely on intrigues, murders, hidden disguises, mistaken identities, and other traditional contrivances of the Victorian novel; his plots employ a very simple mechanism: "one psychological pro-

gression involving two women and a man." Their complexities
derive from the clash between Christopher's (and Ford's) personal dissent ("I stand for monogamy and chastity") and the
artifices that society finds necessary to conceal and justify its
conduct.

On the morrow Tietjens and Macmaster breakfast with an
Anglican clergyman, the Reverend Duchemin, one of "Ruskin's
road-builders" and an authority on the Pre-Raphaelites, some of
whom he has known personally. There, in an eighteenth-century
room with dark wood panels and four Turner seascapes on the
walls, amidst congeries of silver, epergnes, bowls, vases, urns,
kettles, tripods, and surrounded by mounds of food and arrays
of roses and delphiniums, Macmaster will commence, with hands
joined under the table, a liaison with Mrs. Duchemin, Edith
Ethel. It is to be a passionately soulful, spiritually chaste union
of high minds, or so at least they will pretend to themselves and
each other. Yet their union is to entail duplicities of one kind
and another. Valentine Wannop will be duped into chaperoning
Edith Ethel each Friday to Macmaster's literary teas, where
Mrs. Duchemin, who is becoming the Egeria to a number of
literary men, plays hostess. Each Friday night Valentine will
see her to Charing Cross and the train for Rye. Mrs. Duchemin
will get off at Clapham Junction, take a taxicab back to Gray's
Inn, and spend the night with Macmaster (p. 241). Later, Edith
Ethel becomes hysterical and asks Val about the details of abor-
tion; the mask momentarily falls and the coarseness of her
personality is revealed in the vulgarity of her language. "She
raged up and down in the candlelight, before the dark oak panelling, screaming coarse phrases of the deepest hatred for her
lover. Didn't the oaf know his business better than to . . .? The
dirty little Port of Leith fish-handler. . . ." Valentine can only
wonder: "What, then, were tall candles in silver sticks for? And
polished panelling in galleries" (p. 230). What indeed are Pre-
Raphaelite splendors and luxuries for, if not fineness of soul and
spirit?
But Valentine has more personal problems at that moment than
a dispassionate examination of Pre-Raphaelitism. By one of Ford's
peculiar twists of plot, Val is led to believe that Mrs. Duchemin's

lover in this instance has more likely been Tietjens than Macmaster, and she is made miserable by this, as she is genuinely
shocked by Mrs. Duchemin's sexual crudities. (Sylvia, one should
point out, not only accuses Christopher of having Valentine, but
also Mrs. Duchemin, for a mistress.) By a further Fordian irony,
the unborn child becomes attached to Valentine, and Mrs.
Duchemin will accuse her of having had a child by Tietjens.
"I don't see the use," she is ironically made to say to Valentine,
"of keeping on that mask" (p. 259).

"Ethel! Have I gone mad? Or is it you? Upon my word I can't understand. . . ."
Mrs. Duchemin exclaimed:
"For God's sake hold your tongue, you shameless thing! You've
had a child by the man, haven't you?"
Valentine saw suddenly the tall silver candlestick, the dark polished
panels of the rectory and Edith Ethel's mad face and mad hair whirl-
ing before them.
She said:
"No! I certainly haven't. Can you get that into your head? I certainly haven't." She made a further effort over immense fatigue. "I
assure you—I beg you to believe if it will give you any ease—that
Mr. Tietjens has never addressed a word of love to me in his life.
Nor have I to him. We have hardly talked to each other in all the
time we have known each other."
Mrs. Duchemin said in a harsh voice:
"Seven people in the last five weeks have told me you have had a
child by that brute beast: he's ruined because he has to keep you
and your mother and the child. You won't deny that he has a child
somewhere hidden away? . . ."
Valentine exclaimed suddenly:
"Oh, Ethel, you mustn't . . . you *mustn't* be jealous of me! If you
only knew you wouldn't be jealous of me. . . . I suppose the child
you were going to have was by Christopher? Men are like that. . . .
But not of me! You need never, never. I've been the best friend you
can ever have had. . . ."
Mrs. Duchemin exclaimed harshly, as if she were being strangled:
"A sort of blackmail! I knew it would come to that! It always does
with your sort. Then do your damndest, you harlot. You never set
foot in this house again! Go you and rot. . . ."   [pp. 260-261]

The significance of this tragical-grotesque conversation between

Edith Ethel and Valentine, which takes place years after the
morning breakfast at the Duchemin rectory, and is the last talk
they are to have together, is that it both mirrors the events of
that long-ago morning and presents the train of consequences
which have resulted.

On that morning, before the guests arrive, Valentine sits with
Edith Ethel in the rectory. Mrs. Duchemin is examining the
flower arrangements for the purpose, the reader quickly realizes,
of determining whether they will sufficiently conceal the Reverend
Duchemin at breakfast. As it later develops, the nearly insane
Duchemin suffers from a scatological mania which takes the
form of shouting obscenities, largely from Petronius, at his guests.
Valentine quickly senses Mrs. Duchemin's anxiety over the
presence of herself, an innocent young woman, and remarks:
"Look here, Edie. Stop worrying about my mind. If you think that
anything I hear after nine months as an ash-cat at Ealing, with
three men in the house, an invalid wife and a drunken cook, can
corrupt my mind, you're simply mistaken. You can let your
conscience be at rest, and let's say no more about it" (p. 81).
She goes on to explain the financial predicament her father's
death left herself, her mother, and her brother in, and something
of her reasons for becoming a "slavey" (she let drop a remark
to Tietjens the day before on the golf course that she had been
a servant). She also explains how her experiences at Ealing had
made her a suffragette. She concludes: "I'd like you to understand
that in spite of it all I'm pure! Chaste, you know. . . . Perfectly
virtuous" (p. 82).

> Mrs. Duchemin stroked the girl's fair hair and tucked a loose
> strand behind her ear.
> "I wish you'd let me show you how to do your hair," she said.
> "The right man might come along at any moment."
> "Oh, the right man!" Miss Wannop said . . . "The right man for
> me, when he comes along, will be a married man. That's the Wannop
> luck!"   [p. 83]

Valentine's prediction is to prove more than accurate; the final
coming together of Tietjens and Valentine is to be a slow and
gradual meeting, as if the more society rebuffs them and places

obstacles in their way, the more certainly they are to be drawn
to each other.

Tietjens' first serious thought of Valentine is oddly that she
is suited for Macmaster (p. 88), just as Macmaster's first thought
of Mrs. Duchemin is that she is ideally suited for Tietjens (p. 55).
Both of these reflections are peculiarly Fordian ironies (as is Tietjens' comment to Macmaster, early in the novel, that someday he
"might come across another woman," and Father Consett's remark to Mrs. Satterthwaite, Sylvia's mother, that Sylvia's "hell
on earth will come when her husband goes running, blind, head
down, mad after another woman"; see pp. 11 and 42). A further
series of ironies controls the remaining conversation between Mrs.
Duchemin and Valentine, particularly in the light of future
events already foreshadowed.

Valentine goes on talking about Ealing, her family's problems,
and her fears that the police will become involved in the events
of the day before and she will land in prison. Finally she breaks
into tears and is comforted by Mrs. Duchemin. A few moments
later it is Valentine's turn to comfort Mrs. Duchemin, who now
breaks into tears over the perpetual problem her husband presents.

"Why women in your position don't take lovers . . ." the girl said,
hotly. "Or that women in your position *do* take lovers . . ."

Mrs Duchemin looked up; in spite of its tears her white face had
an air of serious dignity:

"Oh, *no*, Valentine," she said, using her deeper tones. "There's something beautiful, there's something *thrilling* about chastity. I'm not nar-
row-minded. Censorious! I don't *condemn!* But to preserve in word,
thought, and action a lifelong fidelity.... It's no mean achievement...."

"You mean like an egg and spoon race," Miss Wannop said.

"It isn't," Mrs. Duchemin replied gently, "the way I should have
put it. Isn't the real symbol Atalanta, running fast and not turning
aside for the golden apple? That always seemed to me the real truth
hidden in the beautiful old legend. . . ."

"I don't know," Miss Wannop said, "when I read what Ruskin
says about it in the *Crown of Wild Olive*. Or no! It's the *Queen of
the Air*. That's his Greek rubbish, isn't it? I always think it seems
like an egg-race in which the young woman didn't keep her eyes in
the boat. But I suppose it comes to the same thing."

Mrs. Duchemin said:

"My *dear!* Not a word against John Ruskin in *this* house." [p. 85]

It is hardly necessary for anyone to say a word against Ruskin. If Valentine's ludicrous analogy of an egg-and-spoon race and her critical remarks about Ruskin's "Greek rubbish" have not been sufficient, there remains the breakfast scene itself in which the Reverend Duchemin, with his delusions and fantasies, becomes both symbol and concrete fact of the crumbling stones of the Victorian edifice. " '*Post coitum tristis!* Ha! Ha! That's what it is?' The voice repeated the words and added sardonically: 'You know what *that* means?' " (p. 93).

The psychological tensions of the scene are held taut by the embarrassment and discomfiture of the hostess and the guests, and by Ford's technical adroitness. The events of the breakfast are broken into minute segments of small action and personal reflection. In a fashion similar to the way a motion-picture camera slowly pans around a room, pausing over various figures to take in bits of the room through their eyes, Ford manipulates point of view, shifting from Macmaster to Mrs. Duchemin to Tietjens, and back again. The effect is to show each of them responding to the situation created by the lunacy of Duchemin: Mrs. Duchemin, with her fears, hopes, and desires; Macmaster with his efforts to be helpful; and Tietjens, whose sympathy and understanding are unwanted and feared by Mrs. Duchemin. Early in the breakfast, before the clergyman's first outburst, Mrs. Duchemin remarks to Macmaster that her husband may not on this occasion prove to be the source of scholarly information on the Pre-Raphaelites that Macmaster desired. "He's apt . . . especially on Saturdays. . . ."

"Oh, dear lady!" (And it seemed to her to be charming to be addressed thus!) "One understands . . . one is surely trained and adapted to understand . . . that these great scholars, these abstracted cognoscenti . . ."

Mrs. Duchemin breathed a great "Ah!" of relief. Macmaster had used the exactly right words.

"And," Macmaster was going on, "merely to spend a short hour; a shallow flight . . . 'As when the swallow gliding from lofty portal to lofty portal' . . . You know the lines . . . in these, your perfect surroundings . . ."

Blissful waves seemed to pass from him to her. It was in this way that men should speak; in that way—steel-blue tie, true-looking gold ring, steel-blue eyes beneath black brows!—that men should look. She was half conscious of warmth; this suggested the bliss of falling asleep, truly, in perfect surroundings. The roses on the table were lovely; their scent came to her.

A voice came to her:

"You *do* the thing in style, I must say."

The large, clumsy, but otherwise unnoticeable being that this fascinating man had brought in his train was setting up pretensions to her notice. [pp. 91-92]

Ford's unique comedy of manners achieves its effect from a coming together of such rather subtle nuances of tone and gesture and attitude with the incongruities of Dickensian comedy and low farce.

At the breakfast there is also present, in addition to Valentine, Mrs. Wannop (who has come unexpectedly and uninvited); Miss Fox, who has been chosen to sit near Duchemin and pour because she is completely deaf; Mr. Horsely, one of Duchemin's three curates; and Parry the Bermondsey light middle-weight, Duchemin's man-in-waiting and keeper. As Duchemin's lapses become more and more unrestrained, Macmaster is less and less able to bring him out of them. The clergyman suddenly rises to his feet, "panting and delighted."

"Chaste!" He shouted. "Chaste, you observe! What a world of suggestion in the word . . ." He surveyed the opulent broadness of his tablecloth; it spread out before his eyes as if it had been a great expanse of meadow in which he could gallop, relaxing his limbs after long captivity. He shouted three obscene words and went on in his Oxford Movement voice: "But chastity . . ." [p. 99]

The guests make do as best they can, trying to drown him out. Mrs. Wannop turns to Mr. Horsley and talks about her writing (Horsley had been prepared to shout a description of an article he had been writing about the *Mosella* of Ausonius). Tietjens begins to talk to Valentine in as loud a voice as possible. Miss Fox, seeing lips moving all around her, joins the conversation. She remarks diagonally to Mrs. Duchemin: "I think we shall have thunder to-day. Have you remarked the number of minute insects. . . ." The scene comes to a noisy close with Duchemin seemingly about to reveal the secrets of his married life.

"When my revered preceptor," Mr. Duchemin thundered on, "drove away in the carriage on his wedding day he said to his bride: 'We will live like the blessed angels!' How sublime! I, too, after my nuptials . . ."

Mrs. Duchemin suddenly screamed:

"Oh . . . no!"   [p. 99]

He is brought up short when, upon the instruction of Macmaster (who, coincidentally, had a friend in college with a mania similar to Duchemin's), Parry the boxer gives the clergyman a kidney punch with his thumb. The Reverend Duchemin falls back into his chair.

Ford's method of composition in the breakfast scene is the method he uses in most of the big scenes in *Parade's End*: the slowing down of time, the multiple points of view, the worrying over minute details of etiquette and conduct, the ironic confrontation of outward appearance with inward reality, and the involvement of more and more coincidences in the pattern of meaning. Comment and scene are so closely interwoven that they merge. Further, the gradual coming together of various strands of narrative and motif serves the order of Ford's meaning. *"I stand for monogamy and chastity.": "I'd like you to understand that in spite of it all I'm pure! Chaste, you know. . . .": "There's something beautiful, there's something* thrilling *about chastity.": "You mean like an egg and spoon race.": " 'Chaste!' He shouted. 'Chaste, you observe! What a world of suggestion in the word. . . .' "* The events of the morning conclude with Mrs. Duchemin and Macmaster privately arranging to meet later in the day.

Their lips met in a passion of pity and tears. He removed his mouth to say: "I must see you this evening. . . . I shall be mad with anxiety about you." She whispered: "Yes! yes! . . . In the yew walk." Her eyes were closed, she pressed her body fiercely into his. "You are the . . . first . . . man . . ." she breathed.

"I will be the only one for ever," he said.

An extreme languor had settled on him, he felt weakened but yet triumphant with the cessation of her grasp. It occurred to him numbly that he would be seeing less of Tietjens. A grief. He heard himself quote:

"Since when we stand side by side!" His voice trembled.

"Ah yes!" came in her deep tones. "The beautiful lines . . . They're true. We must part. In this world . . ." They seemed to her lovely and mournful words to say; heavenly to have them to say, vibrating, arousing all sorts of images.

"You can't say that that isn't great poetry! Great poetry.": "I can't say. I don't read poetry except Byron. But it's a filthy picture . . .": *"Damn it. What's the sense of all these attempts to justify fornication? England's mad about it."* In precisely this manner in *Some Do Not . . .* circumstances and events converge upon one another.

What a long time ago! He heard his own voice saying in the new railway carriage, proudly, clearly, and with male hardness:

"I stand for monogamy and chastity. And for no talking about it. Of course if a man who's a man wants to have a woman he has her. And again no talking about it. . . ." His voice—his own voice— came to him as if from the other end of a long-distance telephone. A damn long-distance one! Ten years . . .

If then a man who's a man wants to have a woman. . . . Damn it, he doesn't! In ten years he had learnt that a Tommie who's a decent fellow. . . . [p. 281]

This is from the last section of *Some Do Not . . .* as Christopher's mind runs *sotto voce* over the events of the evening (his dinner with Macmaster, the party afterward which announced Macmaster's knighthood, and the final part of the evening, spent with Valentine) and the associations they call up. It is 2:30 A.M. and Christopher is sitting in a chair in Sylvia's and his flat in Gray's Inn. In the morning he leaves for France. He has just returned from seeing Valentine and her drunken brother home. The two of them had been about to commence an affair this night, but both circumstances and the place, and the clandestine nature of their course of action, had contrived to make the situation unpropitious.

He had exclaimed:
    "It's perhaps too . . . untidy . . ."
She had said:
    "Yes! Yes . . . Ugly . . . Too . . . oh . . . private!"
He said, he remembered:
    "But . . . for ever . . ."

She said, in a great hurry:

"But when you come back. . . . Permanently. And . . . oh, as if it were in public." . . . "I don't know," she had added. *"Ought* we? . . . I'd be ready. . . ." She added: "I will be ready for anything you ask."

He had said at some time: "But obviously. . . . Not under this roof. . . ." And he had added: We're the sort that . . . *do not!"*

She had answered, quickly too:

"Yes—that's it. We're the sort!"   [p. 283]

This situation, though developed almost totally in dialogue, nevertheless depends for its effect on human consciousness as represented by Tietjens, whose memory holds and filters not merely words and details and events but also feelings, thoughts, emotions.

If technique ultimately seems to loom as less significant in *Parade's End* than in *The Good Soldier,* it is for the very simple reason that it has become for Ford largely automatic, reflexive, and in so doing has become an aspect of style.

The long weekend of Part One of *Some Do Not . . .* comes to a close with Christopher and Valentine traveling in a horse-drawn cart along fog-bound country roads at four-thirty on the morning of the longest day of the year. They are making their return trip from having delivered Valentine's suffragette companion, Gertie Wilson, to safety. As the fog comes up they lose their way. Christopher, striving to find their bearings, tries to read meaning into the "imbecile landscape." Valentine gets down from the cart to search for a road marker. Tietjens sings "John Peel" to let her know the location of the cart, and as he sings, the associative stream carries him into the past: to his family, to the traditional values he upholds, to his present alienation and role as "a lonely buffalo outside the herd" (p. 128). Gradually he turns his attention to the girl, whom he has known less than twenty-four hours, and with whom a convention has already grown up: that "he must play stiff and cold, she warm and cling-ing." But why not break all the conventions? He has forty-eight hours before he will rejoin Sylvia. Why not let them be a holiday? "A holiday from himself above all, a holiday from his standards, from his convention within himself. From clear observation, from exact thought, from knocking over all the skittles of the exacti-

tudes of others, from the suppression of emotions . . ." (p. 129).
With Christopher's decision made, his mind shifts backward to
the events of the trip thus far, reconstructing how, under the
emotional release granted by the fog, which has blocked out the
world about them, the two of them had gradually become attuned
to one another. Their conversation had been ebullient without
being brilliant: light banter about geography, quibbles about
Latin pronunciation and the translation of certain phrases from
Ovid. The particulars proliferate in Tietjen's mind (and are perhaps over-amplified); for the important point is that the scene
(which parallels the scene between Macmaster and Mrs. Duchemin) has become both symbol and fact for a complex event:
the coming together of two people with the restraints of society
temporarily removed. " 'Can't,' he argued with destiny, 'a man
want to kiss a schoolgirl in a scuffle . . .' " (p. 138). He wants
to; but of course he does not.

Shortly after, the sun breaks through and they recognize where
they are. Then, approaching Mountby, where the Sandbachs live,
they are run into by an automobile hurtling out of the treacherous
driveway. Their cart is overturned, their horse badly hurt. The
mechanized twentieth-century has run over the horse-drawn nineteenth century. At the wheel is General Campion, who, "inexpert and very careless," and much more at home with horses,
nevertheless prides himself on his ability to act as his own chauffeur. He is dressed "in full tog. White feathers! Ninety medals!
Scarlet coat! Black trousers with red stripe. Spurs too, by God!"
(p. 141). His inexpert presence at the wheel is a gloomy prophecy
of things to come. As for Valentine and Christopher, the idyll is
over. Lady Claudine had been riding in the car with the General. Valentine's reputation is virtually ruined.

Part Two of *Some Do Not . . .* is built around the afternoon
and evening hours of a single day in London. The events themselves are largely trivial: a long conversation between Tietjens
and Sylvia, interrupted first by Lord Port Scatho, then by Christopher's brother Mark; a walk by Christopher and Mark to the
War Office, where they are joined by Valentine; and a long talk
between Mark and Valentine while Christopher attends to his
affairs. This is really all there is of present tense. (The events
of the evening, as we have already seen, are told through Chris-

topher's mind at 2:30 A.M.) Through these few events of the
afternoon Ford tries to present in both concrete and personal
form the image of an increasingly corrupt society. His attempt,
unique in the literature of his time, is only partially successful.
Ford strains too hard to achieve his effects, for, as has been remarked, the point about such corruption—recorded by professional historians in terms of economic trends, or political coups,
or government policies, or outstanding instances (such as the
Dreyfus case; Tietjens is constantly associated with Dreyfus, particularly by General Campion)—is that it is anonymous, affecting
the individual only remotely or in a far different cultural form
than the original cause might suggest. Ford's attempt is to make
the correspondence direct and to interweave one event with another so that there is no separation: they all form part of the
pattern.

Lord Port Scatho, for example, comes to the Tietjens flat as the
representative of their landlord, the benchers. Sylvia has written
accusing Mrs. Duchemin of serving as Tietjens' mistress in the
flat across the way. But it also develops that Port Scatho's nephew,
"Brownie," has chosen the few hours when Tietjens' bank account
was overdrawn to have his checks returned. (Later Christopher
tells Mark that the bank has made a "mistake." "By God!" Mark
replies, "this is the last of England!") Brownlie has been motivated in part by sexual jealousy (he desires Sylvia), in part by personal malice (what Tietjens calls "the incidental degeneration of
the heroic impulse," produced by the distinction of those in uniform and those who are not). From this one small incident, the
failure to extend credit to a gentleman's overdraft, a whole chain
of consequences develops. Christopher's club asks him to resign,
and he is in serious trouble with the army, where he paid his
monthly mess bill with one of the checks Brownlie returned.
Ford's account of Tietjens' difficulties at this point seems less
than realistic, and more than a little hysterical; yet the effect he
is striving to achieve is easy enough to see, as is his method: to
directly involve Tietjens in a conflict with some organized segment of society by which it becomes necessary for one or both
to make some kind of formal acknowledgement of their positions,
some public statement or gesture. Tietjens will be placed beyond
the reach of social compromise and will violate tradition by inex-

cusable actions. Thus, to follow the pattern out, Tietjens will resign from his club. The club's committee will hold an emergency
meeting, and, in the light of what it has learned from Port Scatho,
it will draft a letter to Christopher asking him to reconsider. He
will then withdraw his resignation—only to resign again the next
morning. Ruggles, who is directly responsible for most of the
misinformation about Christopher, says: "Not that. . . . You
couldn't do that. . . . Not to the *club!* . . . It's never been done.
. . . It's an insult. . . ." Christopher replies: "It's meant to be"
(p. 286).

Ruggles, who is a Scotsman attached to the royal court in a
minor capacity, has for years shared a floor of living quarters
with Mark Tietjens (the situation is meant to parallel that of
Macmaster and Christopher). Ruggles is an inveterate gossip,
and when Marks asks him to find out about Christopher's activities, he undertakes the assignment with more than a little malice.
He makes his inquiries of the priestesses of society (among them,
"the lady known as Glorvina": a Thackerayan touch, as is Ford's
talk of the "book" of society, "kept in a holy of holies, in which
bad marks are set down of men of family and position"), and
in making his investigation he injures Christopher as much as
he can.

And, quite steadily and with, indeed, real belief in much of what he
said, Ruggles had denigrated Tietjens. . . . Ruggles could not see
why Christopher had taken Sylvia back after her elopement with
Perowne; he could not see why Christopher had, indeed, married
Sylvia at all when she was with child by a man called Drake—just as
he wasn't going to believe that Christopher could get a testimonial
out of Lord Port Scatho except by the sale of Sylvia to the banker.
He couldn't see anything but money and jobs at the bottom of these
things. He couldn't see how Tietjens otherwise got the money to support Mrs. Wannop, Miss Wannop, and her child, and to maintain
Mrs. Duchemin and Macmaster in the style they affected, Mrs.
Duchemin being the mistress of Christopher. He simply could see
no other solution. It is, in fact, asking for trouble if you are more
altruist than the society that surrounds you.   [pp. 206-207]

Tietjens makes the point in another way. "You see," he tells Valentine, "in such a world as this, an idealist—or perhaps it's only
a sentimentalist—must be stoned to death. He makes the others

so uncomfortable" (p. 237). Ruggles can only surmise that he has damaged Tietjens. "He had talked in what he considered to be the right quarters, but he hadn't any evidence that what he had said had got through" (p. 207).

The damage to Tietjens' immediate family, however, is unmistakable. For both the elder Tietjens and Mark believe what Ruggles tells them.

. . . Ruggles had told Mr. Tietjens senior that Christopher's wife had been with child when he had married her; he had hushed up her elopement with Perowne and connived at other love affairs of hers to his own dishonour, and was suspected in high places of being a French agent, thus being marked down as suspect in the great book. . . . All this in order to obtain money for the support of Miss Wannop, by whom he had had a child, and to maintain Macmaster and Mrs. Duchemin on a scale unsuited to their means, Mrs. Duchemin being his mistress. The story that Tietjens had had a child by Miss Wannop was first suggested, and then supported, by the fact that in Yorkshire he certainly had a son who never appeared in Gray's Inn.
[p. 209]

The elder Tietjens, to all appearances, commits suicide the next day, after avoiding Christopher at the club on the night before. (It is not until *The Last Post* that we learn that his death most likely was accidental.) Christopher cannot find it in himself to forgive his father, and he does not forgive Mark. " 'But you *must*,' Mark said—and it was a tremendous concession to sentimentality —'take enough to make you comfortable' " (p. 218). But Christopher is neither interested in the Groby money nor in the course of the petty antagonisms surrounding him.

Even though Mark's offer of monetary help is refused by Christopher, Mark's role in *Some Do Not . . .* is nevertheless the Dickensian role of financial savior, particularly to the Wannops, whom the elder Tietjens had supported before his death. And while Christopher is neither young nor helpless, nor morally and politically naïve, as are the heroes of Dickens (Walter Gay, Richard Carstone, Pip), he has close affinities with them. Indeed, there is a heavy nineteenth-century manner about large segments of *Some Do Not . . .* not unfitting in a novel that tells the story of a man's spiritual journey from the nineteenth to the twentieth century. But ultimately Christopher's story is a twentieth-century story, and the theme of alienation, handled by Ford on an epic scale which includes both the personal and the public, is a theme a younger generation of novelists, writing less publicly and more personally, was to make central to their work.

Some Do Not . . . , published in 1924, more clearly indicates Ford's position as a transitional figure in the history of twentieth-century fiction than his earlier *Good Soldier,* the sheer technical brilliance of which has misleadingly suggested to commentators a more modern reading of the novel than its contents will support. Ford's achievement in the art of the novel is not really diminished by its limitations of time and place. Ford extended the range of subject matter of the modern novel and in so doing enlarged the role played by technique. Ultimately, along with a handful of others, such as Joyce, he enlarged the dimensions of modern sensibility and taste.

In *Some Do Not . . .* Ford has things to say about the relationship between the sexes which up to Ford's time had never been said before in English fiction. Ford's technical achievement lies in having found a way to impart the pyschological truths that inform and make real the world of *Parade's End.* But Ford's notion of psychological reality is not one of passive detachment and his artistic labors are not directed, except parenthetically, toward the modern novelist's frequent goal of self-understanding. Another way of suggesting Ford's position in modern letters is to point out that, while Christopher Tietjens predates the heroes of contemporary fiction as a Christ-figure, Ford's handling of his hero's predicament sets Ford a generation apart from the novelist of today. At the root of the difference between Ford and *"les jeunes,"* as he called the younger writers, such as Hemingway and Fitzgerald, is the way he viewed psychological reality.

EIGHT

Towards Tomorrow

> Arts rise and die again, systems rise and die again,
> faiths are born only to die and to rise once more;
> the only thing constant and undying is the human
> crowd.
>
> ENGLAND AND THE ENGLISH

In the curious but informative 1910 Epistolary Epilogue to *A Call*, written, like T. S. Eliot's notes to *The Waste Land,* to fill out needed pages for the publisher, Ford converses with an imaginary opponent (most likely Violet Hunt) concerning the art of fiction. At one point he supplies two specimens of the same conversation, one supposedly the way his unnamed fellow writer would have set it down, the other the way he himself would have handled the conversation. His examples are farcical as usual, but they are none the less revealing for that. "You," he addresses his opponent, "would probably render a conversation thus:

> Extending her hand, which was enveloped in a creamy tulle, Mrs. Sincue exclaimed, 'Have another cup of tea dear?' 'Thanks—two lumps,' her visitor rejoined. 'So I hear Colonel Hapgood has eloped with his wife's French maid!' "

"I" Ford goes on, "should have probably set it down:

> After a little desultory conversation, Mrs. Sincue's visitor, dropping his dark eyes to the ground, uttered in a voice that betrayed neither exultation nor grief, 'Poor Hapgood's cut it with Nanette. Don't you remember Nanette, who wore an apron with lace all around it and those pocket things, and curled hair?' "   [pp. 300-301]

Ford's handling of the scene differs from his fellow writer's in

168

its accentuated though minute drama and its sense of congruity between detail and dialogue. The first specimen characterizes the maid by national type and occupation, makes use of irrelevant detail, and depends on cheap surprise.

Ford's serious handling of situation and detail in *Parade's End* reveals much of the same psychological concerns as his hypothetical example. Here is Tietjens walking in the English countryside with Valentine.

> "God's England!" Tietjens exclaimed to himself in high good humor. "Land of Hope and Glory!—F natural descending to tonic, C major: chord of 6-4, suspension over dominant seventh to common chord of C major. . . . All absolutely correct! Double basses, 'cellos, all violins, all woodwind, all brass. Full grand organ, all stops, special *vox humana* and key-bugle effect. . . . Across the counties came the sound of bugles that his father knew. . . . Pipe exactly right. It must be: pipe of Englishman of good birth; ditto tobacco. Attractive young woman's back. English midday midsummer. Best climate in the world! No day on which man may not go abroad!" [p. 106]

This is not whimsy but a carefully controlled musical analogue which represents the verbal limits of an English gentleman, even of Tietjens' capacities. Ford's use of inner consciousness depends on psychological realism, despite its obvious literary quality. In *No More Parades* Sylvia sits in a hotel lobby in wartime France and makes a silent pact with her deceased spiritual guide, Father Consett. In ten minutes she will search the room for a presentable man. If she finds one, she will go into religious retreat and leave off her habitual tormenting of Christopher. As she waits for the time to pass, her mind roams over the long-ago past, as well as over recent events, particularly those created by her surprise arrival at the military supply depot commanded by General Campion. In her reverie she recalls a bulldog she once lashed with a whip and left outside during the night; the next morning it was dead. The bulldog makes her think of Christopher and his passive acceptance of her abuses, the personal embarrassments and social predicaments she causes him. The particulars multiply in her mind. Then:

> She said: "The ten minutes is up, father . . ." and looked at the round, starred surface between the diamonds of her wrist watch. She

said: "Good God! . . . a minute . . . I understand how hell can be
eternity. . . ."   [p. 417]

Time has become subjective, dependent on inner psychological
processes.

But where physical action is as important as inner consciousness Ford is less successful. In *A Man Could Stand Up—*, Tietjens,
surveying the troops, of which he has lately been second-in-command, and over which he is about to assume control, falls into
reverie while conversing with the first sergeant. He recalls a night
attack in which, having nothing to do as second-in-command, he
went up from the dugout command post into the trenches. A
subaltern only two days out from England, Aranjuez, was having
difficulty loading and firing a Verey gun. The private who had
acted as his loader was dead or wounded at his feet. Tietjens
assumes charge of the gun and sends the young lieutenant for
medical aid.

Tietjens became like a solitary statue of the Bard of Avon, the
shelf for his elbow being rather low. Noise increased. The orchestra
was bringing in *all* the brass, *all* the strings, *all* the wood-wind, *all*
the percussion instruments. The performers threw about biscuit tins
filled with horse-shoes; they emptied sacks of coal on cracked gongs,
they threw down forty-storey iron houses. It was comic to the extent
that an operatic orchestra's crescendo is comic. Crescendo! . . .
C r e s c e n d o! CRRRRRES C. . . . The Hero must be coming! He didn't.

Still like Shakespeare contemplating the creation of say, Cordelia,
Tietjens leaned against his shelf. From time to time he pulled the
trigger of the horse-pistol; from time to time he rested the butt on
his ledge and rammed a charge home. When one jammed he took
another. He found himself keeping up a fairly steady illumination.

The Hero arrived. Naturally he was a Hun. He came over, all legs
and arms going, like a catamount; struck the face of the parados, fell
into the trench on the dead body, with his hands to his eyes, sprang
up again and danced. With heavy deliberation Tietjens drew his great
trench-knife rather than his revolver. Why? The butcher instinct?
Or trying to think himself with the Exmoor stag-hounds. The man's
shoulders had come heavily on him as he had rebounded from the
parados-face. He felt outraged. Watching that performing Hun he
held the knife pointed and tried to think of the German for *Hands*

Up. He imagined it to be *Hoch die Haende!* He looked for a nice spot in the Hun's side.

His excursion into a foreign tongue proved supererogatory. The German threw his arm abroad, his—considerably mashed!—face to the sky.

Always dramatic, Cousin Fritz! Too dramatic really.

He fell, crumbling, into his untidy boot. Nasty boots, all crumpled too, up the calves! But he didn't say *Hoch der Kaiser,* or *Deutschland über alles,* or anything valedictory. [.559]

Here the vast allusiveness of Tietjens' mind reveals a softness in the material which Ford's technique cannot conceal, and the confusion over precisely what has happened strikes the reader as a wrong note, even though on the next page Ford makes clear that the soldiers in a nearby trench had seen the approaching German and had shot him.

But most of the sequences in France, at the supply depot in *No More Parades* and in the trenches in *A Man Could Stand Up*—, do not revolve around physical action. Some of these pages are among the best Ford ever wrote, particularly the opening of *No More Parades,* with the death of O Nine Morgan, the batman. As Ambrose Gordon has remarked, in "A Diamond of Pattern: The War of F. Madox Ford," "there is much cold, much wet, much mud in Ford's landscape, but there is very little action. Ford knew that war was mostly waiting."[1] (Ford was also over forty when in the service, and "action" simply did not interest him as it did, for example, the young Hemingway.) Tietjens thinks to himself, in the third volume of the series:

You hung about and you hung about, and you kicked your heels and you kicked your heels: waiting for Mills bombs to come, or for jam, or for generals, or for the tanks, or transports, or the clearance of the road ahead. You waited in offices under the eyes of somnolent orderlies, under fire on the banks of canals, you waited in hotels, dug-outs, tin sheds, ruined houses. There will be no man who survives His Majesty's Armed Forces that shall not remember those eternal hours when Time itself stayed as the true image of the bloody War! . . . [p. 569]

Ford saw the man at war as a man divided within himself. Personal events at home loom as large in the soldier's mind as

events at the front ("Soldiers are dreamers; when the guns begin / They think of firelit homes, clean beds, and wives"; so run
Sassoon's lines.), and they can disturb him more, produce greater
stress, because he is relatively helpless to do anything about them.

A man at this point is subject, in his interests at home, to exactly
the same disasters or perplexities as his temperament prepares for
him in times of peace. If he is the sort of man to have put up with
treacheries of others his interests at home will suffer from treasons;
if he is the man to incur burdens of debt, debts there will unaccounta-
bly amass themselves; if he is a man destined to be betrayed by women
his women will betray him exaggeratedly and without shame. For all
these vicissitudes will be exaggerated by the more strident note that
in time of war gets into both speeches and events. . . . And he is indeed, then, *homo duplex*: a poor fellow whose body is tied in one
place but whose mind and personality brood eternally over another
distant locality.[2]

Tietjens' worries provide an elaborately intensified version of
every man's worries. Their universality is mocked in the personal
histories of the cousin of Macmaster, Captain McKechnie, whose
madness reflects the psychological state Tietjens barely escapes
and whose domestic troubles continue to make him distraught,
and O Nine Morgan, the private soldier whose wife runs off with
a boxer. Also, Tietjens' commanding officer in *A Man Could
Stand Up*— has financial problems very much like those produced
by Brownlie's refusal to honor Christopher's overdraft in *Some
Do Not . . . .*

Ford designed his hero, "the last megatherium," so that he
would be more critic than participant, more acted upon than
active.

My character would be deprived of any glory. He was to be just
enough of a man of action to get into the trenches and do what he
was told. But he was to be too essentially critical to initiate any daring
sorties. Indeed his activities were most markedly to be in the realm
of criticism. He was to be aware that in all places where they managed things from Whitehall down to brigade headquarters a number
of things would be badly managed—the difference being that in
Whitehall the mismanagement would be so much the result of jeal-
ousies that it would have all the aspect of the most repellent treach-
ery: in brigade headquarters, within a stone's throw of the enemy, it

would be the result of stupidities, shortage of instruments or men, damage by enemy activities, or, as was more often the case, on account of nearly imbecile orders percolating from Whitehall itself.[3]

As with the scenes that take place in peacetime England, the context of the war sequences is always wider than the immediate foreground of a headquarters hut in a supply depot or a trench in the lines. Ultimately Ford is less interested in the war than in what it represents: humanity driven underground, the end of one civilization, its ruling classes no longer capable of leading; the emergence of another governing class, yet unknown but obviously unlike the old order—ruder for one thing. "Tiring people! Without manners! . . . They would presumably run the world now. It would be a tiresome world" (p. 591). Early in the war Tietjens had visited the War Office and there came across a man in a room devising the ceremonial for the disbanding of a Kitchener battalion. It was the one ceremony, according to Tietjens, for which the Edwardian world was prepared.

"Well, the end of the show was to be: the adjutant would stand the battalion at ease; the band would play *Land of Hope and Glory,* and then the adjutant would say: *There will be no more parades.* . . . Don't you see how symbolical it was—the band playing *Land of Hope and Glory,* and then the adjutant saying *There will be no more parades?* . . . For there won't. There won't, there damn well won't. . . . No more Hope, no more Glory, no more parades for you and me any more. Nor for the country . . . nor for the world, I dare say . . . None . . . Gone . . . Na poo finny! No . . . more . . . parades!"

[pp. 306-307]

This passage, central to all four of the Tietjens novels, states openly what Ford's narrative conveys by circumstance and event, by the farcically compounded incidents which crowd around Christopher. In the new world which the war helped to create and Ford records, the military panoply is a boring irrelevance.

Most novels that have dealt directly with the First World War, with "front line action," have today largely become mere footnotes to history. The mechanics of yesterday's war soon become quaint, the language it creates obsolete ("Na poo finny!" echoes across the pages of *Parade's End*), while the emotions behind individual acts of courage and bravery, stupidity and duplicity, become less intelligible when deprived of their immediate historical gloss. Even the best—Barbusse's *Under Fire,* Remarque's *All Quiet on the Western Front,* Aldington's *Death of a Hero,* March's *Company K*—seem today to possess a mass hysteria and paranoia fathomable only in terms of the times. In one sense, personal narrative, such as Robert Graves's autobiographical account of his trench experiences in *Goodbye to All That,* seems to withstand the passing of time better. Another exception to the general rule is David Jones's *In Parenthesis,* first published in 1937. *In Parenthesis* is in part personal narrative (like Graves, and like Ford, Jones served in a Welsh regiment), in part novel, but it is also a good deal more, and if it survives, as it now seems destined to, it will be because of qualities that make universal in another way the experiences of life in the trenches. Jones's book makes use of techniques akin to those of Eliot's in *The Waste Land.* Sentences are constructed in poetic segments; typographical breaks in lines indicate one kind of shift or another; and the author has even appended a series of explanatory notes. The story line itself is skeletal: a journey to the front and battle. Private John Ball, the main figure, an Everyman, is barely distinguishable from the other troops in the ranks. Scene floats into scene, routine merges into other routines, snatches of dialogue crisscross others like barbed wire. The chasm between events and their meaning is filled with a chiaroscuro of fragments from Arthurian legends, Welsh folklore, and the Matter of Britain.

Like *In Parenthesis,* Ford's war novels are also destined to survive, largely because here the chasm between events and their meaning in *Parade's End* is always filled by the synthesizing consciousness of Tietjens, or when not Christopher, one of the lesser figures. As Gordon has noted, there is a "curiously closed-in quality" to Ford's scenes.

Out there and a little beyond is unnamed horror: the horror of what lies beyond the front lines, of No Man's Land, of the unknown, from which for the most part we take cover with varying degrees of success. Were the action placed out there, as it is in much of the *Iliad,* it would be necessarily tragic. But Ford's characters remain enclosed, boxed-up, holed-in. We—the readers and the characters—await the inevitable intrusion, and when it comes it is horrid and macabre, but not tragic. It is more than anything absurd, since in this shut-in scene the norms of a life of reason and common sense (or what passes for them) have, despite all, been preserved, in particular such matters as rank and class. These are simply incommensurate with the intruding horror, and it with them. So, when death enters in the guise of O Nine Morgan, for a brief time the social norms are shattered—for one thing his blood gets on an officer's shoes—but the normal is quickly re-established. It is perhaps this very quickness, indeed, which keeps the rhythm comic.[4]

The pattern, as Gordon points out, applies to Ford's peacetime scenes as well. "Always the scene is an interior (though the walls may be only of vapor) into which there is a violent intrusion, a very brief dispersal, and a quick regrouping. The very recurrences of this pattern suggest a further structural principle: each such boxed-in interior . . . comes to suggest all the rest."[5] But it is also the shut-off, enclosed quality of Ford's scenes which in one sense delineates the limits of his imaginative achievement in the art of the novel. Here, for example, is the fogbound scene from *Some Do Not . . .* in which General Campion's car rams the horse cart that holds Valentine and Christopher.

Not ten yards ahead Tietjens saw a tea-tray, the underneath of a black-lacquered tea-tray, gliding towards them, mathematically straight, just rising from the mist. He shouted, mad, the blood in his head. His shout was drowned by the scream of the horse; he had swung it to the left. The cart turned up, the horse emerged from the mist, head and shoulders, pawing. A stone sea-horse from the fountain of Versailles! Exactly that! Hanging in air for an eternity; the girl looking at it, leaning slightly forward.
The horse didn't come over backwards: he had loosened the reins. It wasn't there anymore. The damndest thing that *could* happen! He had known it would happen. He said:
"We're all right now!" There was a crash and scraping like twenty tea-trays, a prolonged sound. They must be scraping along the mudguard of the invisible car. He had the pressure of the horse's mouth; the horse was away, going hell for leather. He increased the pressure. The girl said:
"I know I'm all right with you." [pp. 139-140]

It is easy to see the extent to which Ford's artistic allegiances are divided between two centuries by setting beside this scene another crash scene, the accident involving Myrtle Wilson on the road to West Egg in *The Great Gatsby.*

The scene in *Gatsby* is recalled through the mind of Michaelis, the operator of a "coffee joint" beside Wilson's garage. Wilson had been quarreling with his wife. Michaelis, standing in the doorway of his own place, hears them.

"Beat me!" he heard her cry. "Throw me down and beat me, you dirty little coward!"
A moment later she rushed out into the dusk, waving her hands and shouting—before he could move from his door the business was over.
The "death car" as the newspapers called it, didn't stop; it came out of the gathering darkness, wavered tragically for a moment, and then disappeared around the next bend. Michaelis wasn't even sure of its color—he told the first policeman it was light green. The other car, the one going toward New York, came to rest a hundred yards beyond, and its driver hurried back to where Myrtle Wilson, her life violently extinguished, knelt in the road and mingled her thick dark blood with the dust.
Michaelis and this man reached her first, but when they had torn open her shirtwaist, still damp with perspiration, they saw that her left breast was swinging loose like a flap, and there was no need to listen for the heart beneath. The mouth was wide open and ripped at the corners, as though she had choked a little in giving up the tremendous vitality she had stored so long.[6]

It is more than the difference of age or nationality that separates Ford and Fitzgerald. It is the difference of generations in the history of the novel. Ford slows time to a near-halt, saturating the moment until the reader, like Christopher, is giddy from wave upon wave of impressions. There is always a domestic quality about Ford's scenes, produced in part no doubt by their bound-in quality, but also partly derived from Ford's tone, which has the quality of good gossip at tea-time (the General's car appears through the mist like a "black-lacquered tea-tray"). Fitzgerald, on the other hand, parcels out his "impressions" much more sparingly and seemingly with much more objectivity. (The seemingly factual report carries with it overtones of the coroner's inquest at which Michaelis testified.) Yet here too the author takes over the scene, though much more quietly: first when the "death car," appearing out of *the gathering darkness*," wavers *"tragically for a moment"*; then when the driver of the second car returns to the spot "where Myrtle Wilson, her life violently extinguished, *knelt in the road and mingled her thick dark blood with the dust"*; finally when Michaelis and the driver bend over Myrtle Wilson's body, her left breast *"swinging loose like a flap"* and "the mouth wide open and ripped at the corners, *as though she had choked a little in giving up the tremendous vitality she had stored so long."* Fitzgerald's conscious restraint of the poetic quality of his prose marks the control he is exercising over his material.

A more critical distinction between Fitzgerald and Ford remains to be observed. In the course of his narrative Fitzgerald breaks up his scene some half dozen times into subjective fragments. Thus, for example, Nick will pass the scene of the accident on the commuter train to New York City the next morning. But he does not view the scene. (Had he looked out of the train window, hours after the accident, it is unlikely that he would have seen anything but a stretch of road, passing cars, and a deserted garage and gasoline pumps.) Instead Nick crosses to the other side of the car. Nevertheless he imagines a curious crowd at the ash heaps, little boys searching for dry spots of blood, and "some garrulous man telling over and over what happened, until it became less and less real even to him and he could tell it no longer, and Myrtle Wilson's tragic achievement was forgotten" (p. 156). Nick's imaginative rearrangement of the landscape, with its heightened tragic overtones, artistically prepares us for the return to the night before in the final sentence of the paragraph: "Now I want to go back a little and tell what happened at the garage after we left there the night before." The crucial point is that Fitzgerald is not bound to his scene, either by chronological sequence or the demands of character. Ford, on the other hand, hangs everything on a single rendering of a scene, and once the scene has been enacted it cannot be gone over again. (There are exceptions to this, of course. At the beginning of *Some Do Not* . . . several scenes are viewed first through Tietjens' eyes, then through Macmaster's. But in general the point holds; echoes and verbal snatches of a scene are all that can occur, and these through the consciousness of one of the characters.) In other words, for all the glamour of innovation attached to the time-shift, Ford is still temporally tied to the episodic, as well as to the subjective consciousness of a leading character.

As we have seen in earlier chapters, the sources of Ford's use of the time-shift are various. The effects he achieved cannot be explained merely by the artistic theories he subscribed to. Other considerations enter the picture, not the least of which is the background of Ford's career, the cultural milieu from which he came and the era which saw him reach adulthood. Ford unintentionally reminds us of this complex derivation at various points in his nonfictional prose. In his 1932 Introduction to the Modern Library edition of Hemingway's *A Farewell to Arms,* for example, he remarks that "Hemingway's words strike you, each one, as if they were pebbles fetched fresh from a brook. . . . The aim—the achievement—of the great prose writer is to use words so that they shall seem new and alive because of their juxtaposition with other words. This gift Hemingway has supremely."[7] "On the other hand," Ford remarks several paragraphs later, "a writer holds a reader by his temperament. This is his true 'gift'—what he receives from whoever sent him into the world. It arises from how you look at things."[8] One is reminded that the hallmarks of the artist during Ford's adolescent years were fantasy, whimsy, eccentricity; Ford's "impressionism" always depends to some extent on such tokens of "genius."

The comparison of a moment ago between Ford and Fitzgerald becomes more pointed if one keeps in mind that *Some Do Not . . .* and *The Great Gatsby* were published within a year of each other, and, more important, that Fitzgerald's achievement depends on techniques that are similar to those of Ford and Conrad. As James E. Miller has pointed out, to Conrad in particular Fitzgerald was indebted both "for a new approach to his craft" and also "for more specific elements: for the use of style or language to reflect theme; for the use of the modified first person narration; and for the use of deliberate 'confusion' by the re-ordering of the chronology of events."[9] Whatever Fitzgerald's debt to Conrad, his narrative art is much more akin to Ford's, particularly in its dependence on the skillful manipulation of transitions, the imaginative movements that accompany such transpositions or shifts in time as Fitzgerald's narrator, Nick Carraway, chooses to make. But Fitzgerald carried the evolution of a method a step farther, and nowhere is this more evident than in Fitzgerald's assurance of form, the very simplicity with which he manipulates time. Such assurance of form Ford could only maintain by talking to himself, as well as his reader, through Dowell and Tietjens. One might add in conclusion that Fitzgerald, unlike Ford, realized that he was the personal author of his own wreckage. It is this awareness that separates Ford's generation from Fitzgerald's. It is not that Fitzgerald was more honest than Ford but that by the time Fitzgerald wrote, it had become possible to accept blame. Self-knowledge had become a human discovery.

In *The Great Gatsby* the southern belle Daisy Fay, the first "nice girl" James Gatz had ever known, is the bright symbol of Gatsby's dreams. Beautiful and rich, she is the incarnation of all his elaborate fantasies, his vision of the American dream. "High in a white palace, the king's daughter, the golden girl." But in *Gatsby,* as Leslie Fiedler points out, "Dark Lady and Fair, witch and redeemer have fallen together."[10] Daisy tumbles far short of Gatsby's dreams, not merely, as Nick puts it, "because of the colossal vitality of his illusion" (p. 97), but because she has been corrupted. In this respect the villain-heroine of *Parade's End* is the precursor of Daisy. Sylvia Tietjens embodies in an earlier form at least one of the two cultural projections found in Daisy, *"La Belle Dame sans Merci."* Together with "The Blessed Damozel," this version of the "fatal woman" represents a cultural figment of the nineteenth century which grew out of romanticism and, metamorphosed and transformed, still dominates our literature today in a curious way. It is as if our century were compelled to live out both in fiction and in real life the foolishnesses of the earlier culture. In *Gatsby* Daisy's doubleness is essentially a reflection of our schizophrenic view of woman: goddess and bitch, Fair Lady and Dark, angel and temptress. (In *Tender is the Night,* as Fiedler points out, Fitzgerald makes his heroine, Nicole, an actual schizophrenic.) Daisy's dark side is reflected in Jordan Baker, the woman athlete who cheats at golf. In *Parade's End* Sylvia's role as a cultural projection is mirrored in Mrs. Duchemin, the Pre-Raphaelite siren whose sexual hypocrisy is revealed in the course of her affair with Macmaster.

Sylvia of course is other things also. She is for Ford a complex personal symbol, a fantasy figure in part identifiable with Violet Hunt. She also represents a segment of upper-class society, the smart set whose names and photographs are frequently seen in the rotogravure sections of newspapers. Ford sets her further off from the herd, making her a Roman Catholic and hence something of an outsider. Ford was not very familiar with the kind of society in which Sylvia supposedly moved, and the existence of this superior social milieu—composed of such friends of Sylvia as Eunice Vanderdecken, Elizabeth B., Queenie James, Di Wilson—is created by a faking process so deft that it takes on the plausibility of high art. We never really see Sylvia moving in this world, except briefly in *The Last Post,* when she is staying with Lord and Lady Fittleworth. (Fittleworth is the name of a Sussex village near Ford's and Stella's cottage.) Yet Sylvia is powerfully drawn both as a symbol and as a human being, particularly in the effect she has on other people.

A complete silence had fallen on the room. Every woman in it was counting the pleats of Sylvia's skirt and the amount of material in it. Valentine Wannop knew that because she was doing it herself. If one had that amount of material and that number of pleats one's skirts might hang like that. . . . For it was extraordinary: it fitted close round the hips, and gave an effect of length and swing—and yet it did not descend as low as the ankles. . . . And from the silence Valentine could tell that every woman and most of the men—if they didn't know that this was Mrs. Christopher Tietjens—knew that this was a personage of *Illustrated Weekly,* as who should say of county family, rank. Little Mrs. Swan, lately married, actually got up, crossed the room and sat down beside her bridegroom. It was a movement with which Valentine could sympathize.   [p. 248]

Ultimately Sylvia's power over men is sexual. She is "man-mad," like all her set. But in her case Ford complicates the motivation, for she plays the "fatal woman" to men's imaginations, then practises "every kind of 'turning down' on these creatures" (p. 146). She discovers that her power over them increases as she is cold toward them. After her return to Christopher, she becomes chaste; "she cherished her personal chastity much as she cherished her personal cleanliness and persevered in her Swedish exercises after her baths before an open window, her rides afterwards, and her long nights of dancing which she would pursue in any room that was decently ventilated" (p. 149). Her own sexual desires are largely sublimated in her revenge against the male sex. In *The Last Post* young Mark Tietjens, her son, thinks to himself: "The dominion of women over those of the opposite sex was a terrible thing. He had seen the old General [Campion] whimper like a whipped dog and mumble in his poor white moustache. . . . Mother was splendid. But wasn't sex a terrible thing" (p. 713).

Sylvia's ruses and perversities seem inhumanly cruel, outrageous, grotesque. Her presence at the military base in France in *No More Parades* produces a sequence of events which ends with a drunken general, as well as Perowne, trying to enter her bedroom late at night, only to be ejected by Christopher, who is ironically placed under military arrest for his conduct. On the night of the Armistice, Sylvia claims to have cancer and purposely falls down a flight of stairs. "She had come for the purpose of telling them that she was going to be operated on for cancer, so that with their sensitive natures they could hardly contemplate going to bed together at that moment" (p. 776). Valentine, however, sees through the ruse.

For all its preposterousness, Sylvia's conduct rings true, for one thing partly because it is based on what Christopher at one point thinks of as the "impossible complication" (p. 224): that she loves him. Through the design of Christopher's rejection of Sylvia, Ford reconstructs on paper his own painful separation from the era and the society that gave birth to both his social idealism and his artistic creed.

In *The Last Post* Sylvia continues to harass Christopher and Valentine, now living in the Sussex countryside. Christopher has become a dealer in antiques and furniture. Valentine is carrying his child. With them are Mark Tietjens and Marie Léonie, Mark's mistress of years whom he married on Armistice Day. Mark lies ill and dying in an outdoor thatched shelter, unable or unwilling to communicate with those who attend him except by movements of the eyes. It is through Mark's interior monologues that crucial sections of the fourth book are rendered. (Christopher is absent until the last pages; he has flown to Groby to see what damage has resulted from the cutting-down of Groby Great Tree. The

tenant, Mrs. de Bray Pape, a rich American, has had the tree
cut down at the instigation of Sylvia. Mrs. Pape then becomes
worried over what legal action Christopher might take.) Christopher's absence from the Sussex scene is in part no doubt a sign
of Ford's growing detachment from his material, though the details of *The Last Post* reflect Ford's personal life more intimately
than those of the earlier volumes, which may be one reason he
personally liked it least. More important, Ford seems to have
needed the additional distance from his material which Mark
provides. Thus it is through his eyes that the reader views in
panoramic retrospect significant major events of the earlier volumes, and it is through him that Ford voices both his sentimental
hopes and his satiric reservations about the future.

Ford's pastoral scene is crowded. While Christopher is away,
Sylvia, together with Mrs. Pape, young Mark (or Michael, as he
is also called), and Helen Lowther (a young American), invades
the premises. General Campion and Lord Fittleworth (Christopher's landlord and also host to Sylvia and her party) refuse to
trespass. By the end of the book Sylvia realizes that she has forever lost Christopher to Valentine and stops tormenting him. She
has decided to seek a divorce with the sanction of Rome, and she
is already contemplating marrying General Campion, who is about
to be appointed to some high post in India. Marriage to Campion,
she realizes, will give her continued social position. But Sylvia
also recognizes that her social milieu is on the wane. "In her
world there was the writing on the wall" (p. 809). When Christopher returns from Groby he brings with him a piece of Groby
Tree; the curse, set upon the Tietjens hundreds of years ago for
usurping the land (Christopher repeatedly mentions *Splenden on
Sacrilege* through the four volumes), has been symbolically lifted.
Christopher, at last unfettered, can now fashion out of the ruins
of his world a future life with Valentine.

By the end of *A Man Could Stand Up—*, with which Ford
originally intended to end the series, the future had already
emerged in bold outline. "Feudalism was finished" (p. 668); so
was the nineteenth century for him. Christopher separates himself
from both. But his violation of conventional moral attitudes is

made at the expense of all the assurances of wealth, rank, and honor offered the man-in-society. "People would talk. About him. It was his fate. And hers" (p. 667).

Ford's fable is an expansive metaphor for his own venture into the twentieth century, but while his vision is both highly personal and somewhat eccentric, the pattern of its meaning is not. The story of Christopher and Valentine, their retreat from society and their roles as new Adam and Eve, is one archetypal version of romance in the twentieth century. Christopher, quixotic and Christ-like, is an early prototype of the picaresque saint of today's literature. The young, athletic, emancipated Valentine is a twentieth-century incarnation of the Jamesian innocent. Unlike Nancy in *The Good Soldier,* who was victimized by Leonora's sexual talk, Valentine withstands a double sexual shock, once in Ealing, where as a maid she was subjected to the coarseness and crudities of the men of the house, and later in the Duchemin parlor, where Edith Ethel lets her mask slip and reveals the vulgarities of her private life with Macmaster. (In *The Last Post,* once again a widow, Edith Ethel makes a brief appearance, ironically with a slightly deranged Ruggles by her side whom she is training as "a consort.")

Valentine is the daughter of an enlightened Victorian novelist and a classical scholar of advanced views. "Like most of her young friends, influenced by the advanced teachers and tendential novelists of the day, she would have stated herself to advocate an, of course, enlightened promiscuity. That, before the revelations of Mrs. Duchemin! Actually she had thought very little about the matter" (p. 264). Valentine penetrates the maze of this cultural labyrinth, with its seeming contradictions. She realizes that the "bright beings" who publicly advocated enlightened promiscuity in general practised absolute continence. And when people slipped, the facade was still there to protect them. "She remembered the long—call it 'liaison' of Edith Ethel Duchemin and little Vincent Macmaster. Edith Ethel, swathed in opaque crêpe, creeping widow-like along the very palings she could see across the square, to her high-minded adulteries, amidst the whispered applause of mid-Victorian England. So circumspect and

right!" (pp. 661-662). The life together which Christopher and
Valentine are openly about to undertake violates the established
codes of decorum.

Nowhere is the cultural predicament made clearer than in the
position in which Mrs. Wannop finds herself. Valentine thinks:

The Mid-Victorians had had to loosen the bonds. Her mother, to be
in the van of Mid-Victorian thought, had had to allow virtue to "irregular unions." As long as they were high-minded. But the high-
minded do not consummate irregular unions. So all her books had
showed you high-minded creatures contracting irregular unions of
the mind or of sympathy; but never carrying them to the necessary
conclusion. They would have been ethically at liberty to, but they
didn't. They ran with the ethical hare but hunted with the ecclesiasti-
cal hounds. . . . Still, of course, she could not go back on her premises just because it was her own daughter!   [p. 661]

Ultimately it is Mrs. Wannop who brings Christopher and Valentine together, talking to each of them over the telephone, making
them aware that each of them wants what the other has been
hesitant to mention. (Valentine thinks of herself: "Why did she
take it that they were going to live together? She had no official
knowledge that he wanted to. But *they* wanted to TALK. You
can't talk unless you live together"; p. 651.) Valentine's unblush-
ing acceptance of sex and her awareness of the social consequences of what she is about to do is the mark that she, like
Christopher, still has her personal integrity intact. "On an elephant. A dear, meal-sack elephant. She was setting out on . . ."
(p. 674).

Thus ends the third volume of the Tietjens series. *The Last
Post* Ford always considered an ill-conceived afterthought. Yet
the fourth volume fulfills a function too, particularly in the story
of Mark Tietjens who, along with Sylvia, dominates the book.
Both Mark and Sylvia are mythic components in Ford's fictional
universe, and each in his own way signals the end of something.
Learning the terms of the German surrender on Armistice Day,
in which the Allies agree not to go on to Berlin, Mark officially
resigns his government post as head of the Office of Transport.
He also resigns from society, resolving never to speak again.
Mark's symbolic gesture is one more sign of the alienation of

Christopher (and Ford) from postwar England. Like Ezra Pound's soldiers, Ford felt he had come

> . . . home, home to a lie,
> home to many deceits,
> home to old lies and new infamy;
> usury age-old and age-thick
> and liars in public places.[11]

Mark Tietjens' separate peace reflects Ford's separate peace. Ford's disposition to feel himself split between two centuries is nowhere more clear than in the doubling of Christopher and Mark.

Mark's (and Ford's) compassion for Sylvia in *The Last Post* is oddly moving. If Sylvia has given up Christopher, then "his, Mark's, occupation was gone. He would no longer have to go on willing against her; she would drop into the sea in the wake of their family vessel and be lost to view. . . . But damn it, she must have suffered to be brought to that extreme . . ." (p. 830). "Sylvia," as William Carlos Williams has remarked, "is the dead past in all its affecting glamor."[12] It was not easy for Ford to part with the past, and indeed he never did so completely.

Ford's writing career did not end with *The Last Post*. A decade filled with novels and volumes of reminiscences remained to him. But *Parade's End* nevertheless seems the proper book on which to close a study of Ford. For, like Henry James, Ford spent the last years defining and refining his "sense of the past." Perhaps one might close a study of Ford by simply recalling the last words of his own study of James, *and changing* only *the titles of two novels:* "Looking upon the immense range of the books written by this author, upon the immensity of the scrupulous labours, upon the fineness of the mind, the nobility of the character, the highness of the hope, the greatness of the quest, the felicity of the genius and the truth that is at once beauty and more than beauty —of this I am certain, that such immortality as mankind has to bestow . . . will rest upon the author of /*The Good Soldier*/. It will rest also with the author of /*Parade's End*/."

NOTES

AND

BIBLIOGRAPHY

NOTES

(*See also the* BIBLIOGRAPHY, *pp.* 195-197, *and the*
CHRONOLOGICAL LIST OF FORD'S BOOKS, *pp.* 197-201.)

CHAPTER ONE

1. *Paris Was Our Mistress* (N.Y., 1947), p. 120.
2. For a general biographical account of Ford's life see Douglas Goldring's *Trained for Genius* (N.Y., 1949), published in England as *The Last Pre-Raphaelite* (London, 1948). Most of Ford's reminiscences of childhood are in the volume *Memories and Impressions* (published in England as *Ancient Lights*).
3. *Memories and Impressions,* p. 78.
4. *Ibid.,* p. 3. The account of Madox Brown which follows is taken from pp. 247-248 of the same book.
5. *Ibid.,* p. 9.
6. *The Lost Childhood and Other Essays* (N.Y., 1952), p. 90.
7. *Memories and Impressions,* p. 18.
8. *Mightier than the Sword,* p. 126.
9. *Memories and Impressions,* p. 216.
10. *Return to Yesterday,* p. 347.
11. *Rude Assignment* (London, 1950), p. 122.
12. *Return to Yesterday,* p. 348.
13. *Memories and Impressions,* p. xviii.
14. Quoted by Lillian Gilkes in *Cora Crane* (Bloomington, Ind., 1960), p. 112.
15. *Experiment in Autobiography* (N.Y., 1934), p. 526.
16. *Joseph Conrad: A Critical Biography* (London, 1960), pp. 214-215.
17. *Thus to Revisit,* p. 82.
18. *The Twentieth Century Novel* (N.Y., 1932), p. 161.
19. *It Was the Nightingale,* p. 212.
20. *Poetry,* IV (June, 1914). Reprinted as "The Prose Tradition in Verse," in his *Literary Essays* (N.Y., 1944), p. 371.
21. *Parade's End,* p. 447. All references to the four Christopher Tietjens volumes are to the single-volume edition published by Alfred A. Knopf (N.Y., 1950), with an Introduction by Robie Macauley.

22. *Henry James: A Critical Study,* p. 9.
23. Published in America as *Ring for Nancy* (N.Y., 1913). See p. 29 of the American edition.
24. *Joseph Conrad: A Personal Remembrance,* pp. 186-187.
25. See chapter iii of the Scribner edition (N.Y., 1946), p. 54.
26. *Thus to Revisit,* p. 114.
27. Preface to *Collected Poems* (London, 1916), p. 13.
28. *Henry James,* p. 22.
29. *Ibid.,* p. 48.
30. Greene's remarks were made for the publicity pamphlet that announced the 1950 re-publication of the four "Tietjens" novels in the omnibus edition, *Parade's End.*
31. *The Notebooks of Henry James* (N.Y., 1947), p. 170.
32. Preface to *Collected Poems,* p. 22.
33. Reprinted in the Knopf Vintage edition (N.Y., 1957), which also contains An Interpretation by Mark Schorer.
34. *The English Novel* (N.Y., 1957), p. 395.
35. *It Was the Nightingale,* pp. 86-87.
36. *Drawn from Life* (London, 1941), p. 79.
37. *It Was the Nightingale,* p. 23.
38. Section X of "Hugh Selwyn Mauberley," in *Personae,* 2d ed. (N.Y., 1949), p. 195. The ascription of these lines to Ford was first made by Hugh Kenner.
39. *Drawn from Life,* p. 80.
40. 14 August 1923. By permission of T. S. Eliot and the current owner, Mrs. Julia Loewe.
41. 4 October 1923. By permission of T. S. Eliot and the current owner, Mrs. Julia Loewe.
42. *Paris Salons, Cafés, Studios* (Philadelphia, 1928), p. 121.
43. *The Autobiography of Alice B. Toklas* (N.Y., 1933), p. 271.
44. This and the remarks that follow by Mrs. Loewe were made during the broadcast "Memories of Ford Madox Ford," *WBAI Program Folio,* II, #22, 6 (Oct. 30-Nov. 12, 1961). Mrs. Loewe's remarks are drawn from her private script. For details of the broadcast, which included the reminiscences of a good number of Ford's friends, see Harvey's *Bibliography,* p. 472.
45. Reprinted by permission of the owner, Mrs. Julia Loewe.
46. Macauley, Introduction to *Parade's End,* p. v.
47. Preface to *Collected Poems,* p. 13.

CHAPTER TWO

1. *The English Novel,* pp. 91-92.
2. "A Victorian Son," in *The Living Novel* (London, 1949), p. 102.
3. In his Dedicatory Letter Ford quotes John Rodker, the English poet, who once remarked that *The Good Soldier* "is the finest French novel in the English language!"
4. The Loewe Manuscript Collection contains a portion of the novel bearing that title (listed in Harvey's *Bibliography,* p. 118, as unpublished). The Epigraph to *The New Humpty-Dumpty* reads: "There be summer queens and dukes of a day, / But the heart of another is a dark forest." According to Richard A. Cassell the phrase "Another person's heart, you know, is a dark forest" appears in the W. R. S. Ralston translation of Turgenev's *Liza* (London, 1915), p. 84. See Cassell's *Ford Madox Ford: A Study of His Novels* (Baltimore, 1961), p. 147, n.
5. In *England and the English* (N.Y., 1907), p. 338. This volume contains all three of Ford's books on the English landscape: *The Soul of London* (1905), *The Heart of the County* (1906), and *The Spirit of the People* (1907).
6. *Sober Truth* (London, 1932), p. 18.
7. *Joseph Conrad,* pp. 136-137.
8. *Ibid.,* p. 137.
9. *Ibid.,* p. 136.
10. Preface to *The Ambassadors.* See *The Art of the Novel: Critical Prefaces by Henry James,* with an introduction by Richard P. Blackmur (N.Y., 1948), p. 320.
11. *Joseph Conrad,* pp. 218-219.
12. One point should be made about this and the following two chapters. They do not deal with the reliability or veracity of the narrator because for this reader of Ford they are not problems. My own conclusion, based on the detailed analysis of the novel in these chapters, is that Ford would not have created a problem that it took a Sherlock Holmes forty years to uncover; he was quite capable of having built the problem into his structure, had he wanted it to be one. I might add that, for me, Samuel Hynes in his excellent article, "The Epistemology of *The Good Soldier"* (see Bibliography), has satisfactorily examined and resolved the issue.
13. *Henry James,* p. 130.

CHAPTER THREE

1. (N.Y., 1926), p. 242. Published in London in 1926 as *The Flurried Years*.

CHAPTER FOUR

1. *Those Earnest Victorians* (N.Y., 1930), p. 95.
2. *Ibid.*, p. 96.
3. *Ibid.*, p. 160.
4. *Ibid.*, p. 156.
5. *The Allegory of Love* (London, 1938), p. 12.
6. ELH, XXVIII (December, 1961), 384-385.
7. *Those Earnest Victorians*, p. 158.
8. *The Sun Also Rises*, Scribner Library Edition, p. 9.
9. *Ibid.*, p. 23.

CHAPTER FIVE

1. Douglas Goachu, "Pictures of Ezra Pound," *Nimbus*, III (Winter, 1956), p. 31.
2. *Memories and Impressions*, p. 216.
3. *Ibid.*, pp. 254-255.
4. *Ibid.*, p. 263.
5. *Ibid.*, p. 268.
6. *Ibid.*, p. 206.
7. "In Tenebris," *Collected Poems*, p. 163.
8. Preface to *Collected Poems*, p. 27.
9. *Ibid.*, p. 27.
10. Chapter ii of *The Mystery of Edwin Drood*.
11. See chapter ii of Book Two.
12. *Thus to Revisit*, p. 39.
13. *Ibid.*, p. 52.
14. *Joseph Conrad*, p. 208.
15. *Ibid.*, pp. 210-211.
16. *Thus to Revisit*, p. 39.
17. *Ibid.*, p. 119.
18. *Ibid.*, p. 39.
19. *Ibid.*, p. 161.
20. *Joseph Conrad*, p. 208.
21. "On Impressionism," *Poetry and Drama*, II (June, 1914), p. 171.
22. *Joseph Conrad*, p. 211.
23. *Ibid.*, p. 109.

24. Vol. II, chap. xv.
25. *The March of Literature* (London, 1939), p. 769. (U.S. ed.; N.Y., 1938).
26. *The English Novel,* p. 129.
27. *The March of Literature,* p. 766.
28. *Joseph Conrad,* pp. 192-193.
29. *Ibid.,* p. 199.
30. "On Impressionism," p. 173.
31. *Ibid.,* pp. 170-171.
32. *The Art of Fiction and Other Essays* (N.Y., 1948), p. 8.
33. "On Impressionism," p. 173.
34. *Ibid.,* p. 173.
35. *Ibid.,* p. 174.
36. *The Portable Conrad,* ed. M. D. Zabel (N.Y., 1947), p. 708. Ford remarks in *The March of Literature:* "Perhaps more than anything else it [Impressionism] was a matter of giving visibility to your pages; perhaps better than elsewhere, Conrad with his 'It is above all to make you see!' expressed the aims of the New World" (p. 732).
37. *The March of Literature,* p. 734.
38. *The Poetry of Ezra Pound* (Norfolk, Conn., 1953), p. 268.
39. *Thus to Revisit,* p. 44.
40. *The March of Literature,* p. 767.
41. *The English Novel,* pp. 131-132.
42. *The March of Literature,* p. 738.
43. *Ibid.,* p. 740.
44. *Ibid.,* p. 744.
45. *Ibid.,* p. 740.
46. *Ibid.,* p. 766.
47. See Richard A. Cassell's *Ford Madox Ford: A Study of His Novels* (Baltimore, 1961), pp. 127-128, and Paul L. Wiley's *Novelist of Three Worlds: Ford Madox Ford* (Syracuse, 1962), pp. 144-145.

CHAPTER SIX

1. *Henry James,* pp. 90-91.
2. *Wings of the Dove,* chapter iii of the Scribner edition (N.Y., 1946), p. 54.
3. *Henry James,* p. 147.
4. *Joseph Conrad,* p. 200.
5. *The March of Literature,* p. 750.
6. *Ibid.,* p. 752.

CHAPTER SEVEN

1. *It Was the Nightingale*, p. 206.
2. *The Georgian Novel and Mr. Robinson* (N.Y., 1929), p. 34.
3. "Remember that I Have Remembered," in *Gnomon* (N.Y., 1958), p. 150. Originally published in the *Hudson Review*, III (Winter, 1951).
4. *It Was the Nightingale*, pp. 208-209. The account of Ford's plans which follows draws upon pp. 207-227 of this volume.
5. *The English Novel*, p. 397.
6. *Drawn from Life*, pp. 164-165.
7. See especially J. J. Firebaugh, "Tietjens and the Tradition," *Pacific Spectator*, VI (Winter 1952), 23-32.
8. *Coleridge's Miscellaneous Criticism*, ed. T. M. Raysor (Cambridge, Mass., 1936), p. 99.

CHAPTER EIGHT

1. Ambrose Gordon, Jr., "A Diamond of Pattern: The War of F. Madox Ford," *Sewanee Review*, LXX (Summer, 1962), 471.
2. *It Was the Nightingale*, p. 217.
3. *Ibid.*, pp. 217-218.
4. Gordon, *op. cit.*, pp. 478-79.
5. *Ibid.*, p. 479.
6. *The Great Gatsby*, Scribner Library Edition, p. 138. All page references are to this edition.
7. p. xvi.
8. p. xvii.
9. *The Fictional Technique of Scott Fitzgerald* (The Hague, 1957), pp. 80-81.
10. *Love and Death in the American Novel* (N.Y., 1960), p. 301.
11. From "Hugh Selwyn Mauberley," in *Personae*, p. 190.
12. Review of *Parade's End* in *Sewanee Review*, LIX (Winter, 1951), p. 159.

BIBLIOGRAPHY

The standard reference work for those interested in Ford is David Dow Harvey's *Ford Madox Ford: 1873-1939; A Bibliography of Works and Criticism* (Princeton University Press, 1962). In addition, a running bibliography with annotation is maintained by *English Literature in Transition: 1880-1920,* edited by Helmut E. Gerber and published at Purdue University. The special Ford Madox Ford number of *Modern Fiction Studies* (Spring, 1963) also contains a selected checklist, as do the pamphlets and critical books listed below:

1. BIOGRAPHICAL

Bowen, Stella. *Drawn from Life.* London: Collins, 1941.

Goldring, Douglas. *The Last Pre-Raphaelite.* London: MacDonald, 1948. Published in America as *Trained for Genius.* New York: Dutton, 1949.

————. *South Lodge: Reminiscences of Violet Hunt, Ford Madox Ford, and the "English Review" Circle.* London: Constable, 1943.

Harvey, David D. *"Pro Patria Mori:* The Neglect of Ford's Novels in England." *Modern Fiction Studies,* IX (Spring, 1963), 3-16.

Hunt, Violet. *The Flurried Years.* London: Hurst & Blackett, 1926. Also published as *I Have This To Say.* New York: Boni & Liveright, 1926.

Ludwig, Richard M. "The Reputation of Ford Madox Ford." *PMLA,* LXXVI (Dec., 1961), 544-551.

2. BOOK-LENGTH CRITICAL STUDIES OF FORD

Cassell, Richard A. *Ford Madox Ford: A Study of his Novels.* Baltimore: Johns Hopkins Press, 1961.

Meixner, John A. *Ford Madox Ford's Novels: A Critical Study.* Minneapolis: University of Minnesota Press, 1961.

Wiley, Paul L. *Novelist of Three Worlds: Ford Madox Ford.* Syracuse, New York: Syracuse University Press, 1962.

3. PAMPHLETS ON FORD

Gordon, Caroline. *A Good Soldier: A Key to the Novels of Ford Madox Ford.* University of California Library, Davis: Chapbook No. 1, 1963.

Young, Kenneth. *Ford Madox Ford.* (Writers and Their Work, No. 74). London: Longmans, Green, 1956.

4. GENERAL STUDIES

Blackmur, R. P. "The King Over the Water: Notes on the Novels of Ford Madox Hueffer." *Princeton University Chronicle,* IX (April, 1948), 123-127. Reprinted in Mark Schorer, ed., *Modern British Fiction* (Oxford University Press, 1961), pp. 137-142.

Greene, Graham. "Ford Madox Ford." In his *The Lost Childhood and Other Essays.* London: Eyre & Spottiswoode, 1951. Pp. 89-91.

Hynes, Samuel, "Ford and the Spirit of Romance." *Modern Fiction Studies,* IX (Spring, 1963), 17-24.

Kenner, Hugh. "Conrad and Ford." *Shenandoah,* III (Summer, 1952), 50-55. Reprinted in his *Gnomon: Essays on Contemporary Literature.* New York: McDowell, Obolensky, 1958. Pp. 162-170.

5. STUDIES OF *The Good Soldier*

Cox, James Trammel. "Ford's 'Passion for Provence.' " *ELH, XVIII* (Dec., 1961), 383-398.

———. "The Finest French Novel in the English Language." *Modern Fiction Studies,* IX (Spring, 1963), 79-63.

Gose, Elliott B., Jr. "The Strange Irregular Rhythm: An Analysis of *The Good Soldier.*" *PMLA,* LXII (June, 1957), 494-507.

Hafley, James. "The Moral Structure of *The Good Soldier.*" *Modern Fiction Studies,* V (Summer, 1959), 121-128.

Hynes, Samuel. "The Epistemology of *The Good Soldier.*" *Sewanee Review,* LXIX (Spring, 1961), 225-235.

Moser, Thomas. "Towards *The Good Soldier*—Discovery of a Sexual Theme." *Daedalus,* XCII (Spring, 1963), 312-325.

Schorer, Mark. "The Good Novelist in *The Good Soldier.*" *Princeton University Library Chronicle,* IX (April, 1948), 128-133. Reprinted in *Horizon,* XX (August, 1949), 132-138; and as "An Interpretation" in *The Good Soldier* (New York: Knopf [Vintage Books], 1951), pp. v-xv.

Weisenfarth, Joseph. "Criticism and the Semiosis of *The Good Soldier.*" *Modern Fiction Studies,* IX (Spring, 1963), 39-49.

6. STUDIES OF *Parade's End*

Firebaugh, Joseph J. "Tietjens and the Tradition." *Pacific Spectator,* VI (Winter, 1952), 23-32.

Gordon, Ambrose, Jr. "A Diamond of Pattern: The War of F. Madox Ford." *Sewanee Review,* LXX (Summer, 1962), 464-483.

————. *"Parade's End:* Where War Was Fairy Tale." *Texas Studies in Literature and Language,* V (Spring, 1963), 25-41.

Gose, Elliott B., Jr. "Reality to Romance: A Study of Ford's *Parade's End." College English,* XVII (May, 1956), 445-450.

Kenner, Hugh. "Remember That I Have Remembered." *Hudson Review,* III (Winter, 1951), 602-611. Reprinted in his *Gnomon: Essays on Contemporary Literature,* pp. 144-161.

Macauley, Robie. "Introduction." *"Parade's End."* New York: Knopf, 1950. Pp. v-xxii.

Mizener, Arthur. "A Large Fiction." *Kenyon Review,* XIII (Winter, 1951), 142-147.

Walter, E. V. "The Political Sense of Ford Madox Ford." *New Republic,* CXXXIV (March 26, 1956), 17-19.

Williams, William Carlos. *"Parade's End."* In his *Selected Essays.* New York: Random House, 1954. Pp. 315-323.

7. SPECIAL STUDIES

Bradbury, Malcolm. "The English Review." *London Magazine,* V (August, 1958), 46-57.

Cassell, Richard A. "The Two Sorrels of Ford Madox Ford." *Modern Philology,* LIX (November, 1961), 114-121.

MacShane, Frank. "The Transatlantic Review." *London Magazine,* VII (Dec., 1960), 49-59.

————. "The English Review." *South Atlantic Quarterly,* LX (Summer, 1961), 311-320.

CHRONOLOGICAL LIST OF FORD'S BOOKS (INCLUDING COLLABORATIONS AND FORD'S OWN TRANSLATIONS)

After David Dow Harvey's *Ford Madox Ford: 1873-1939; a Bibliography of Works and Criticism.* Princeton University Press, 1962.

Date given is actual year of publication, not necessarily year on title page. If the two differ, the date on the title page follows the name of the publisher.

1891. *The Brown Owl.* London: T. Fisher Unwin, 1892. Children's fairy-tale.

1892. *The Feather*. London: T. Fisher Unwin. Children's fairy-tale.

1892. *The Shifting of the Fire*. London: T. Fisher Unwin. Novel.

1893. *The Questions at the Well*. [pseud. "Fenil Haig"]. London: Digby. Poems.

1894. *The Queen Who Flew*. London: Bliss, Sands, and Foster. Children's fairy-tale.

1896. *Ford Madox Brown*. London: Longmans, Green. Biography.

1900. *Poems for Pictures*. London: John MacQueen. Poems.

1900. *The Cinque Ports*. London: Blackwood. "A Historical and Descriptive Record" (sub-title) of Kent and Sussex port towns.

1901. *The Inheritors*. London: Heinemann. Novel, written in collaboration with Joseph Conrad.

1902. *Rossetti*. London: Duckworth. Art criticism and biography.

1903. *Romance*. London: Smith and Elder. Novel (historical adventure story), written in collaboration with Joseph Conrad.

1904. *The Face of the Night*. London: John MacQueen. Poems.

1905. *The Soul of London*. London: Alston Rivers. Sociological impressionism.

1905. *The Benefactor*. London: Brown, Langham. Novel.

1905. *Hans Holbein*. London: Duckworth. Art criticism.

1906. *The Fifth Queen*. London: Alston Rivers. Novel (historical romance; first of the "Katherine Howard" trilogy).

1906. *The Heart of the Country*. London: Alston Rivers. Sociological impressionism.

1906. *Christina's Fairy Book*. London: Alston Rivers. Children's fairy-tales.

1907. *Privy Seal*. London: Alston Rivers. Novel (historical romance; second of the "Katherine Howard" trilogy).

1907. *England and the English*. New York: McClure, Phillips. Sociological impressionism; published only in America; composed of the previously published *The Soul of London* and *The Heart of the Country* plus *The Spirit of the People*.

1907. *From Inland*. London: Alston Rivers. Poems.

1907. *An English Girl*. London: Methuen. Novel.

1907. *The Pre-Raphaelite Brotherhood*. London: Duckworth. Art criticism.

1907. *The Spirit of the People*. London: Alston Rivers. Sociological impressionism; previously published, only in America, in *England and the English*.

1908. *The Fifth Queen Crowned*. London: Nash. Novel (historical romance; third of the "Katherine Howard" trilogy).

1908. *Mr. Apollo*. London: Methuen. Novel.

1909. *The "Half Moon"*. London: Nash. Novel (historical romance).

1910. *A Call.* London: Chatto and Windus. Novel.
1910. *Songs from London.* London: Elkin Mathews. Poems.
1910. *The Portrait.* London: Methuen. Novel (historical romance).
1911. *The Simple Life Limited* [pseud. "Daniel Chaucer"]. London: John Lane. Novel (satire).
1911. *Ancient Lights.* London: Chapman and Hall, 1910. Reminiscences; published in America in 1911 as *Memories and Impressions.* New York: Harper.
1911. *Ladies Whose Bright Eyes.* London: Constable. Philadelphia: Lippincott, 1935 (revised). Novel (historical fantasy).
1911. *The Critical Attitude.* London: Constable. Essays in literary criticism.
1912. *High Germany.* London: Duckworth, 1911. Poems.
1912. *The Panel.* London: Constable. Novel (farce). Published in America in 1913 as *Ring for Nancy.* Indianapolis: Bobbs-Merrill. New York: Grosset and Dunlap.
1912. *The New Humpty-Dumpty* [pseud. "Daniel Chaucer"]. London and New York: John Lane. Novel (satire).
1913. *This Monstrous Regiment of Women.* London: Women's Freedom League. Suffragette pamphlet.
1913. *Mr. Fleight.* London: Howard Latimer. Novel (satire).
1913. *The Desirable Alien.* London: Chatto and Windus. Impressions of Germany, written in collaboration with Violet Hunt.
1913. *The Young Lovell.* London: Chatto and Windus. Novel (historical romance).
1913. *Collected Poems.* London: Goschen; Martin Secker, 1916.
1914. *Henry James.* London: Martin Secker, 1913. New York: Albert and Charles Boni, 1915. Critical essay.
1915. *Antwerp.* London: Poetry Workshop. Long Poem (pamphlet).
1915. *The Good Soldier.* London and New York: John Lane. New York: Alfred A. Knopf, 1951; Vintage Books, 1957. Novel.
1915. *When Blood is Their Argument.* New York and London: Hodder and Stoughton. War propaganda (anti-Prussian essays).
1915. *Between St. Dennis and St. George.* London: Hodder and Stoughton. War propaganda (pro-French and anti-Prussian essays).
1915. *Zeppelin Nights.* London: John Lane. Historical sketches (told Decameron-fashion against the background of the War), written in collaboration with Violet Hunt.
1917. *The Trail of the Barbarians.* London: Longmans, Green. Translation of the war pamphlet *L'Outrage des Barbares* by Pierre Loti.
1918. *On Heaven.* London: John Lane. Poems.

1921. *A House. The Chapbook*, No. 21. London: Poetry Bookshop. Long poem (pamphlet).

1921. *Thus to Revisit.* London: Chapman and Hall. New York: Dutton. Literary criticism and reminiscence.

1923. *The Marsden Case.* London: Duckworth. Novel.

1923. *Women & Men.* Paris: Three Mountains Press. Essays.

1923. *Mister Bosphorus and the Muses.* London: Duckworth. Long narrative and dramatic poem.

1924. *Some Do Not. . . .* London: Duckworth. New York: Albert and Charles Boni. Novel (first of the "Tietjens" tetralogy).

1924. *The Nature of a Crime.* London: Duckworth. New York: Doubleday. Novella, written in collaboration with Joseph Conrad; previously published in 1909 in *English Review*.

1924. *Joseph Conrad: A Personal Remembrance.* London: Duckworth. Boston: Little Brown. Biography, reminiscence, and criticism.

1925. *No More Parades.* London: Duckworth. New York: Albert and Charles Boni. Novel (second of the "Tietjens" tetralogy).

1926. *A Mirror to France.* London: Duckworth. Sociological impressionism.

1926. *A Man Could Stand Up—.* London: Duckworth. New York: Albert and Charles Boni. Novel (third of the "Tietjens" tetralogy).

1927. *New Poems.* New York: Rudge.

1927. *New York is Not America.* London: Duckworth. New York: Albert and Charles Boni. Essays in sociological atmospheres.

1927. *New York Essays.* New York: Rudge.

1928. *The Last Post.* London: Duckworth. New York: Literary Guild of America. Novel (last novel of the "Tietjens" tetralogy; titled *Last Post* in England).

1928. *A Little Less Than Gods.* New York: Viking Press. Novel (historical romance).

1928. *Perversity.* Chicago: Pascal Covici. Translation of a novel by Francis Carco; possibly not by Ford.

1929. *The English Novel.* Philadelphia and London: J. B. Lippincott. London: Constable, 1930. Essay in literary criticism and history.

1929. *No Enemy.* New York: Macaulay. Disguised autobiography (concerning the war years; written shortly after the war).

1931. *Return to Yesterday.* London: Gollancz. New York: Horace Liveright, 1932. Reminiscences (up to 1914).

1931. *When the Wicked Man.* New York: Horace Liveright. London: Jonathan Cape, 1932. Novel.

1933. *The Rash Act.* New York: Long and Smith. London: Jonathan Cape. Novel.

1933. *It Was the Nightingale.* Philadelphia and London: J. B. Lippincott. Autobiography and reminiscences (from 1918).

1934. *Henry for Hugh.* Philadelphia and London: J. B. Lippincott. Novel.

1935. *Provence.* Philadelphia and London: J. B. Lippincott. London: Allen and Unwin, 1938. Impressions of France and England.

1936. *Vive le Roy.* Philadelphia and London: J. B. Lippincott. "Mystery" novel.

1936. *Collected Poems.* New York: Oxford University Press.

1937. *Great Trade Route.* New York: Oxford University Press. London: Allen and Unwin. Impressions of France, the United States, and England.

1937. *Portraits from Life.* Boston: Houghton Mifflin. Essays in personal reminiscence and literary criticism about ten *prosateurs* and one poet; published in England in 1938 as *Mightier than the Sword.* London: Allen and Unwin.

1938. *The March of Literature.* New York: Dial Press. London: Allen and Unwin, 1939. My references are to the Allen and Unwin edition. Survey of literature "From Confucius to Modern Times."

* * *

1950. *Parade's End.* Introduction by Robie Macauley. New York: Alfred A. Knopf. Posthumous publication in America of the "Tietjens" tetralogy in one volume.

1962. *The Bodley Head Ford Madox Ford.* Edited and introduced by Graham Greene. London: The Bodley Head. Two-volume republication of *The Good Soldier,* selected reminiscences and poems, and the *Fifth Queen* trilogy.

1963. *The Fifth Queen.* New York: Vanguard Press.